# THE OPTICAL ILLUSIONS

## COLORING BOOK

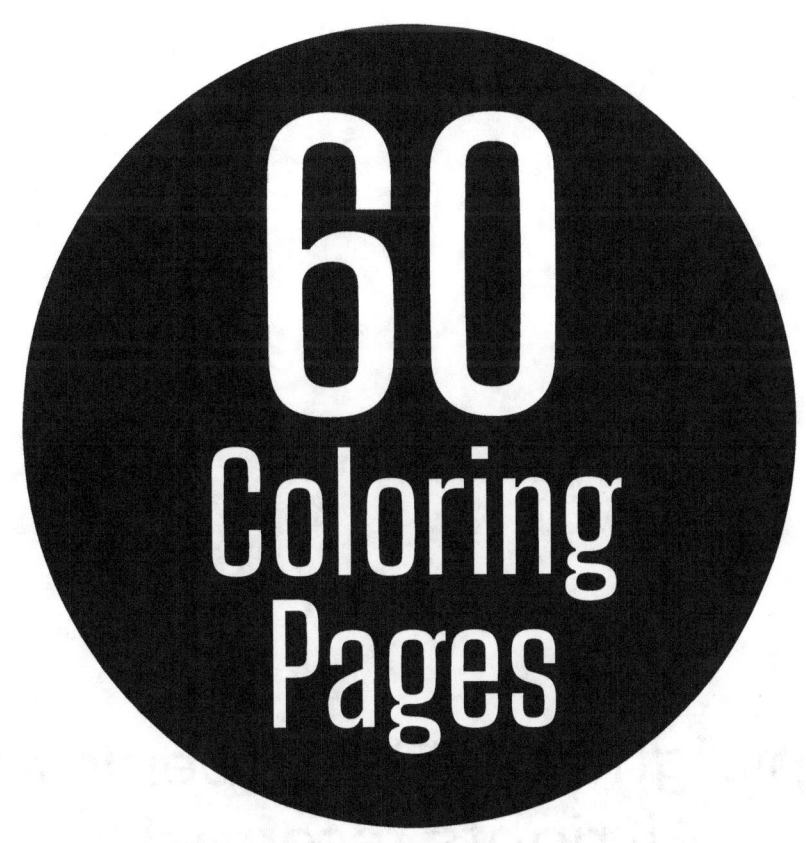

Copyright © 2021 CH.benloway
All rights reserved.
ISBN:9798637446964

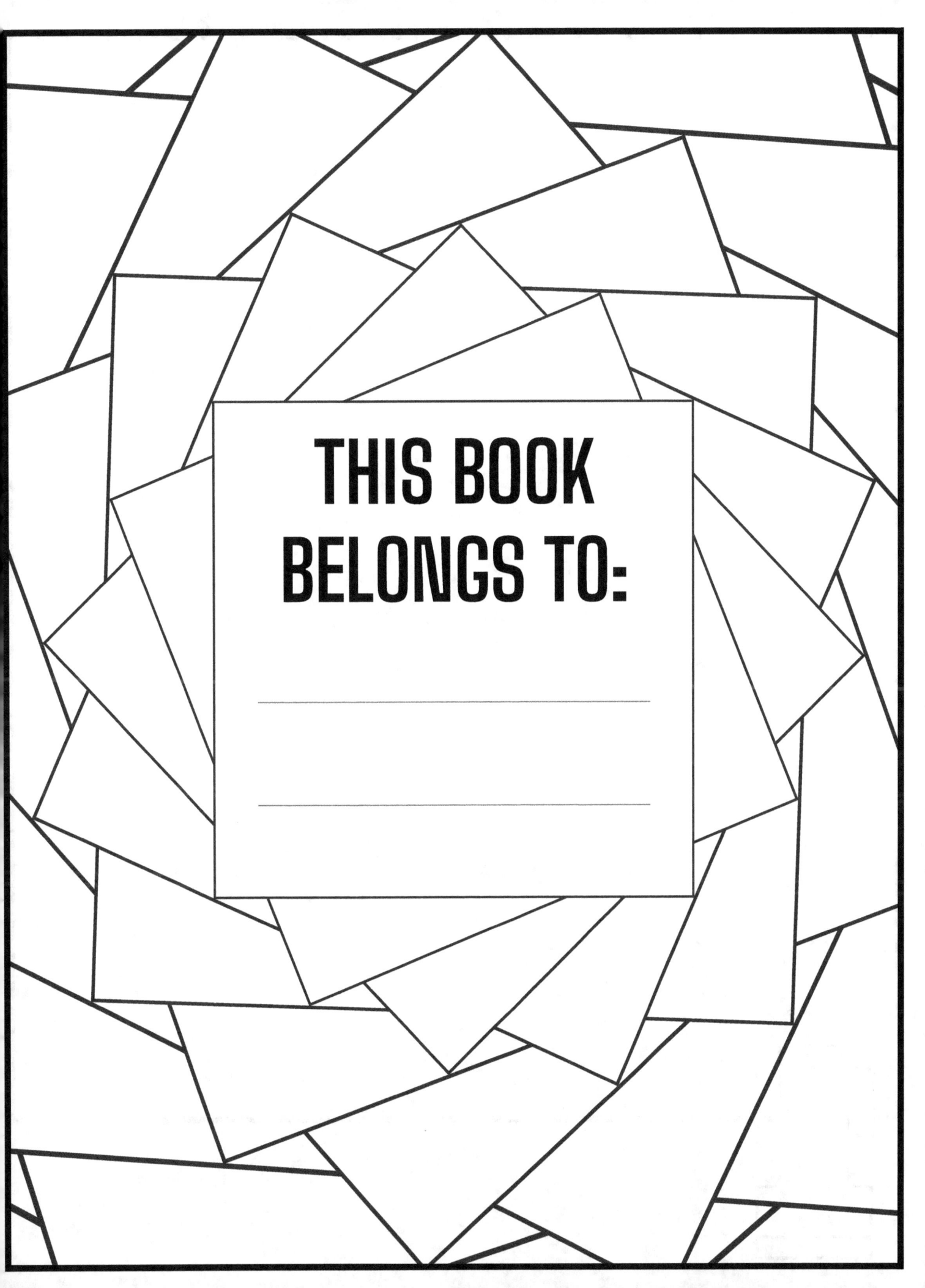

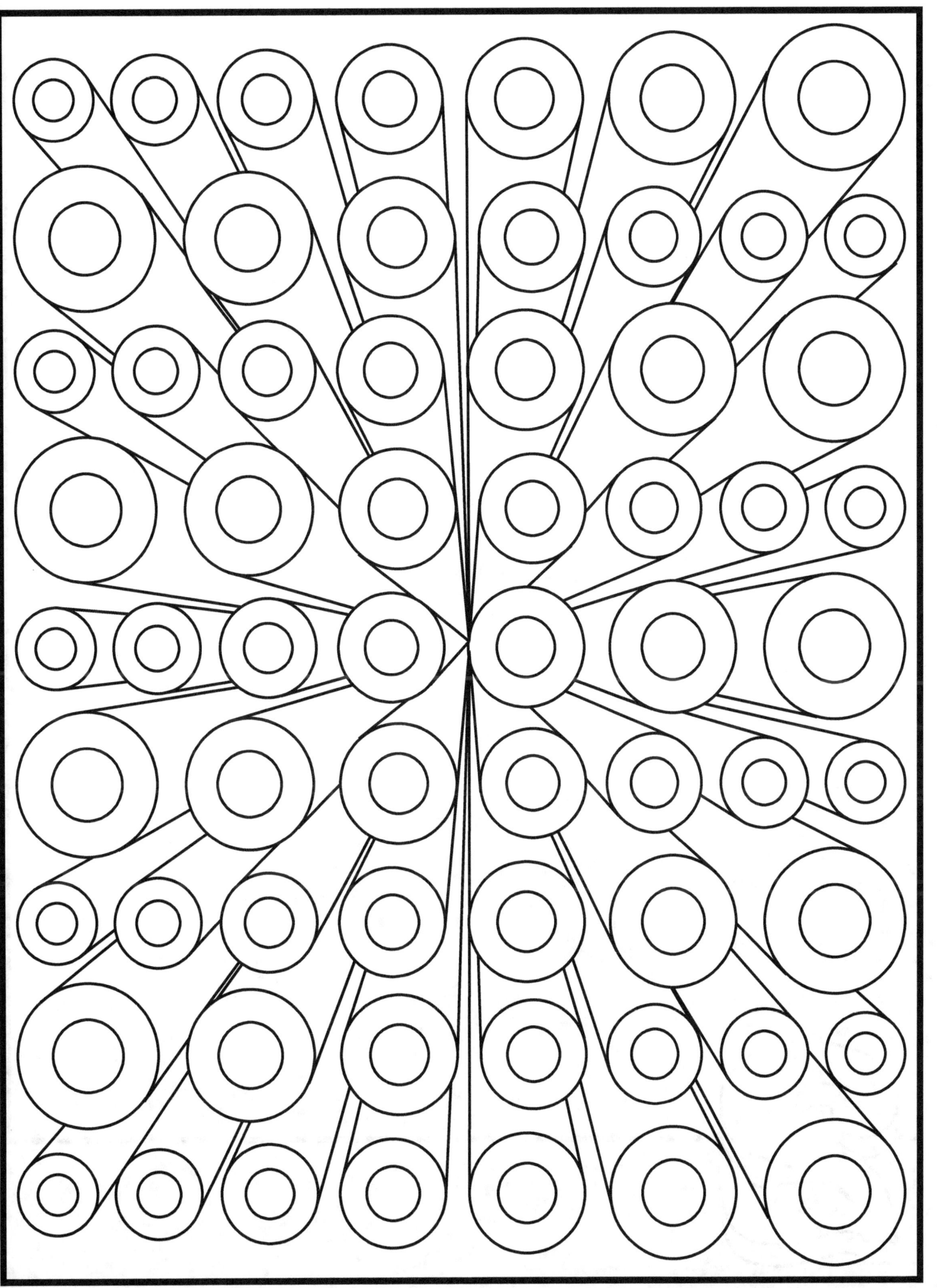

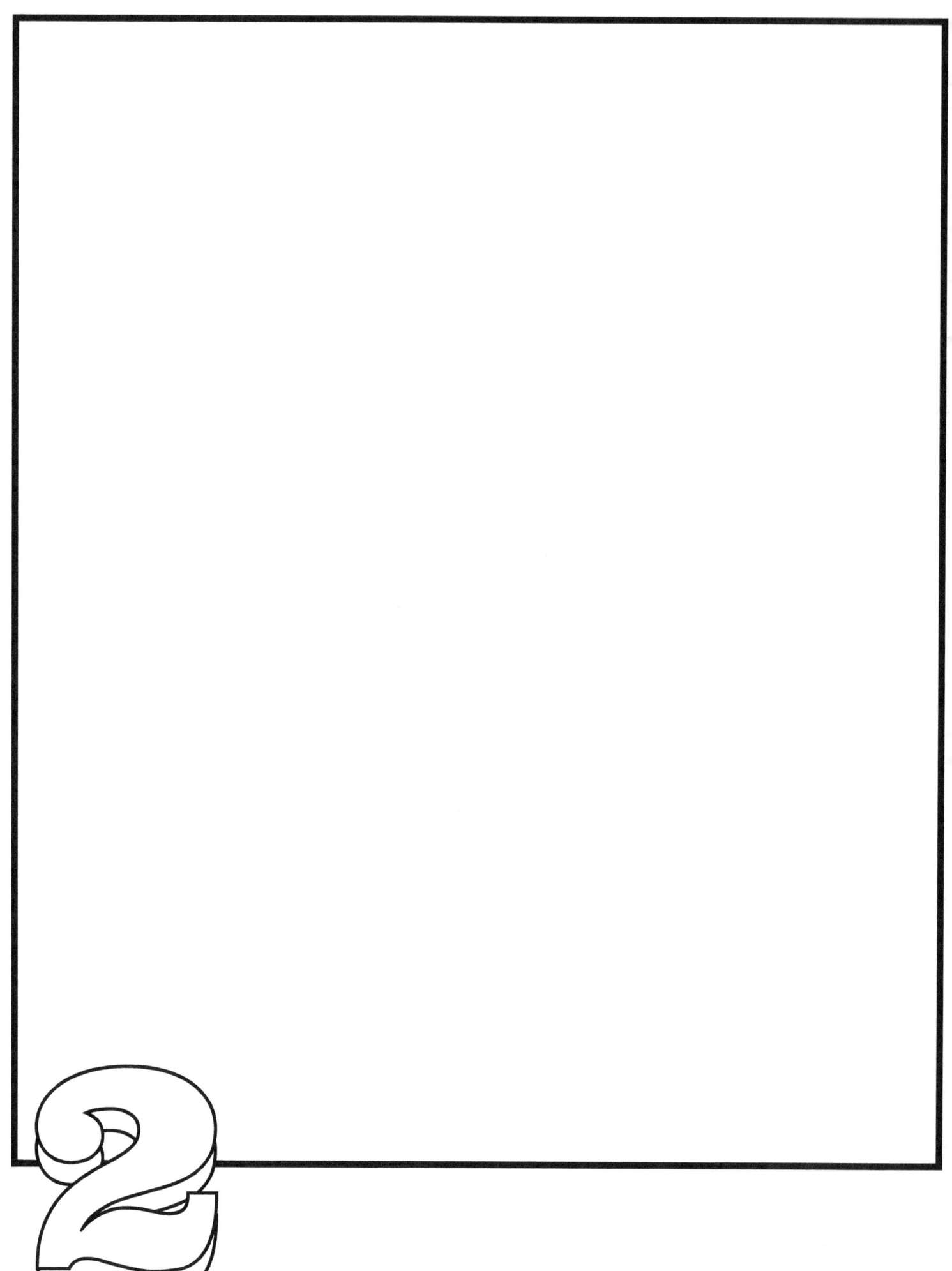

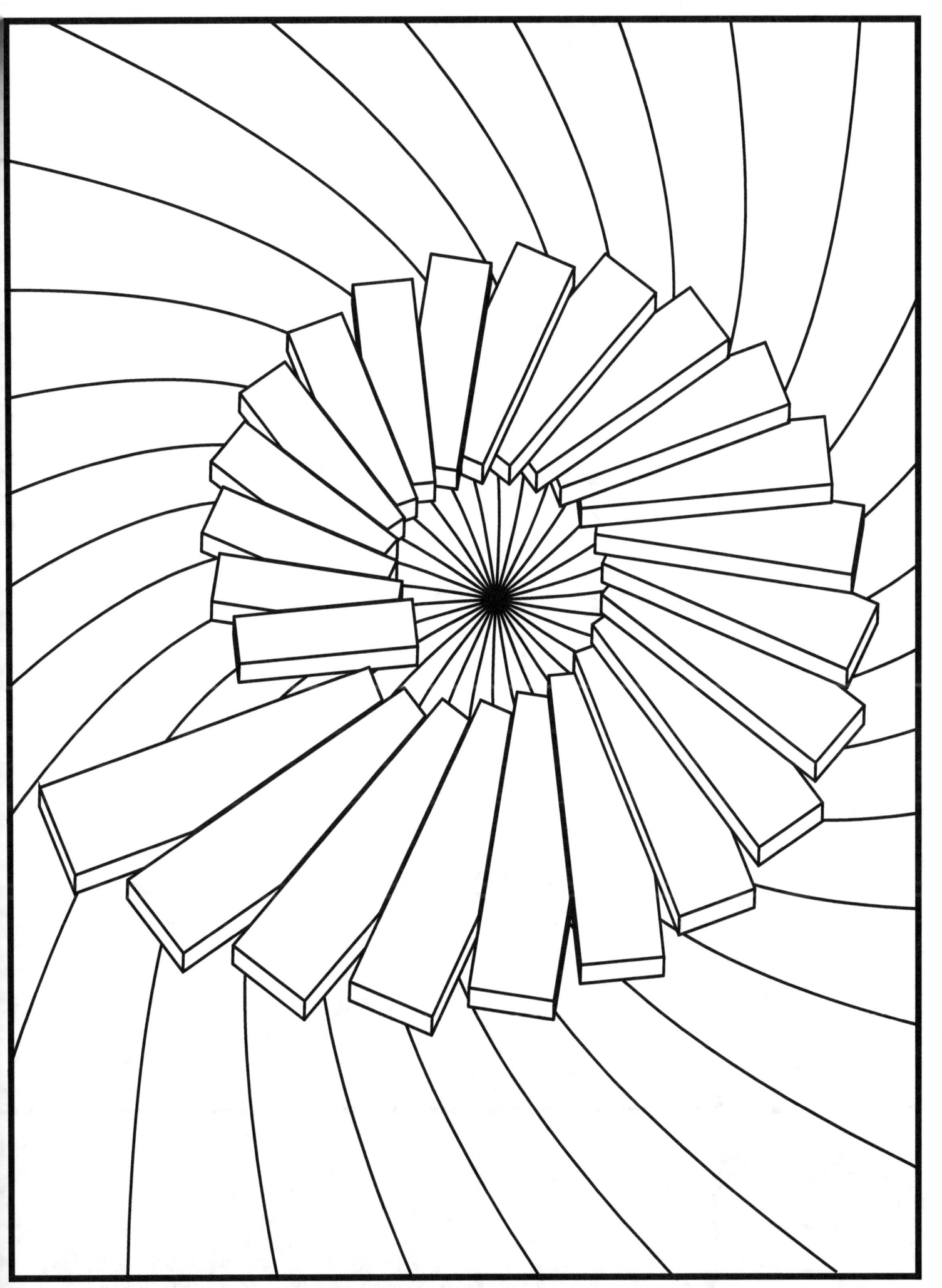

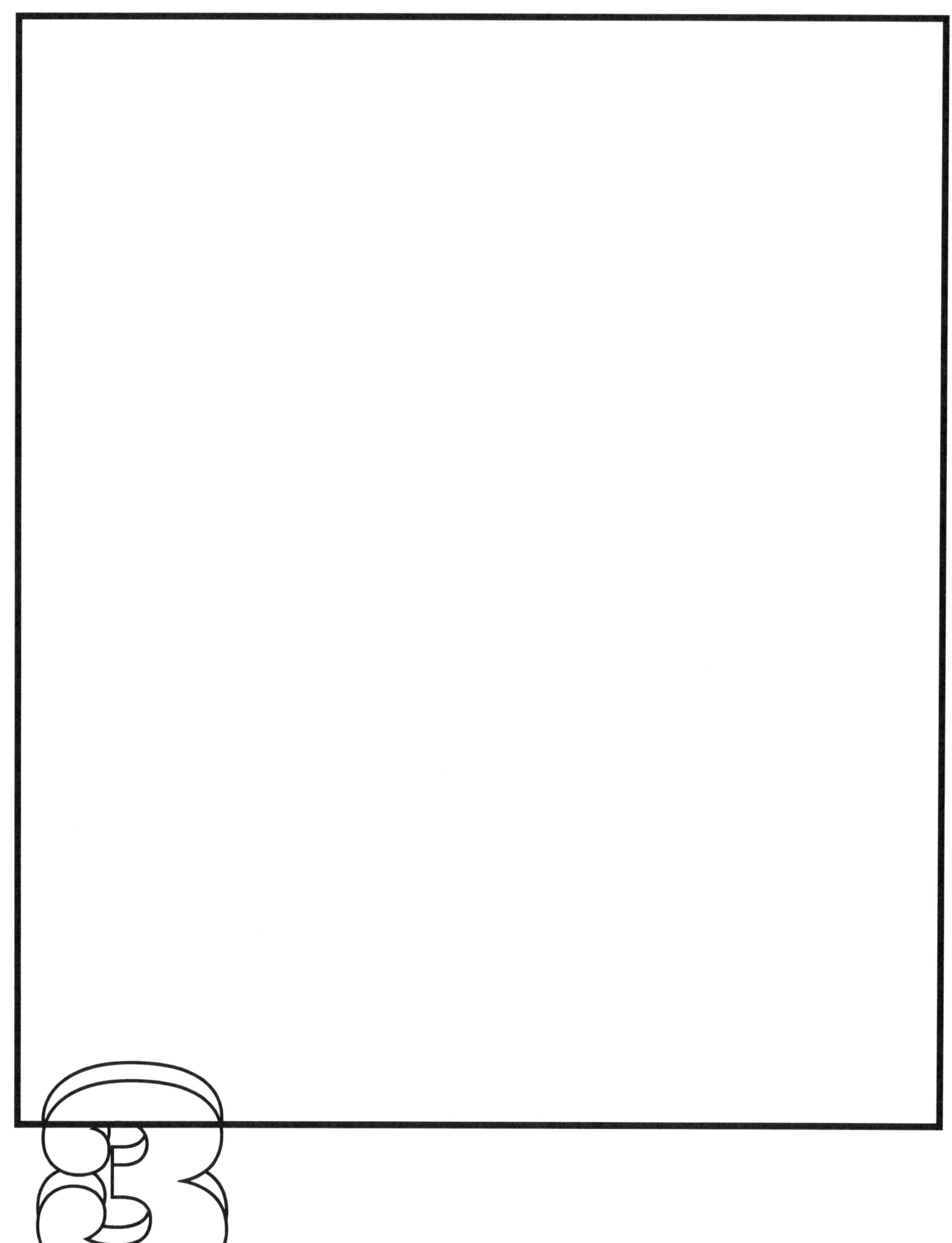

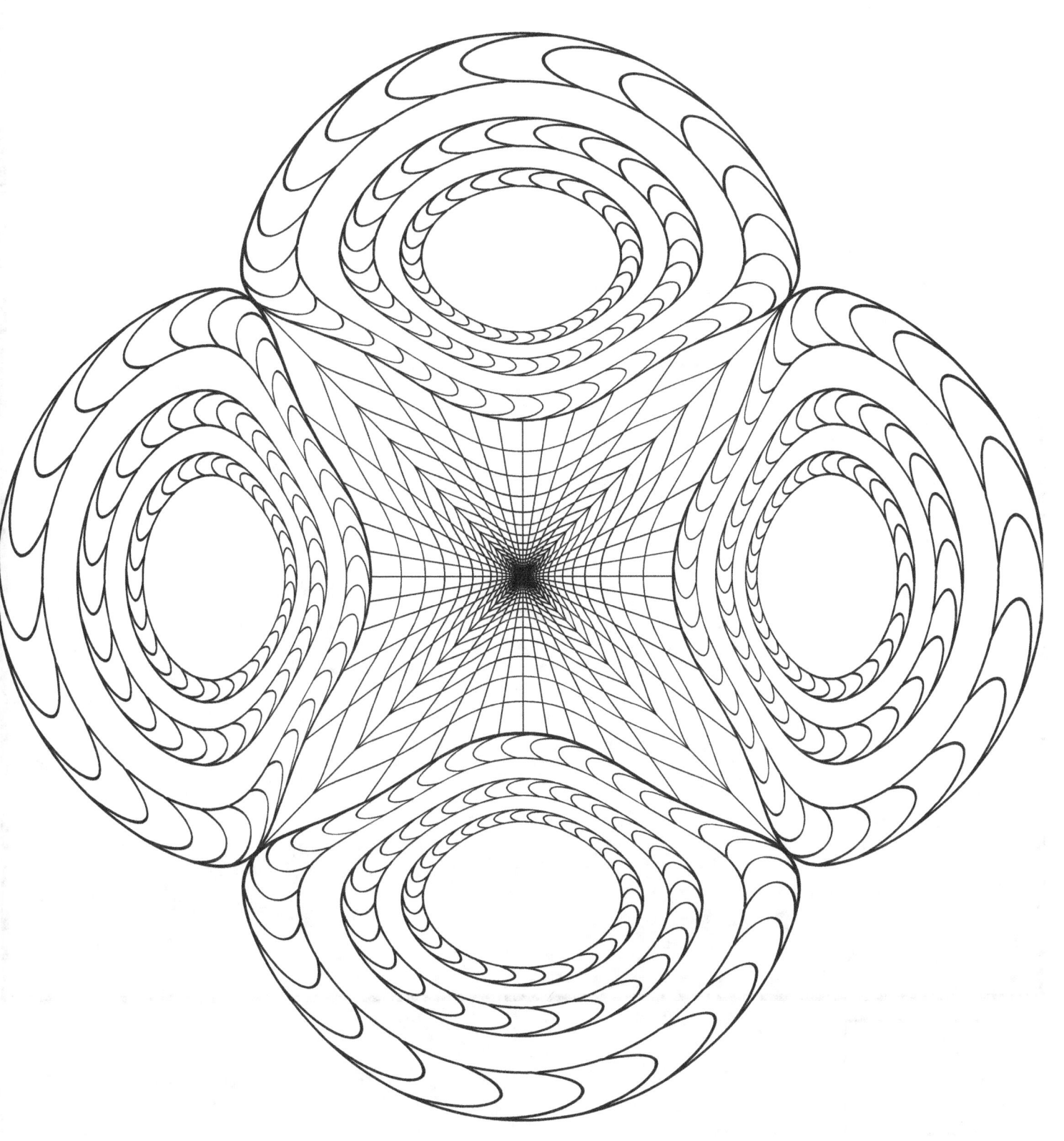

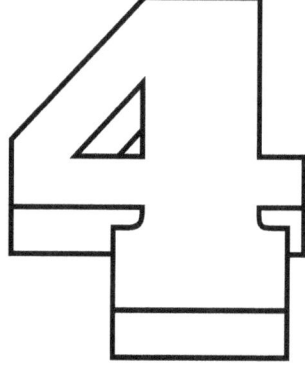

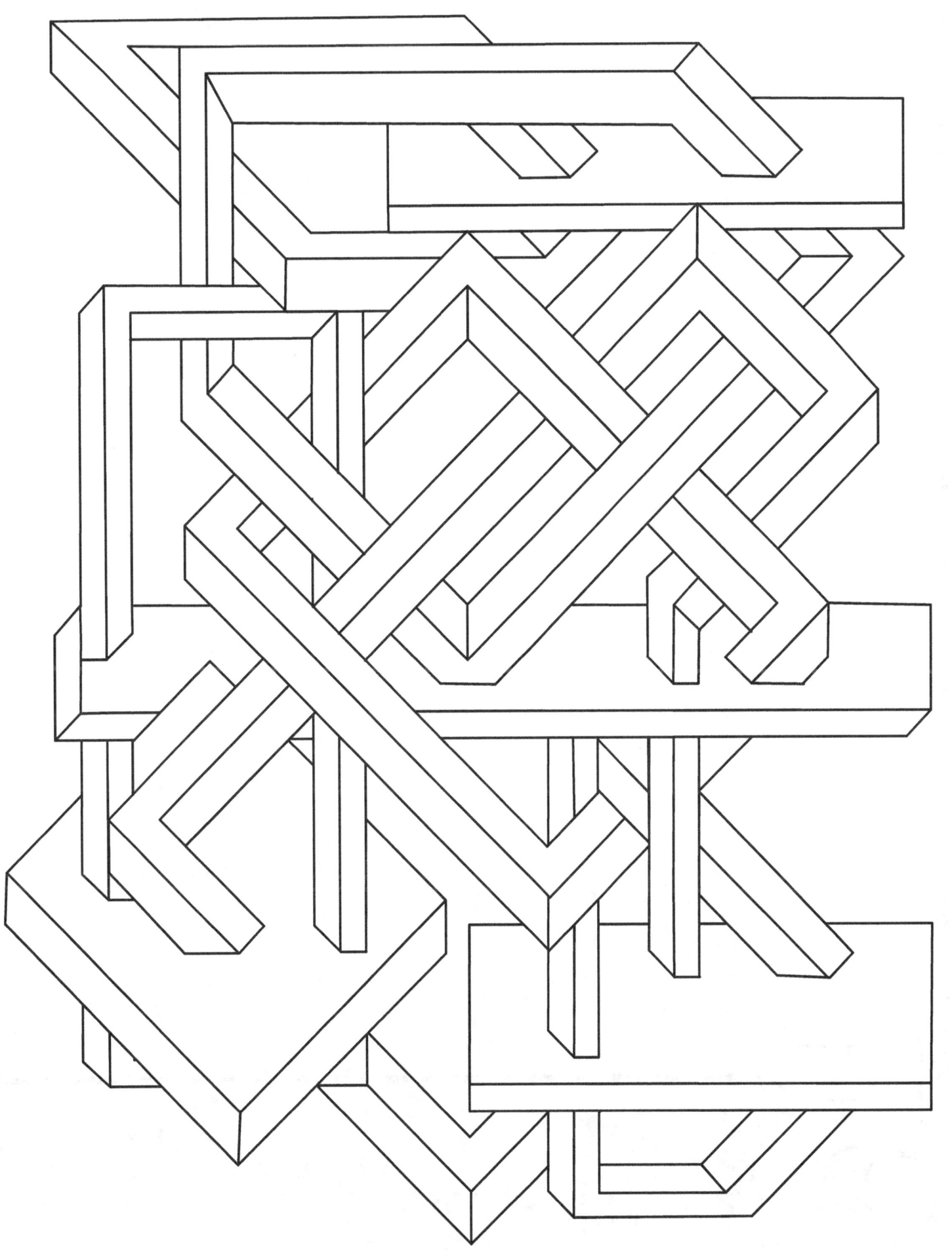

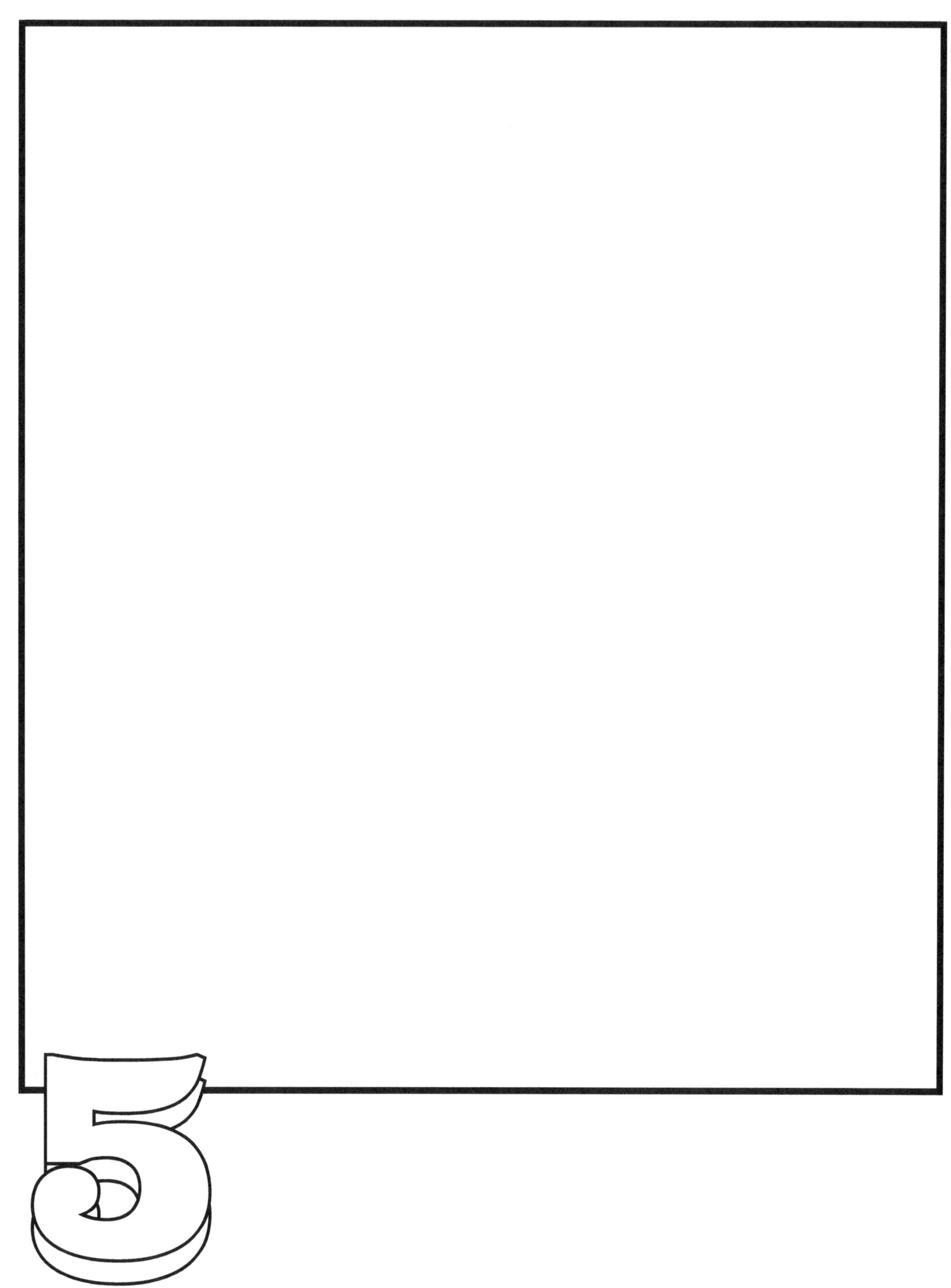

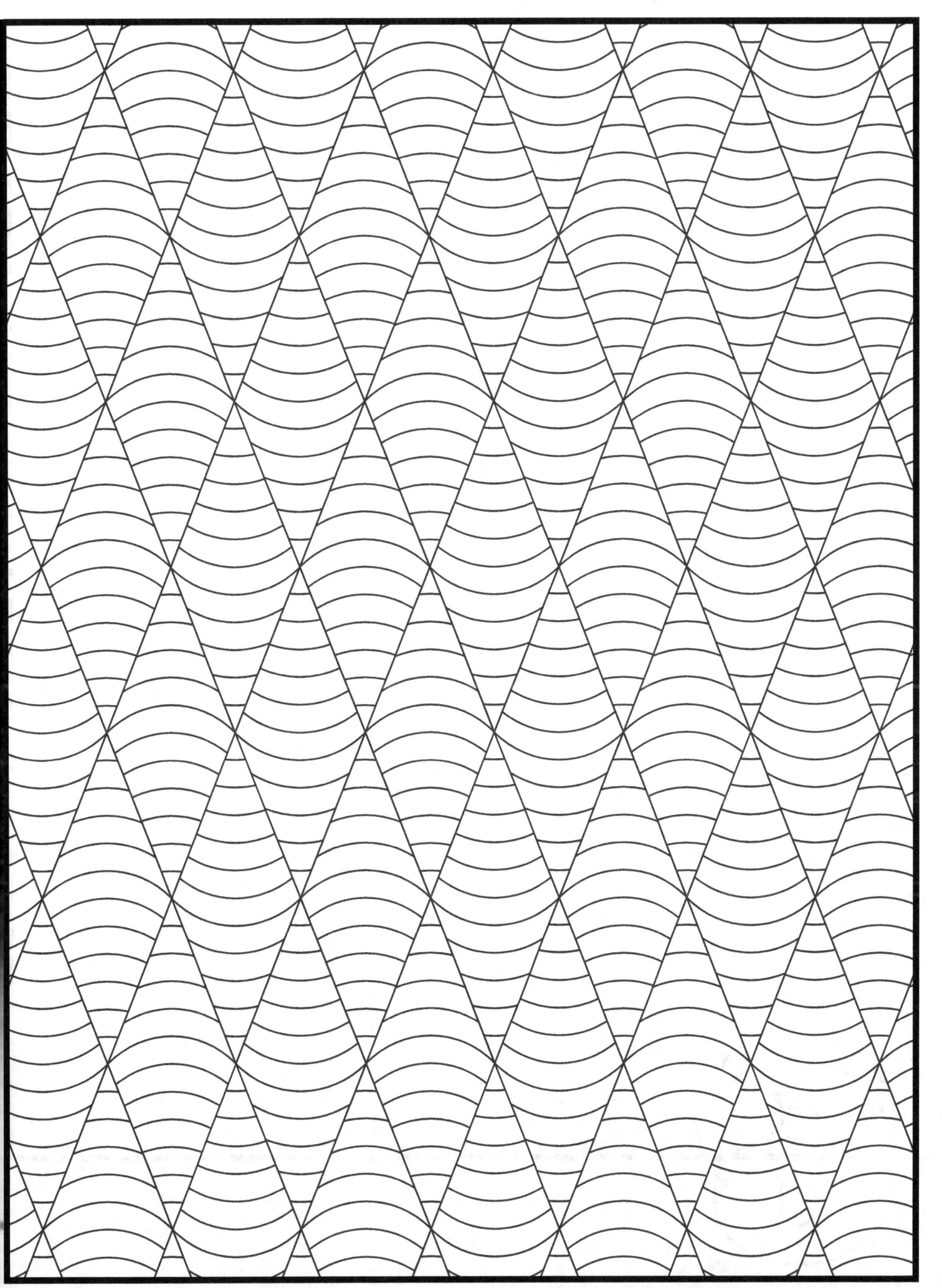

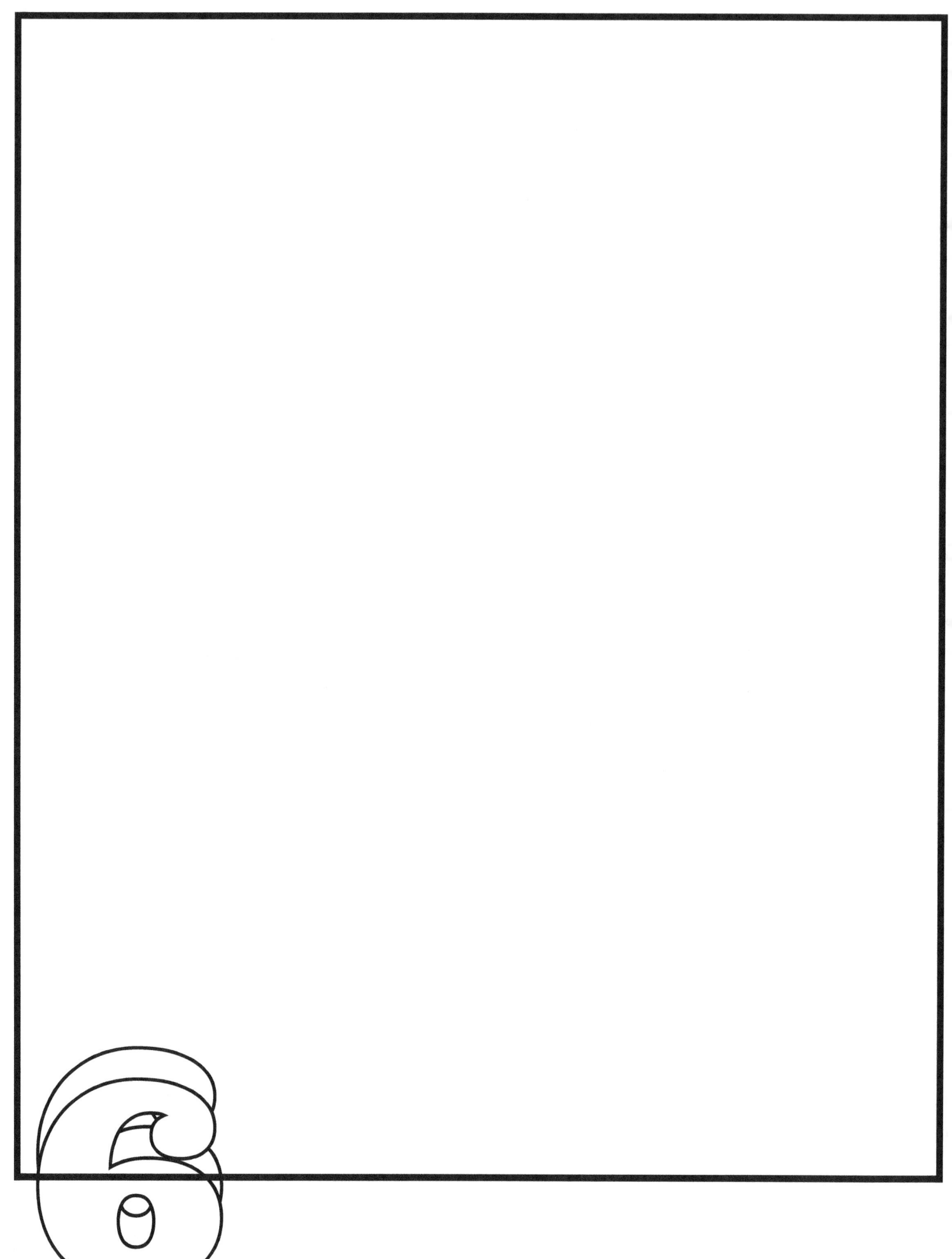

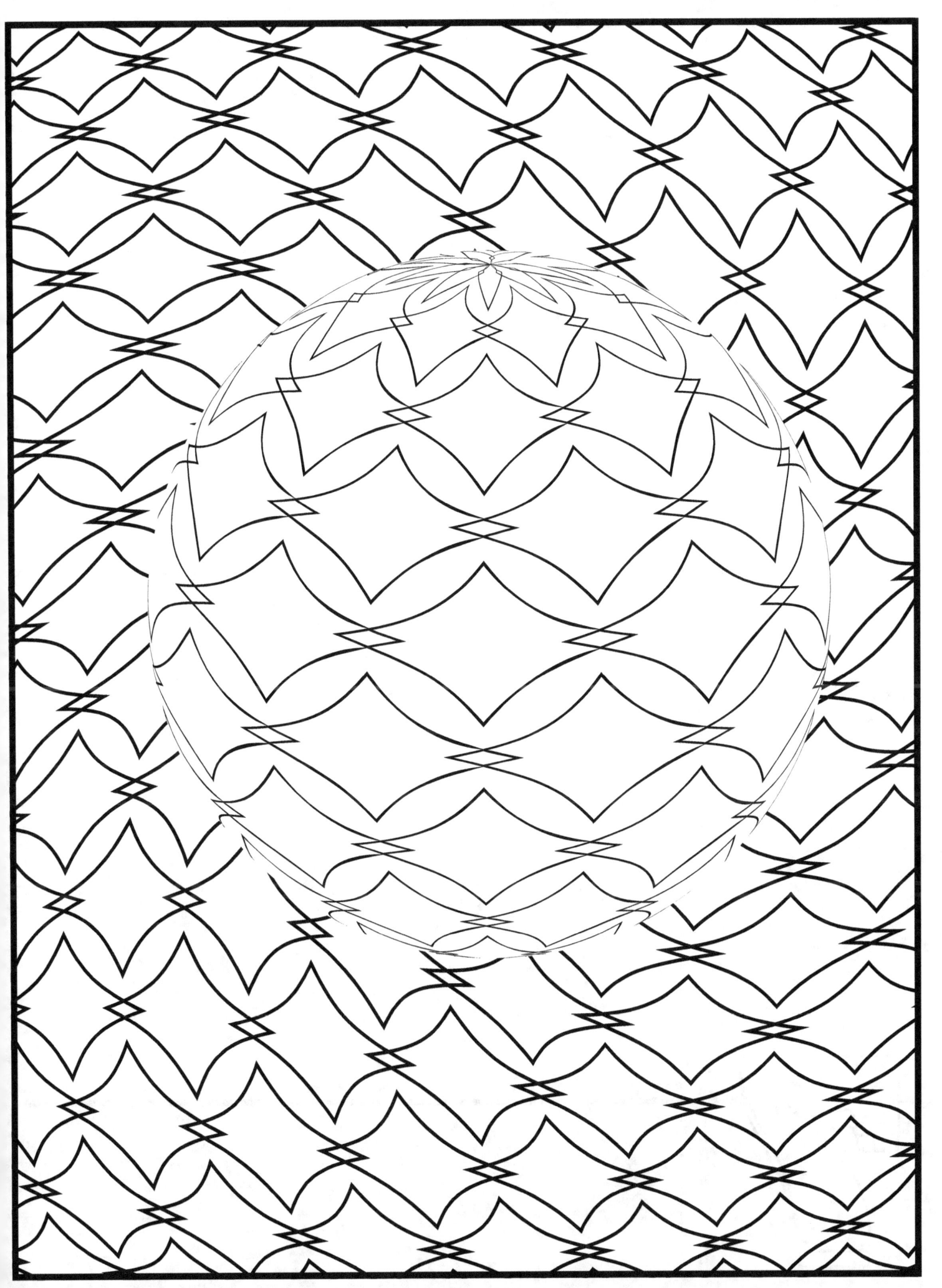

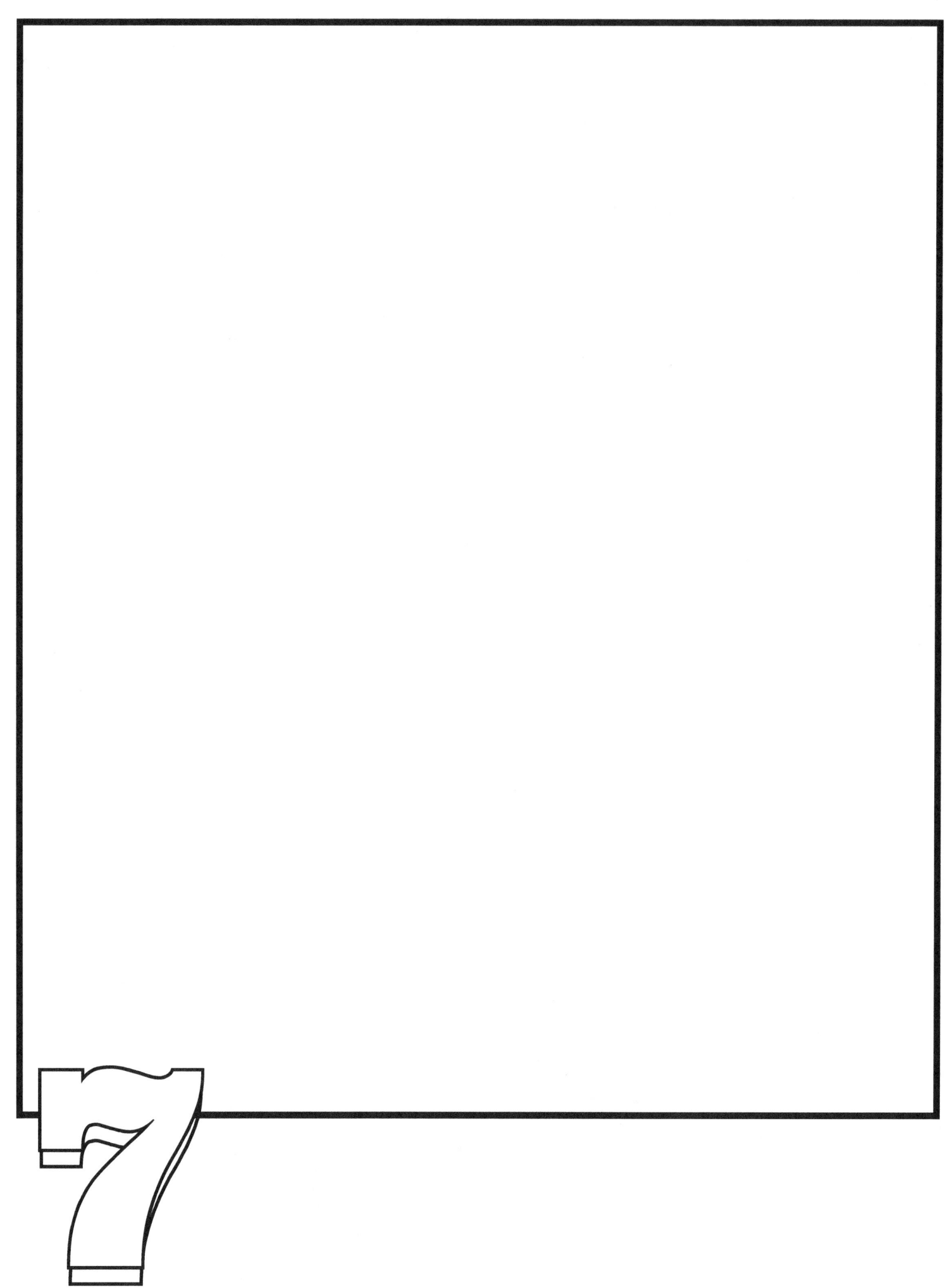

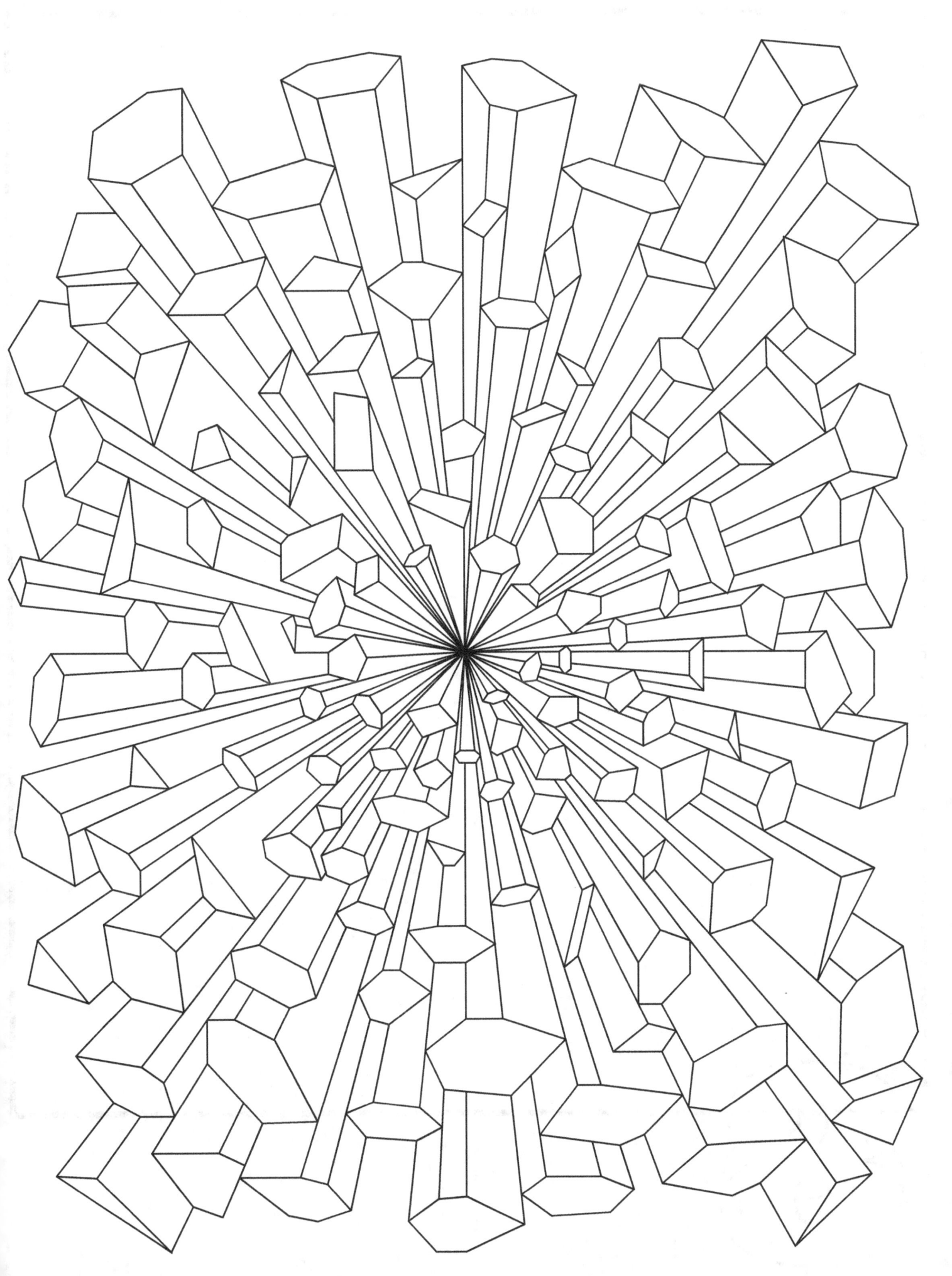

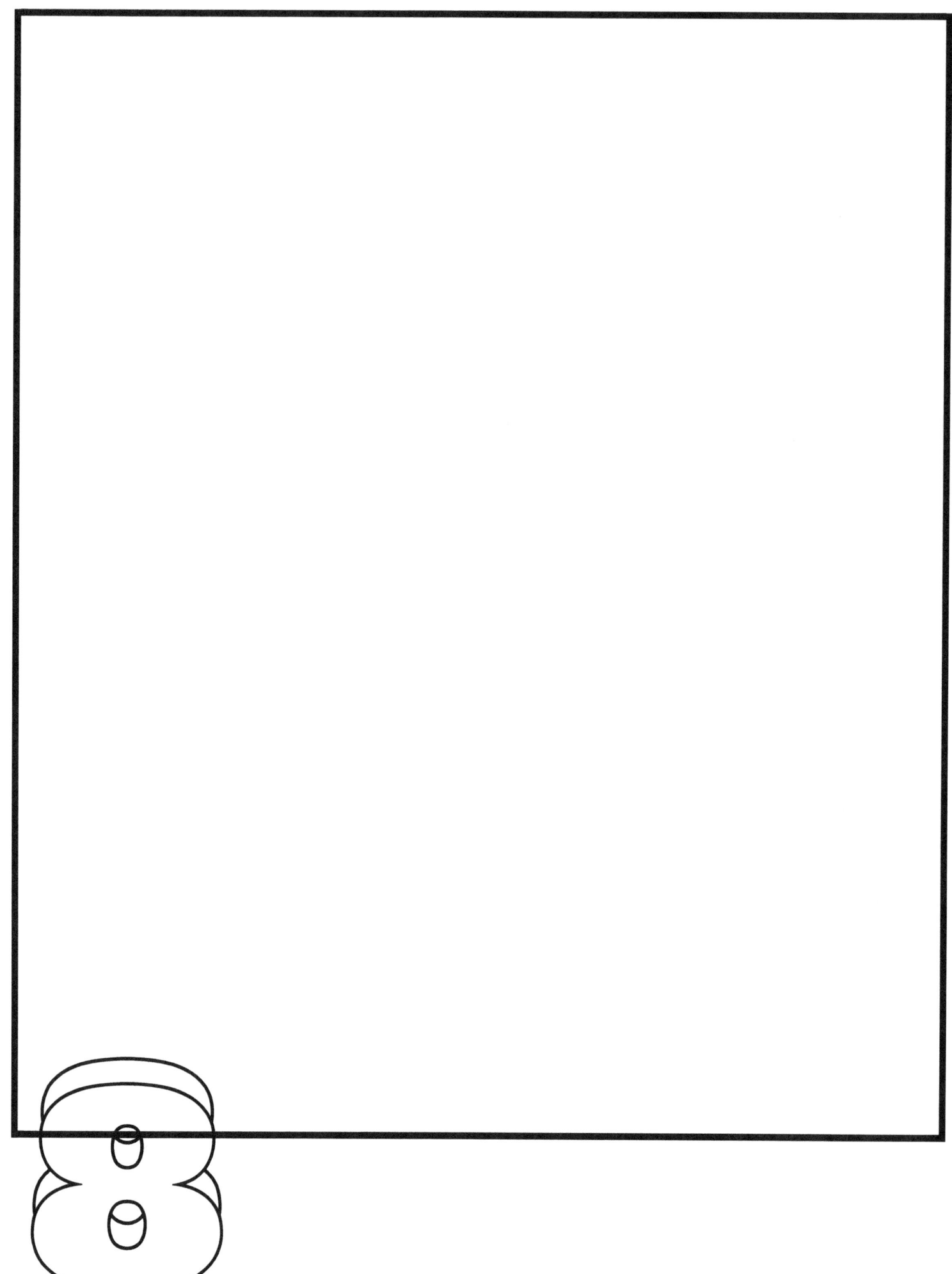

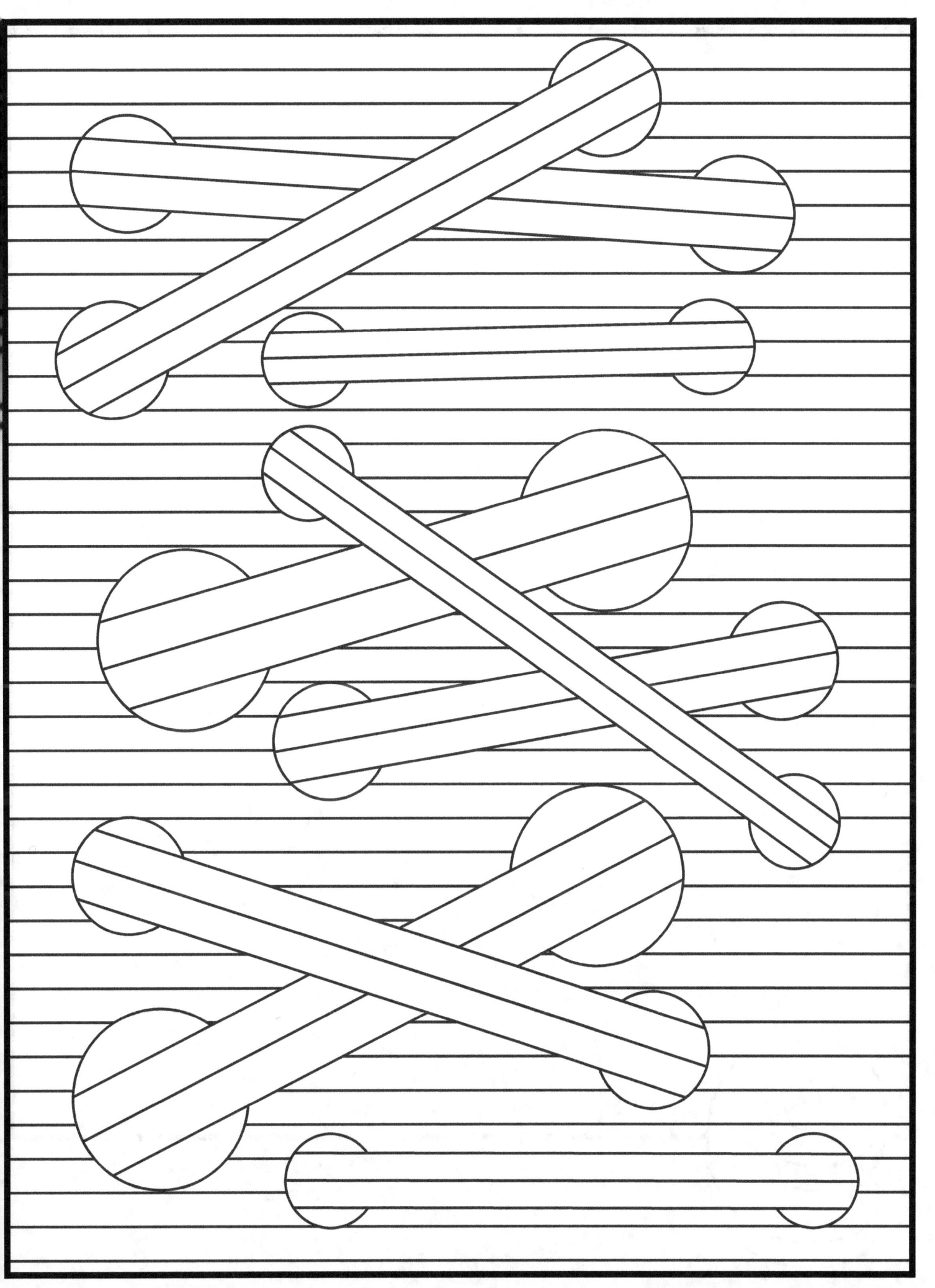

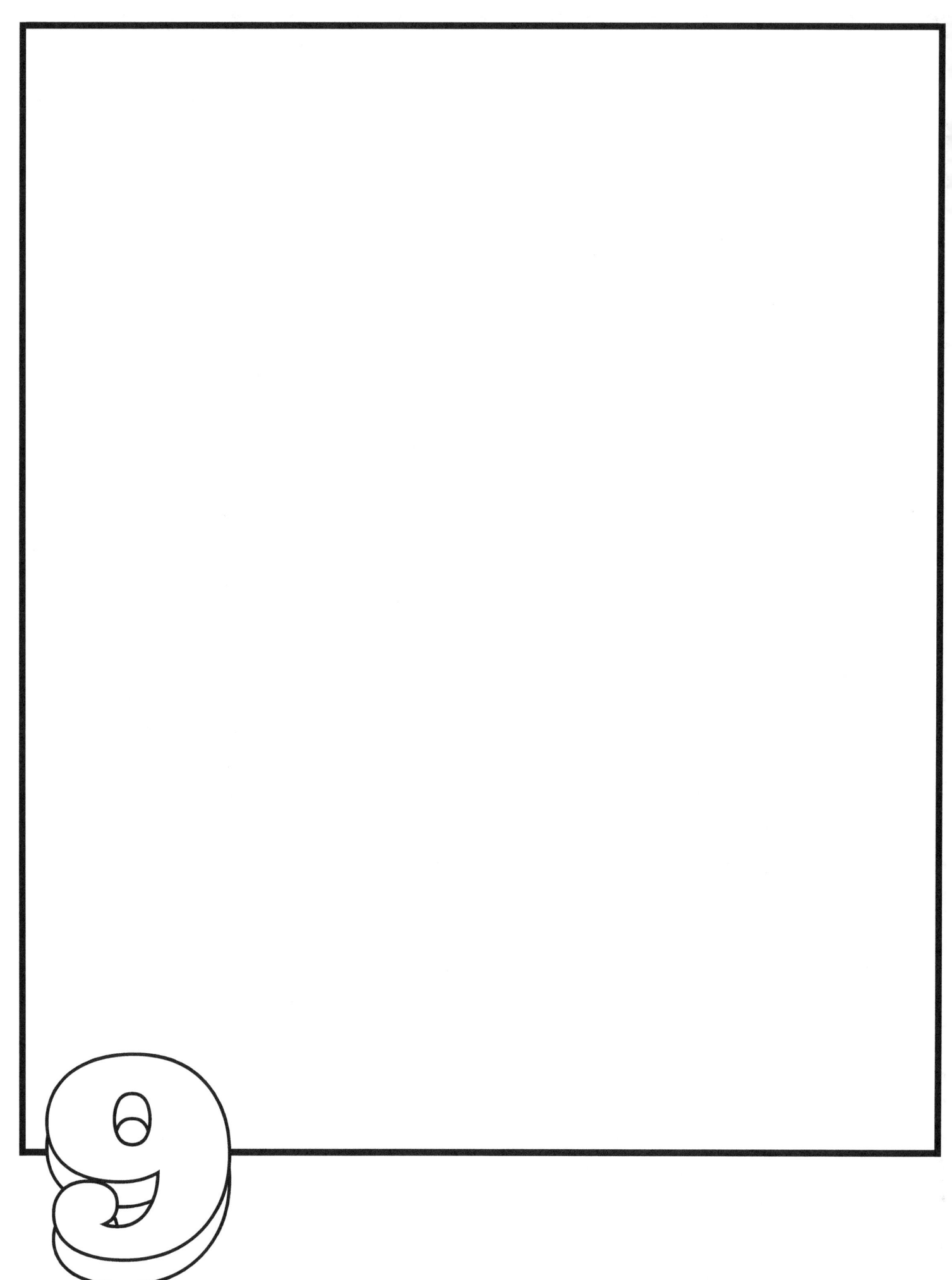

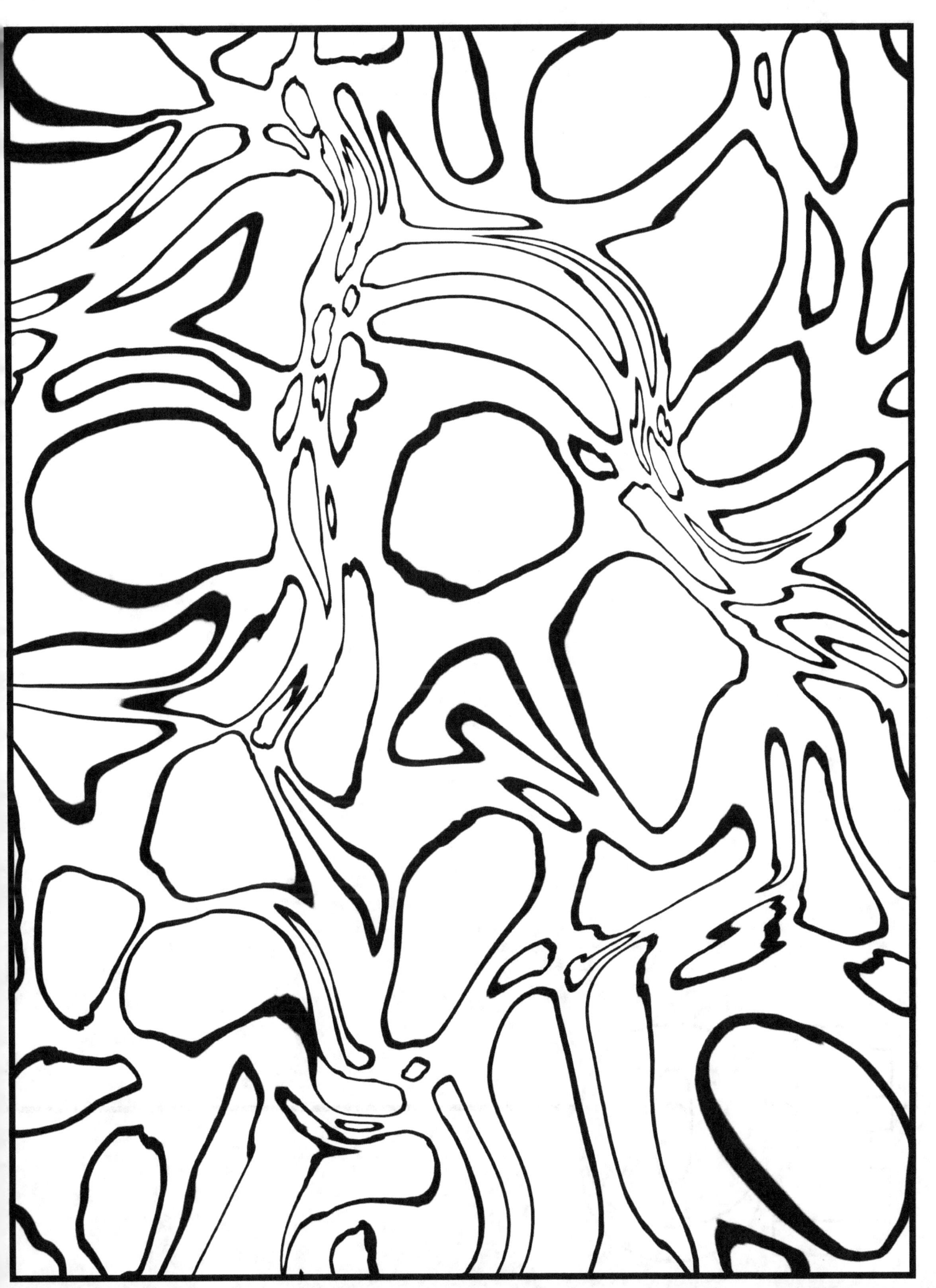

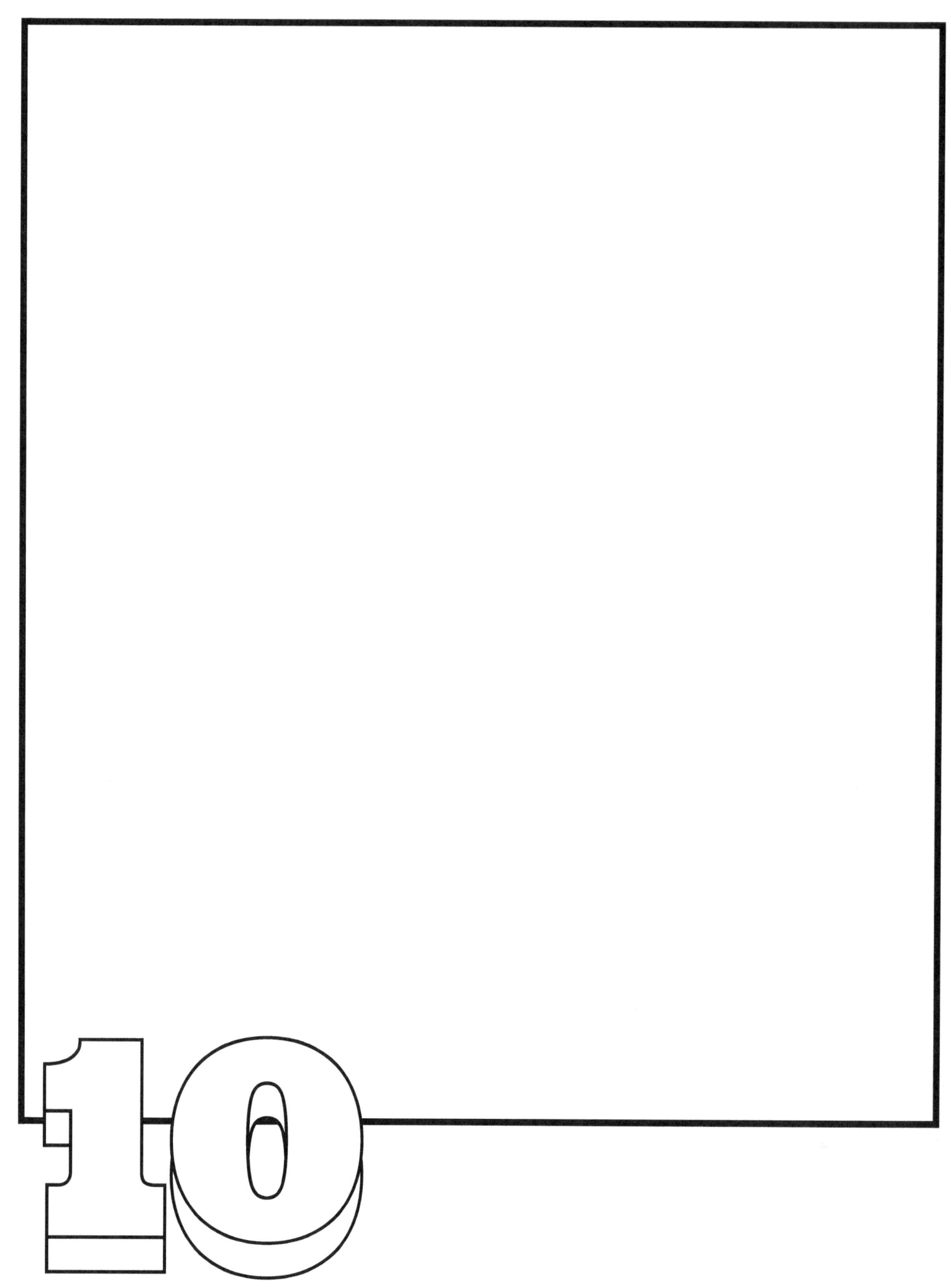

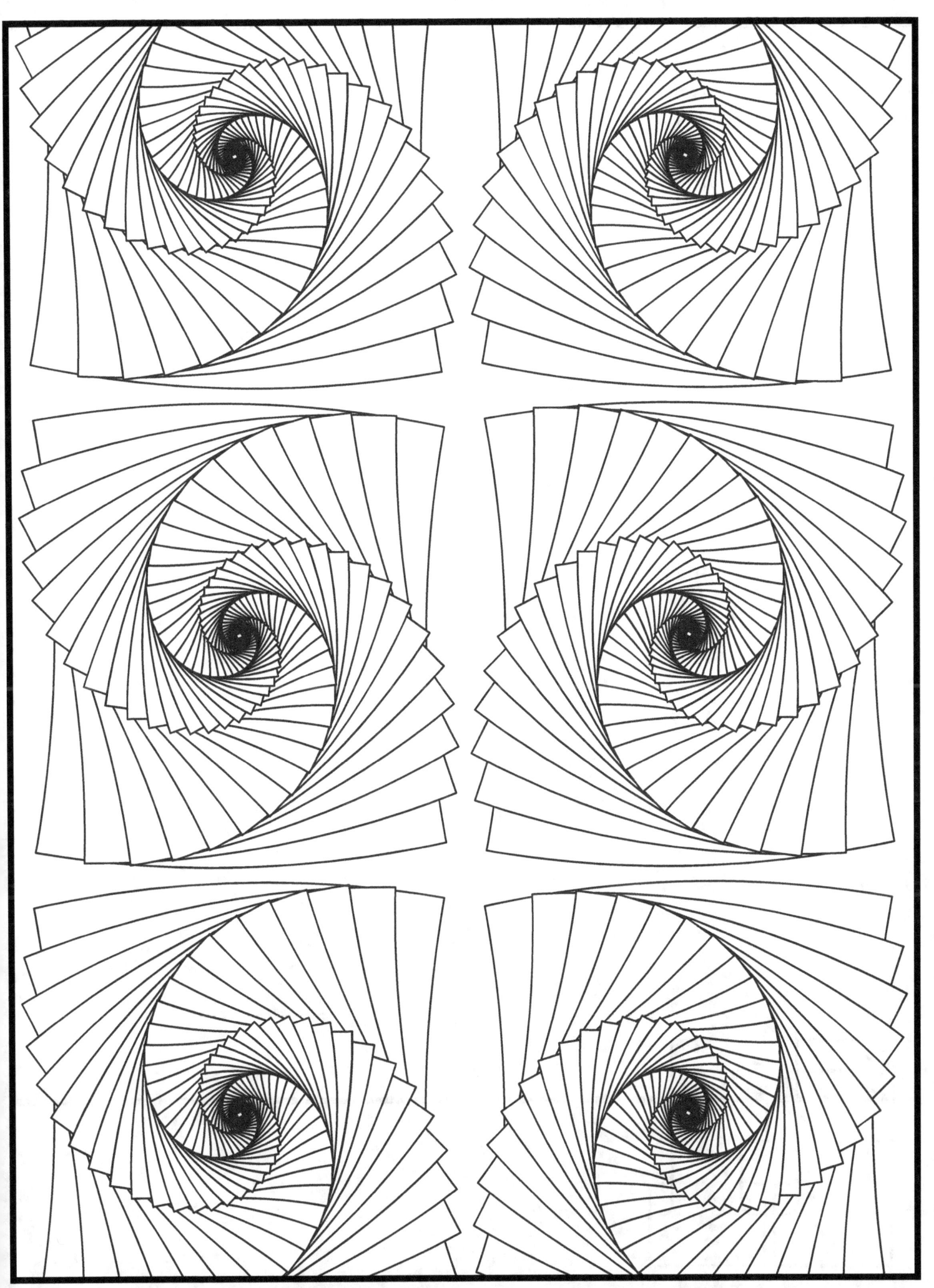

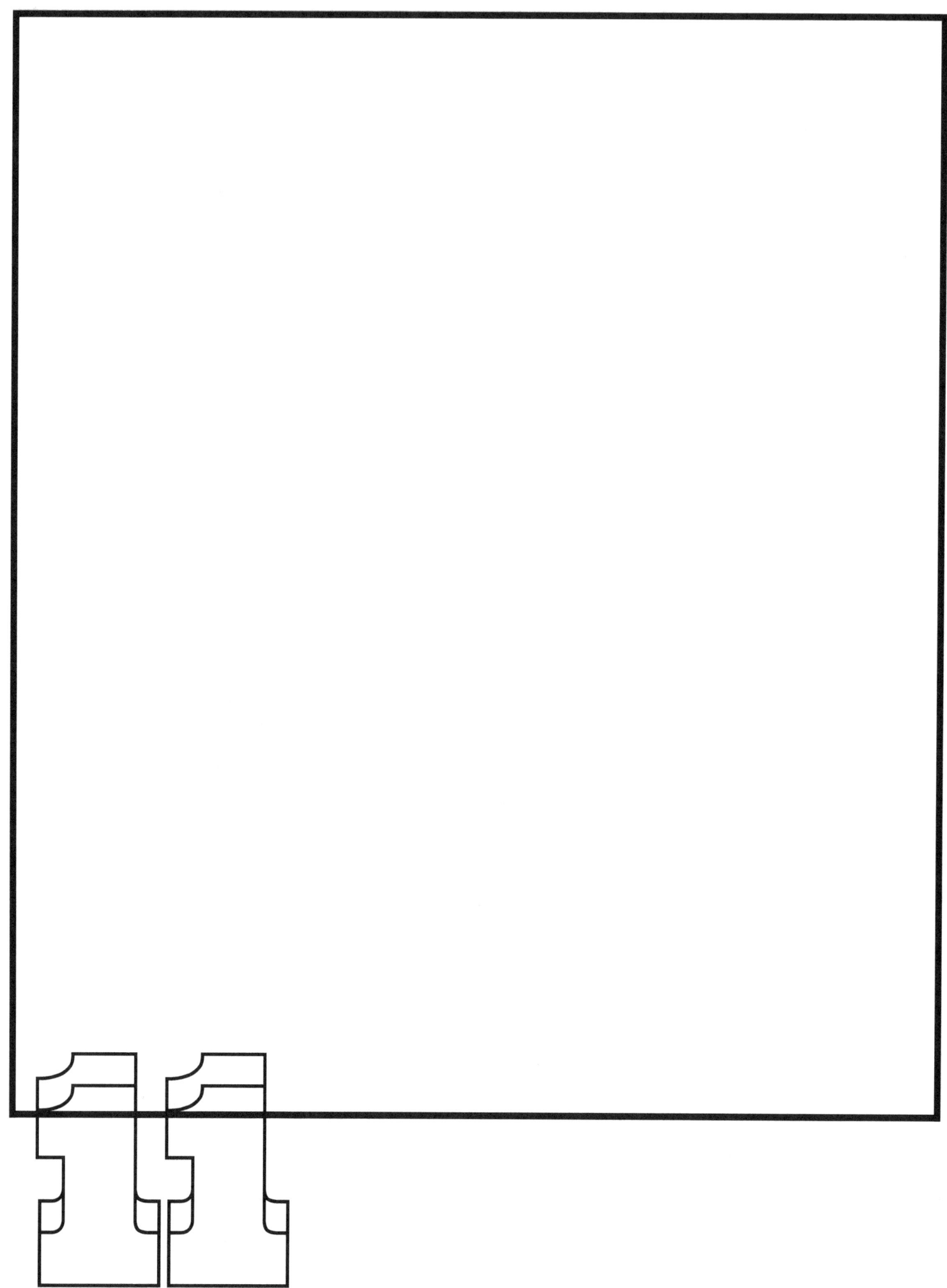

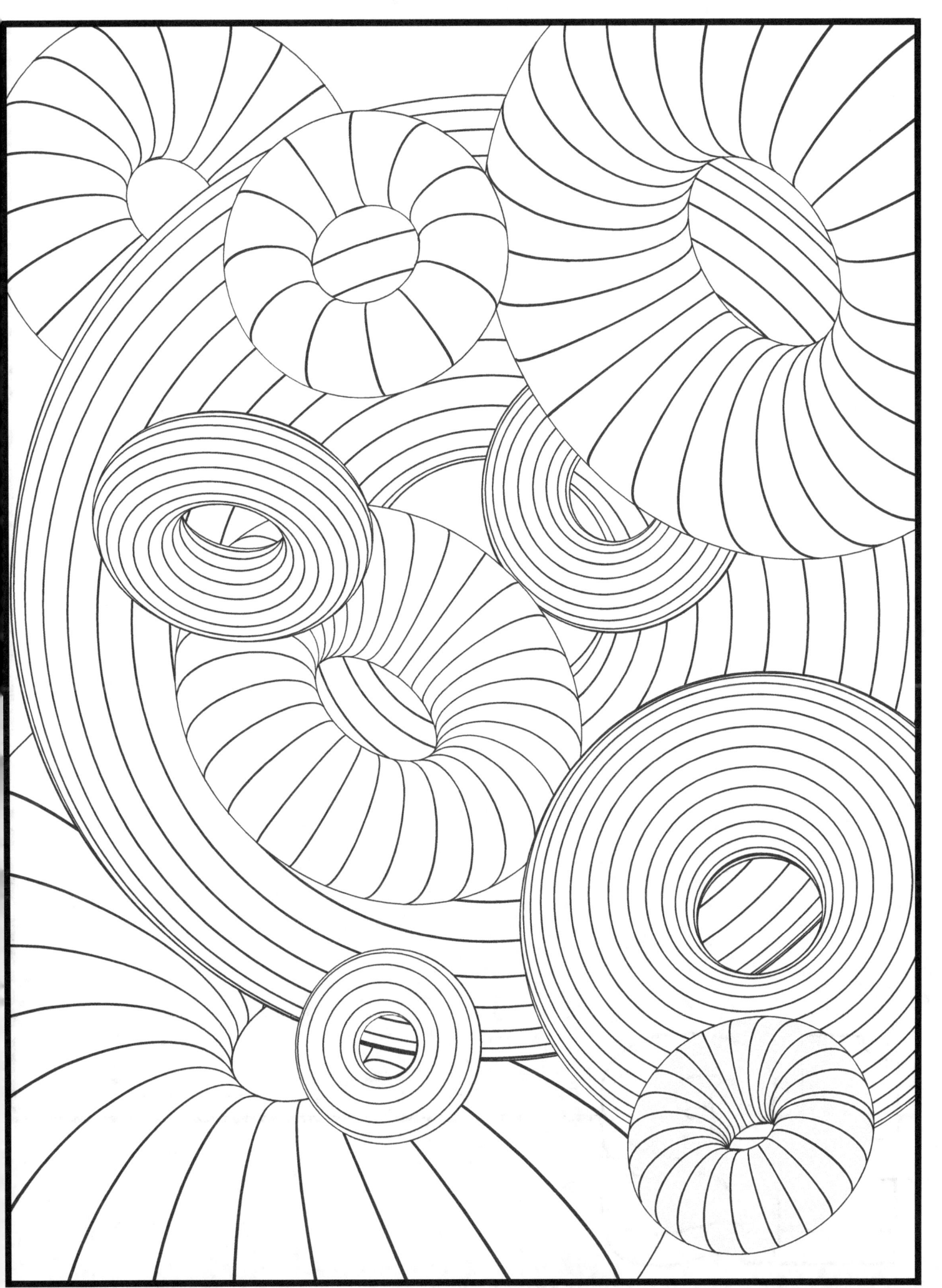

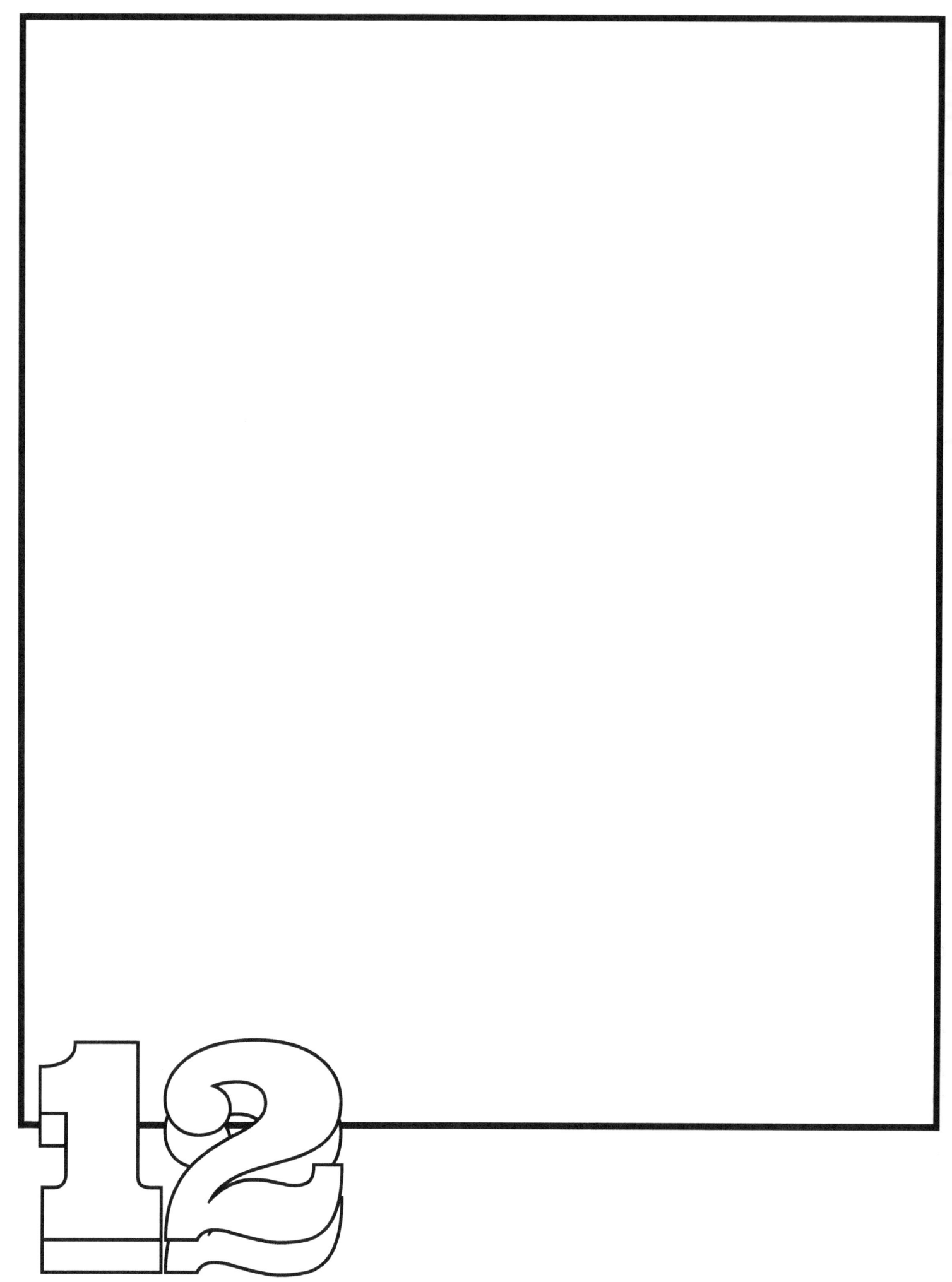

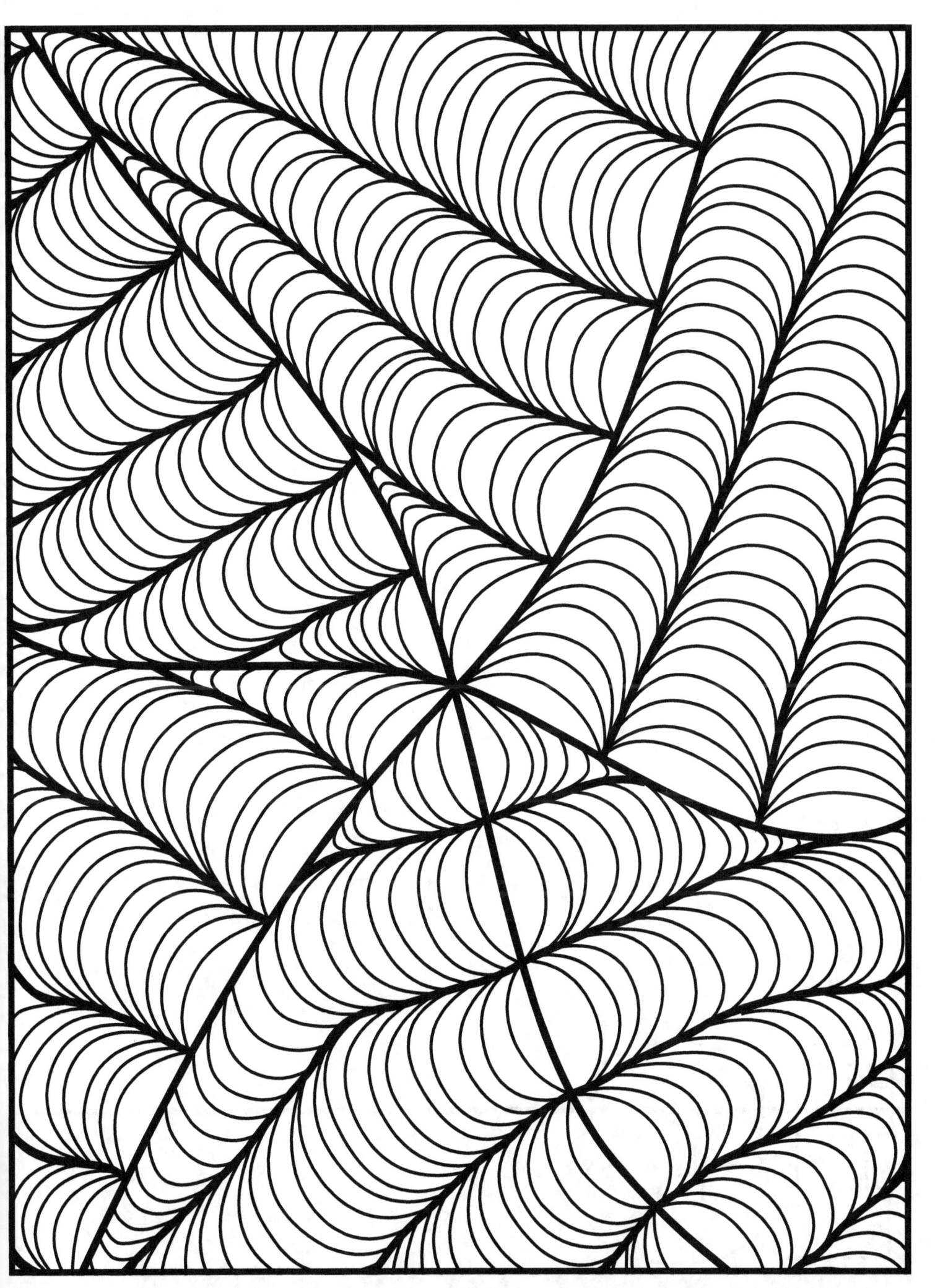

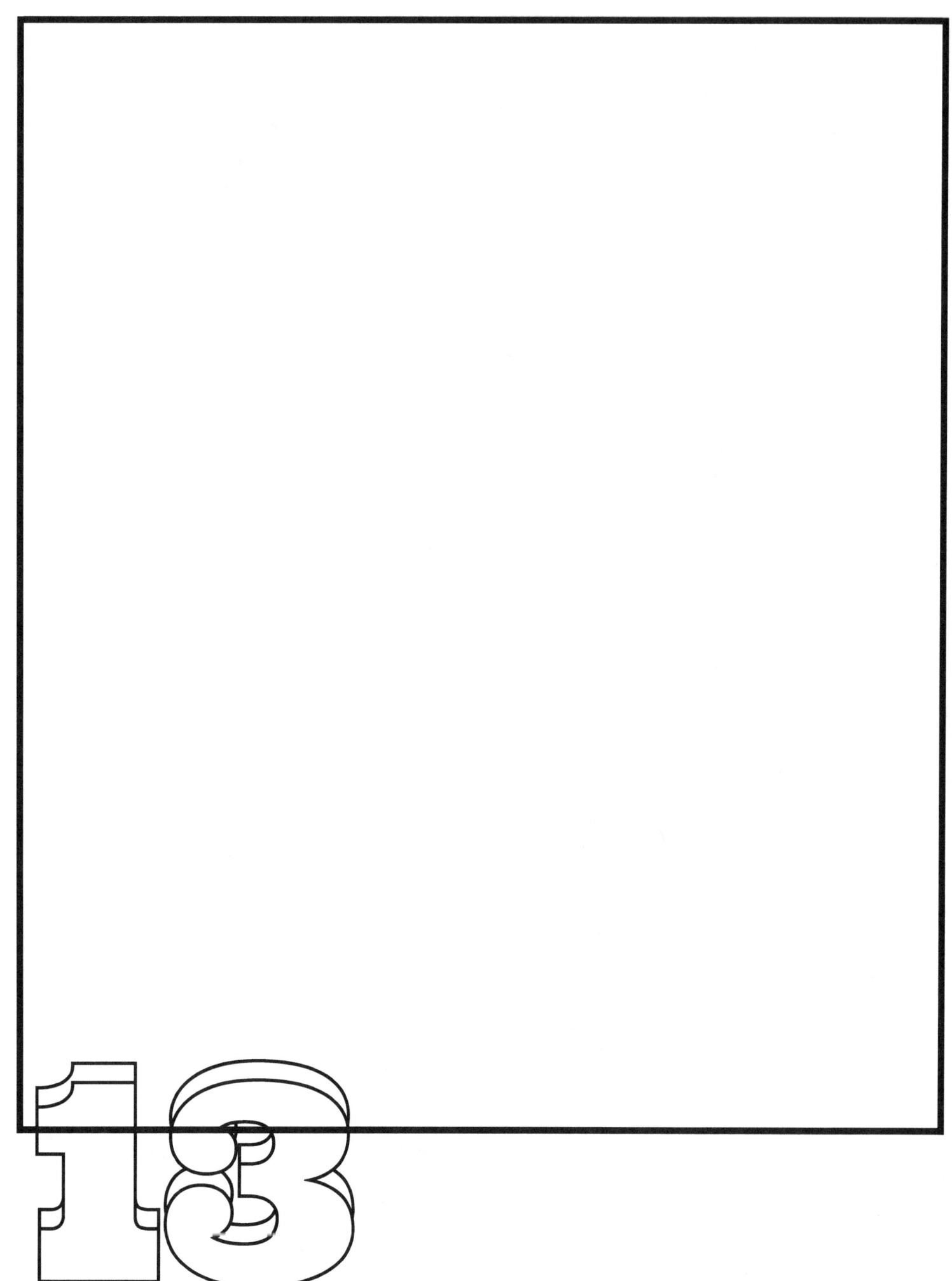

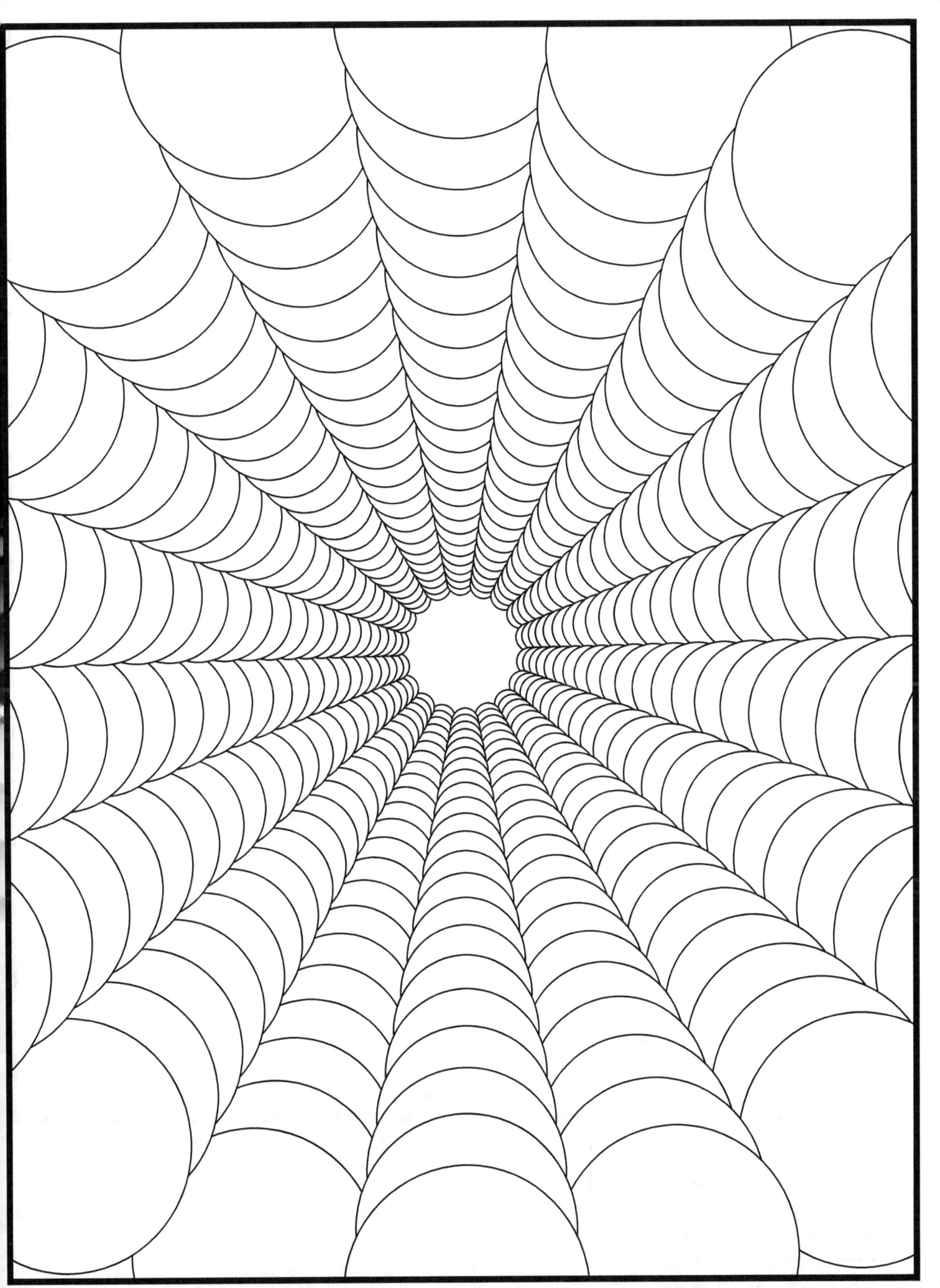

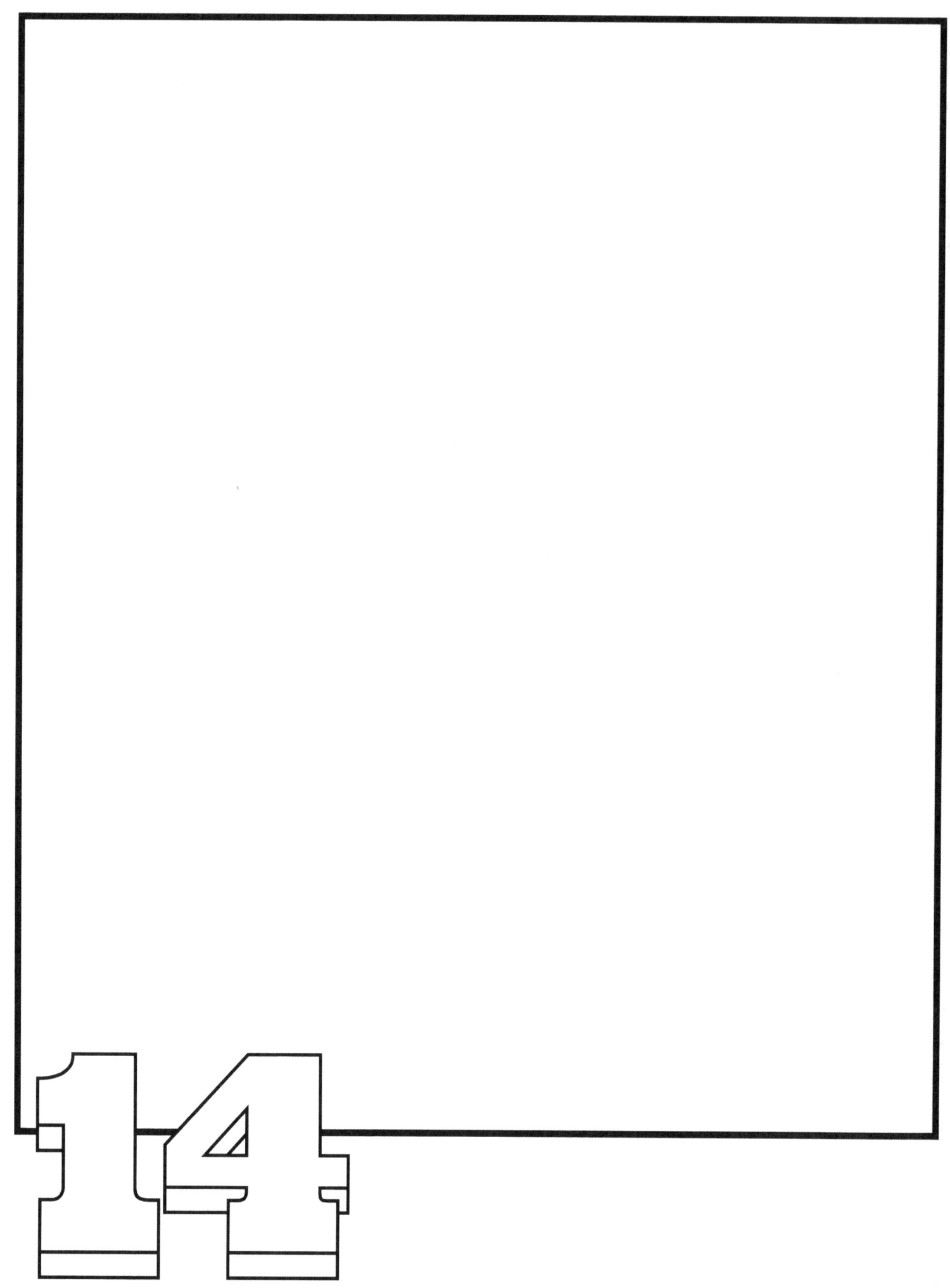

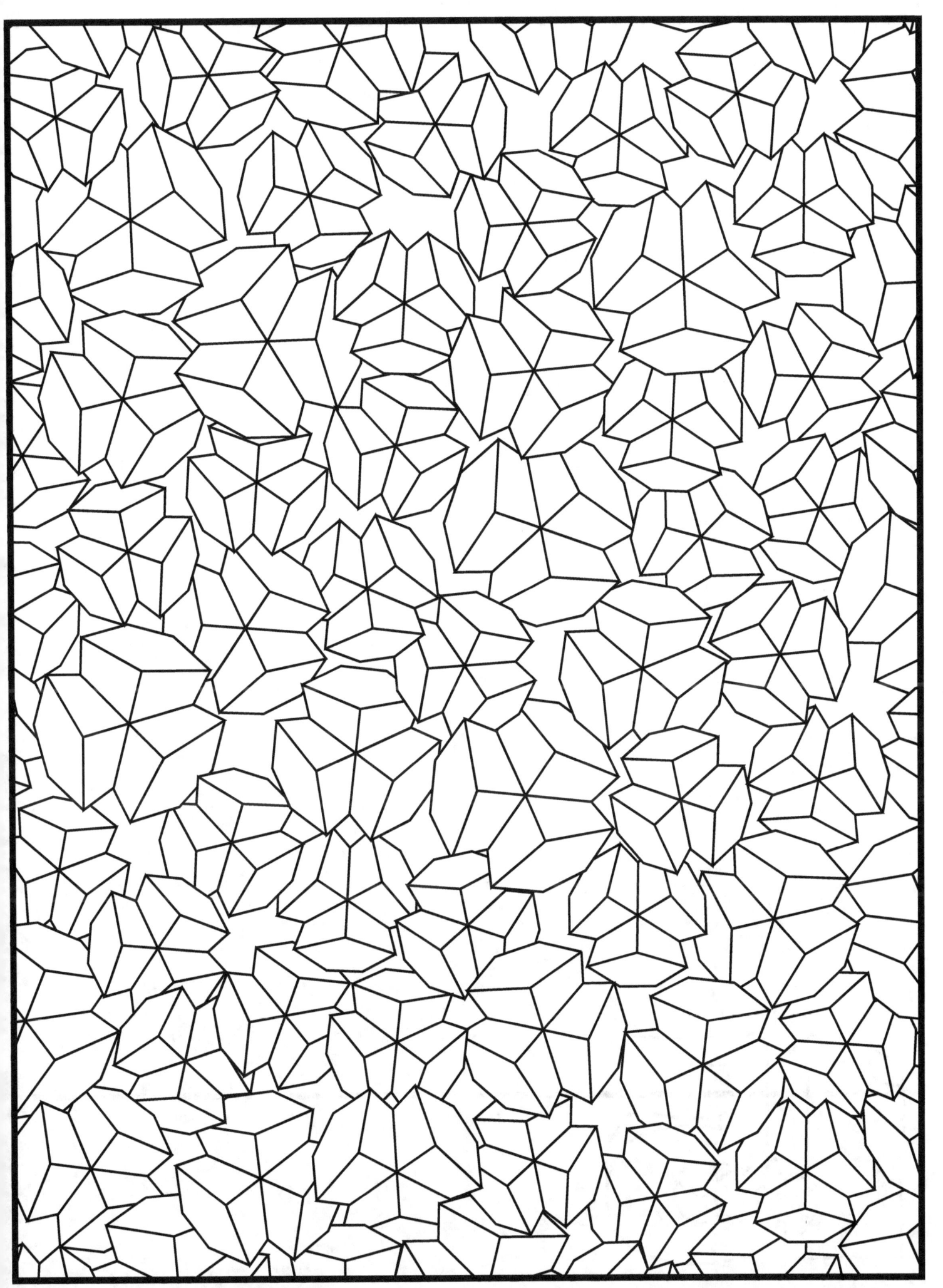

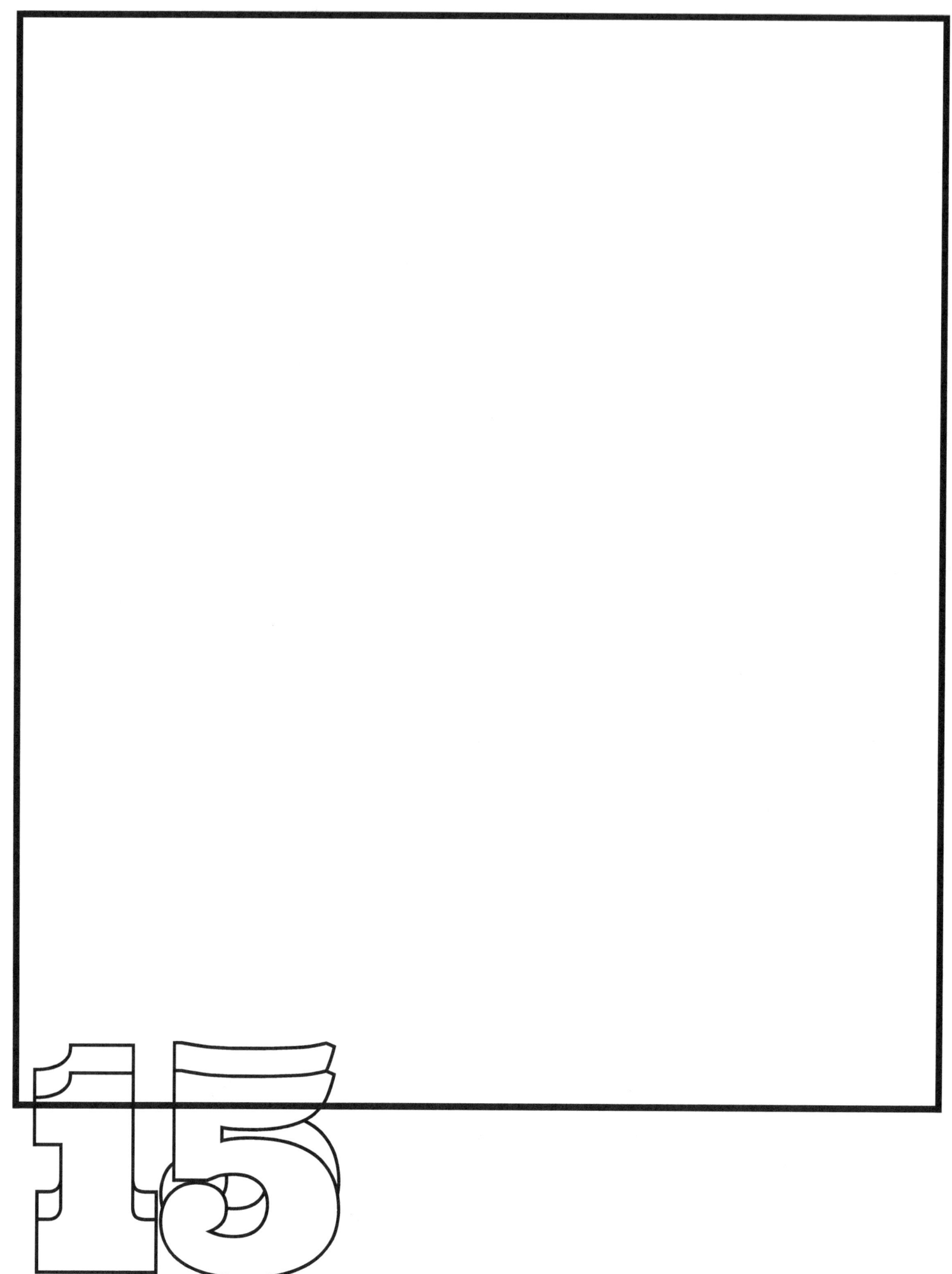

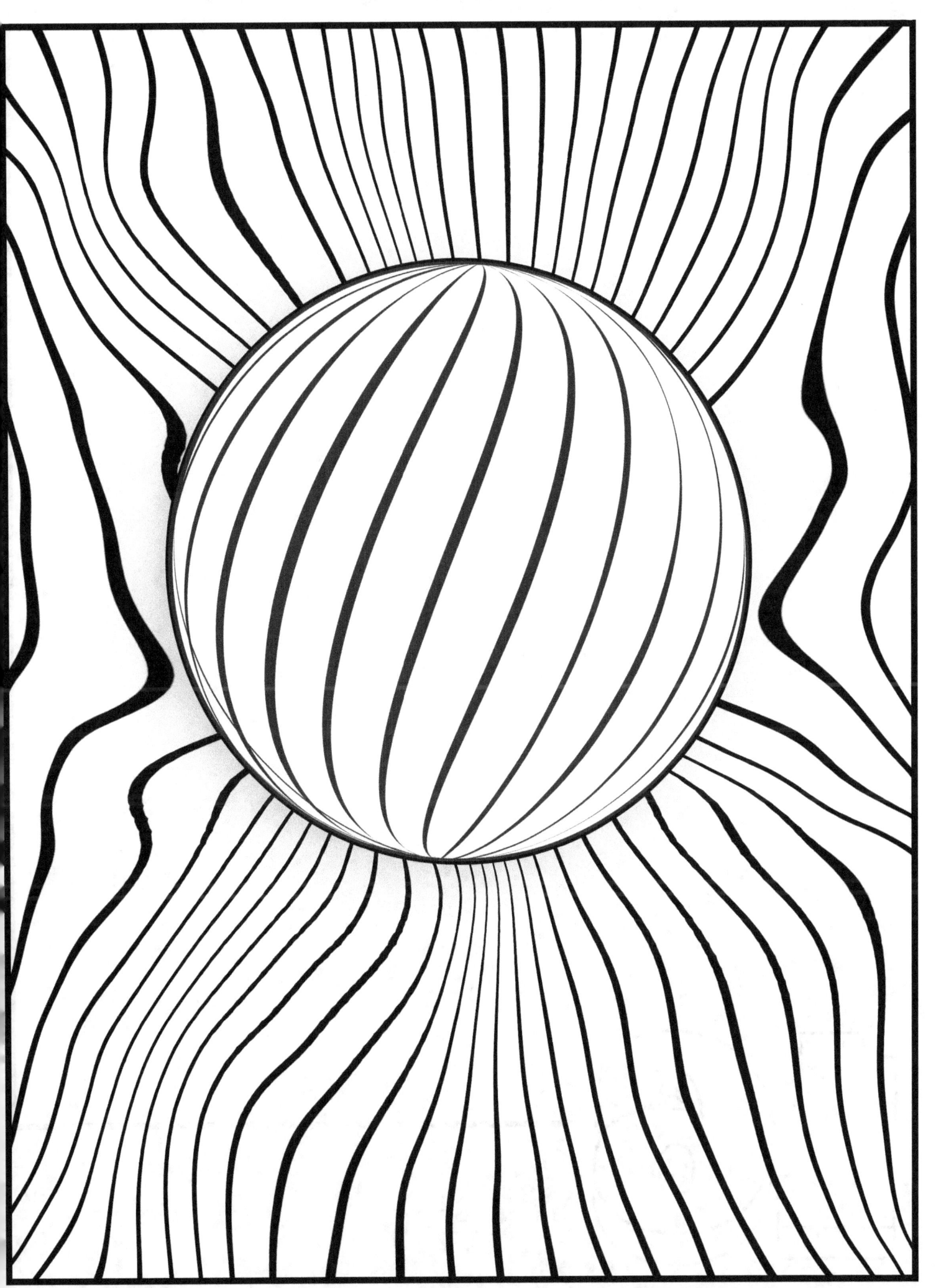

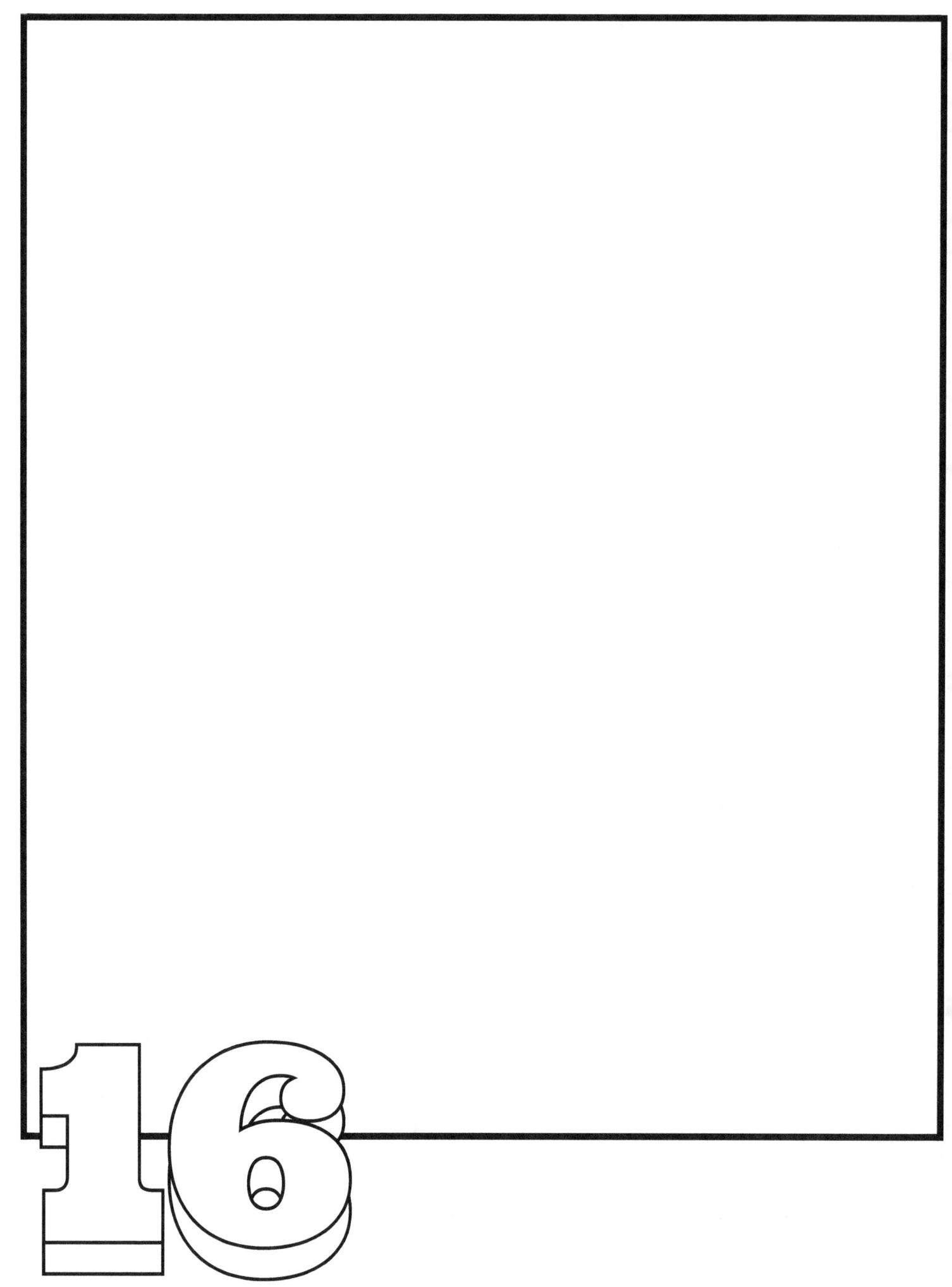

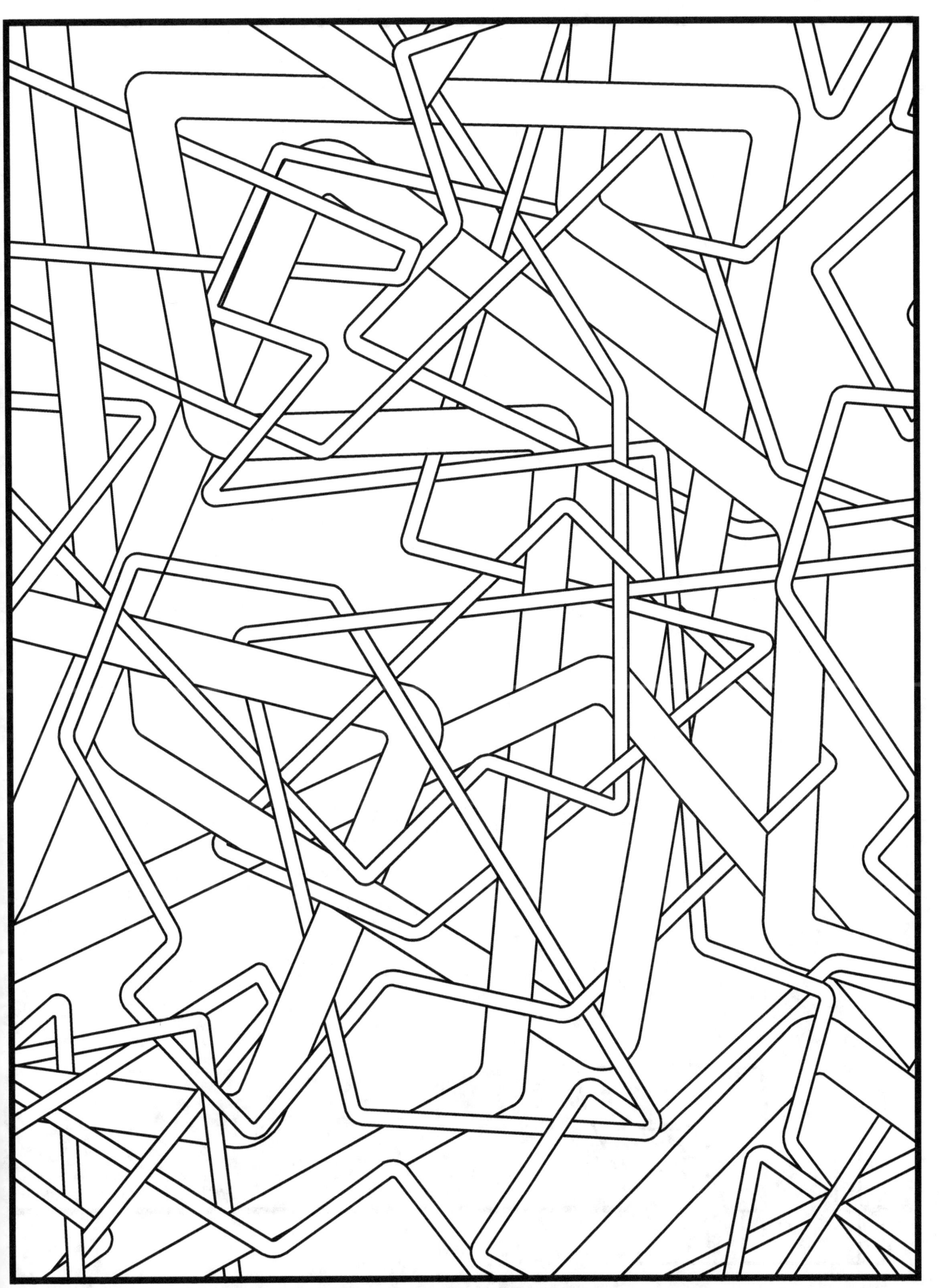

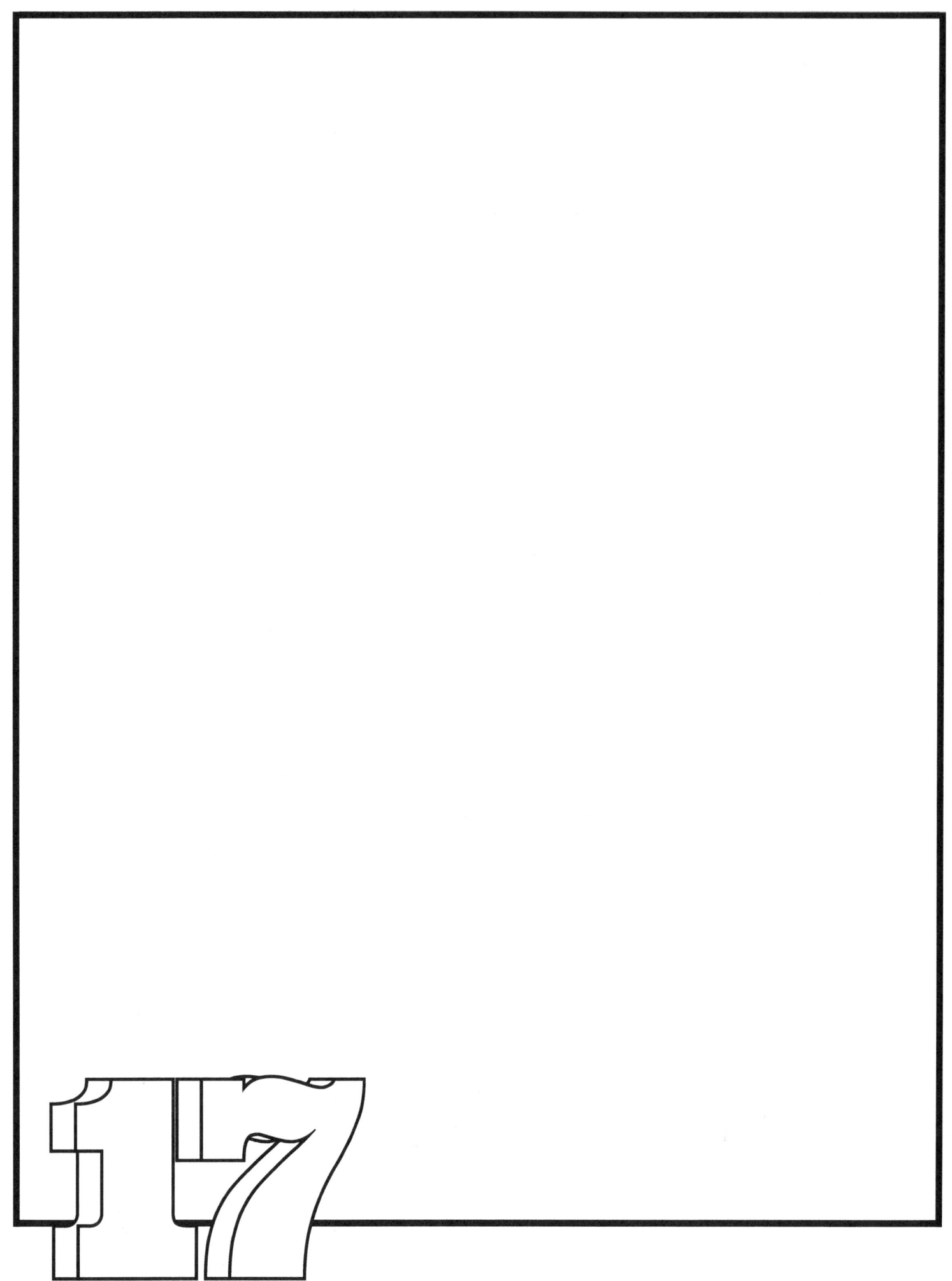

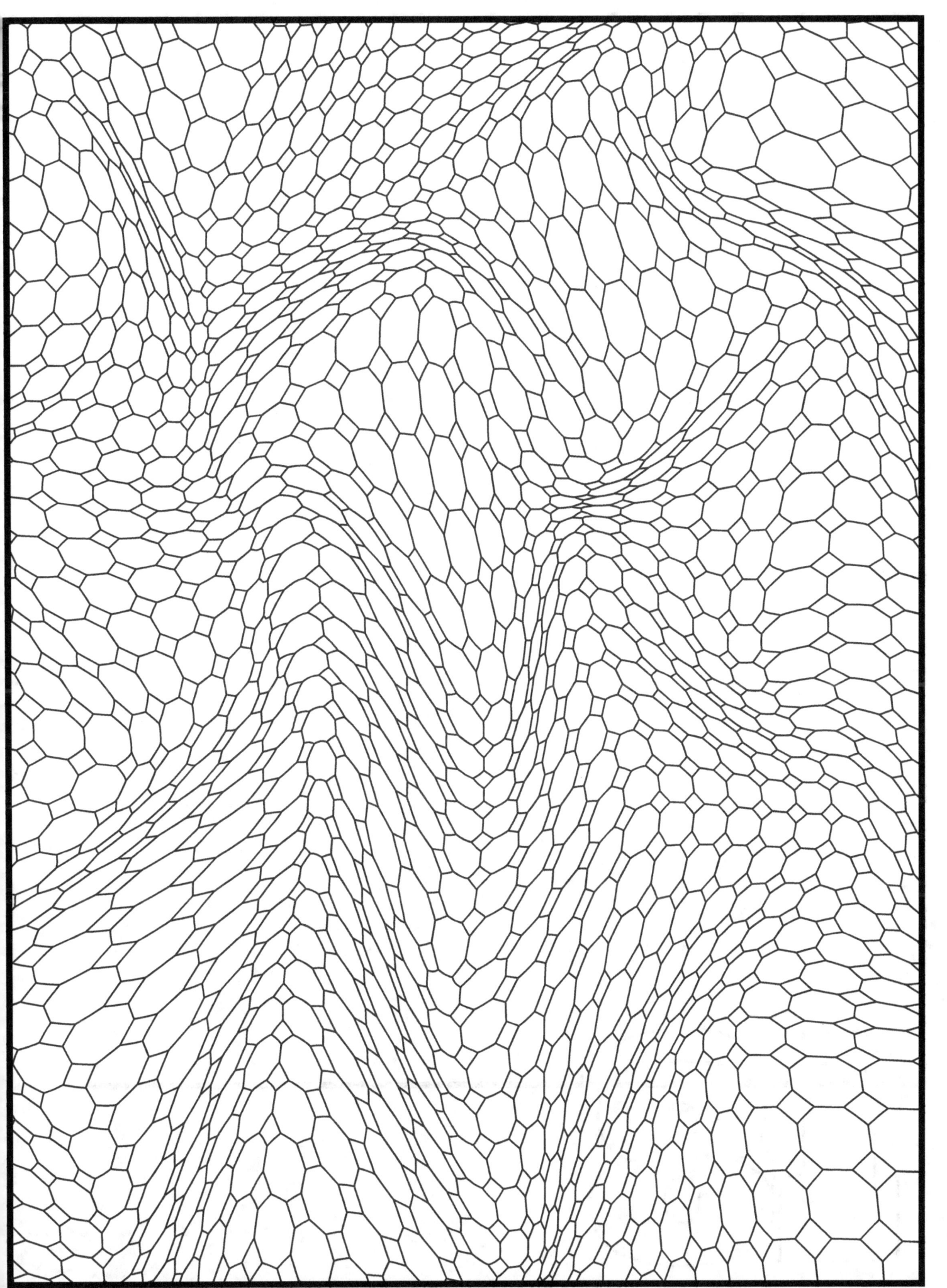

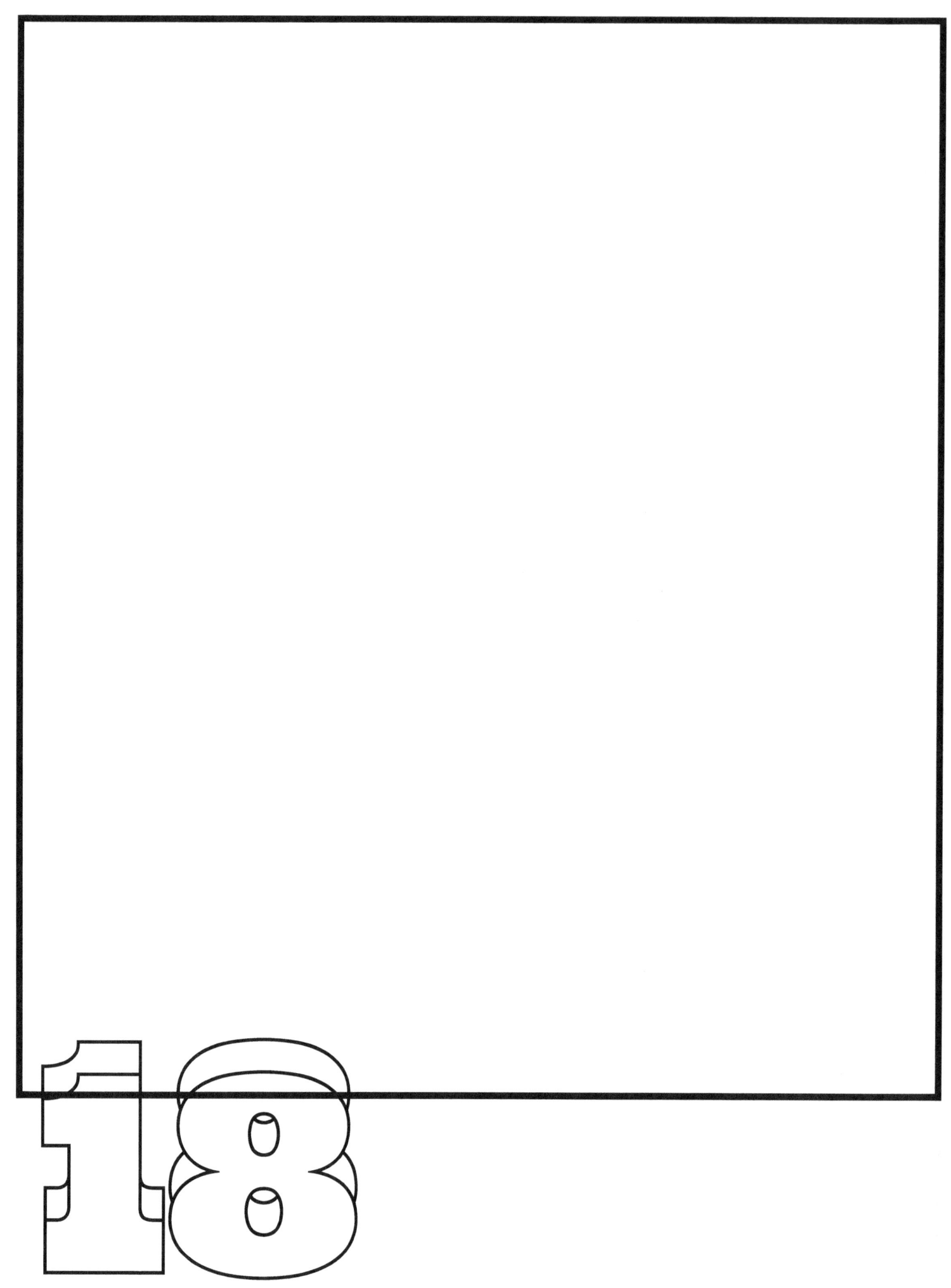

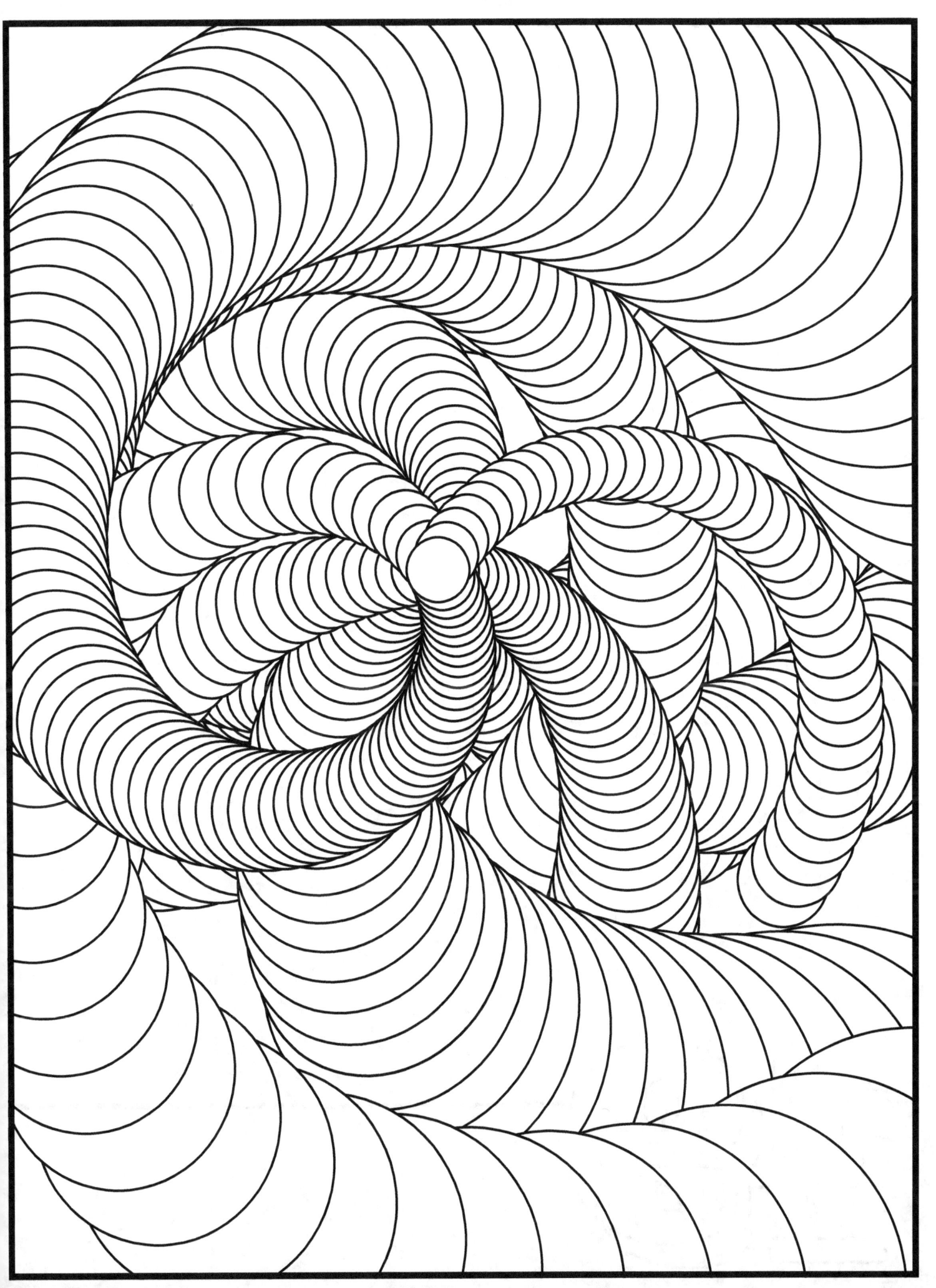

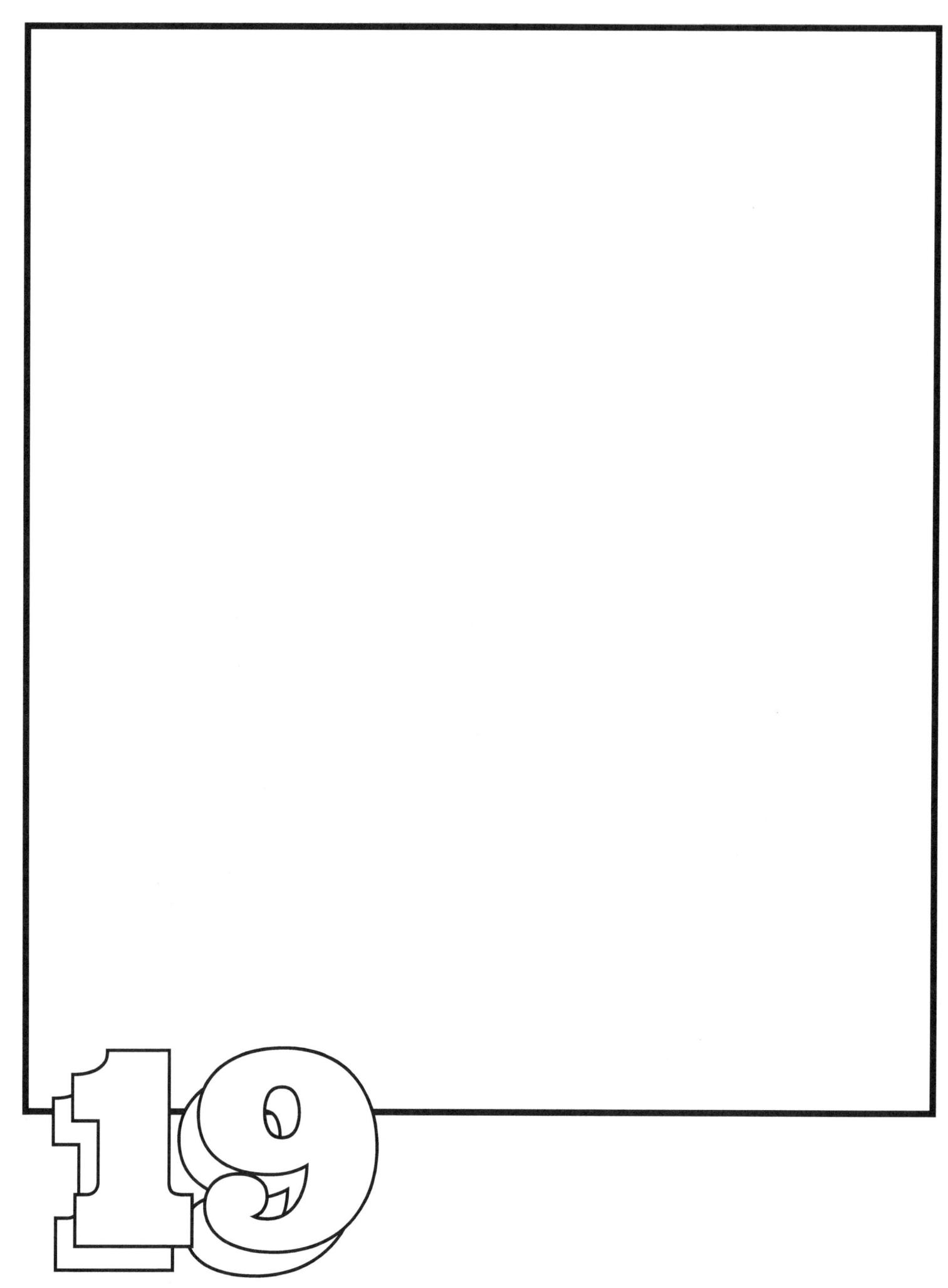

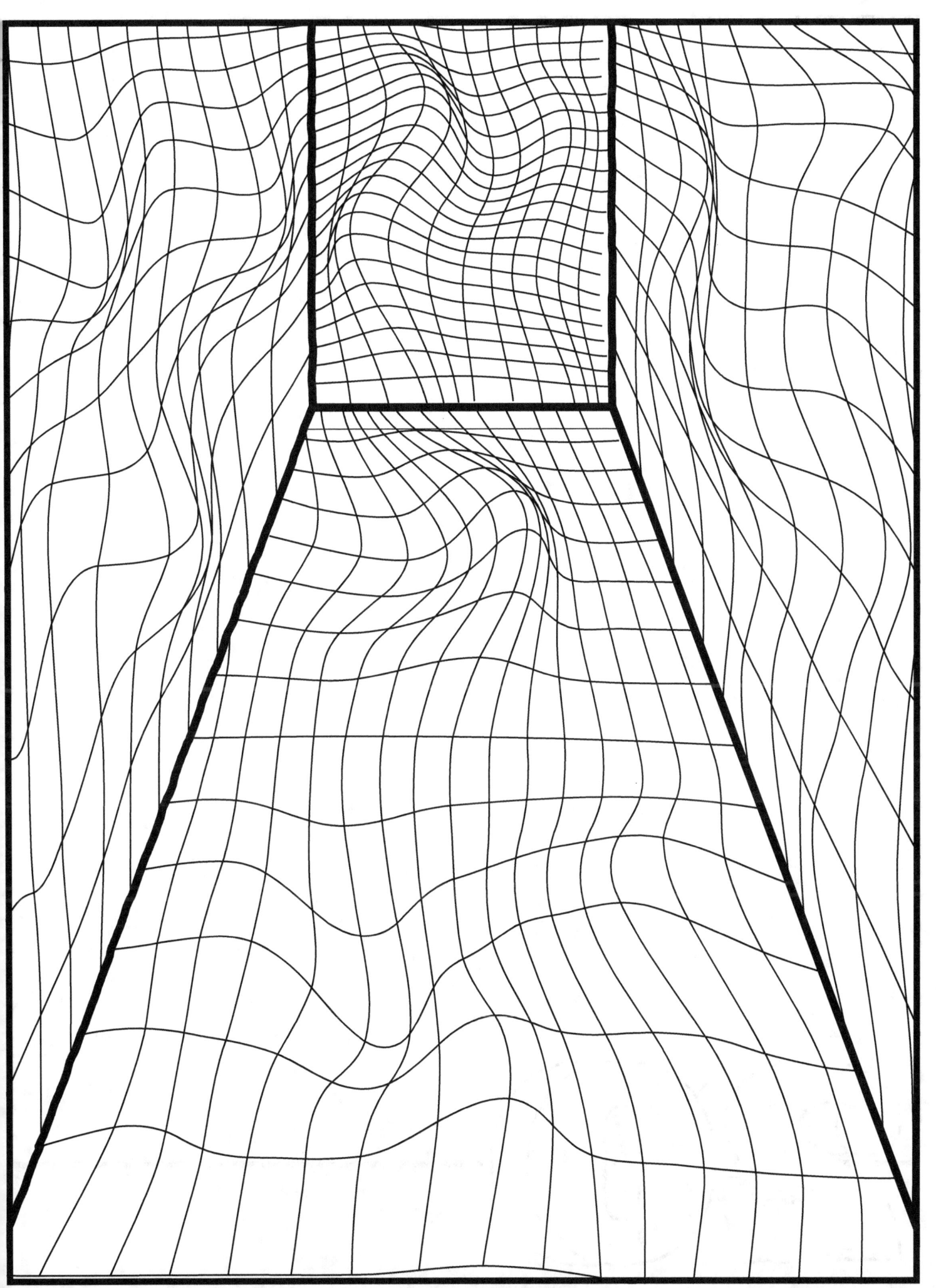

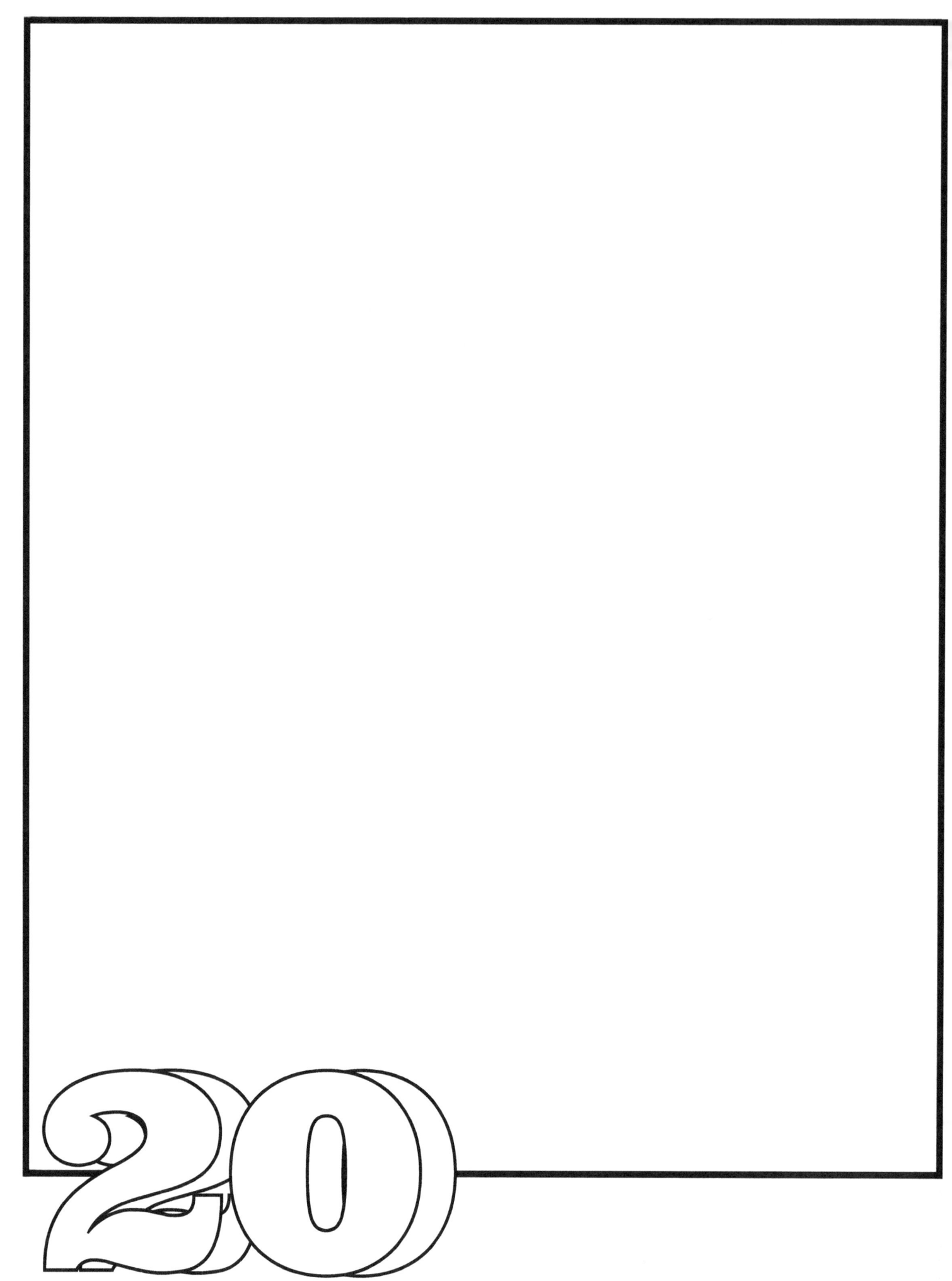

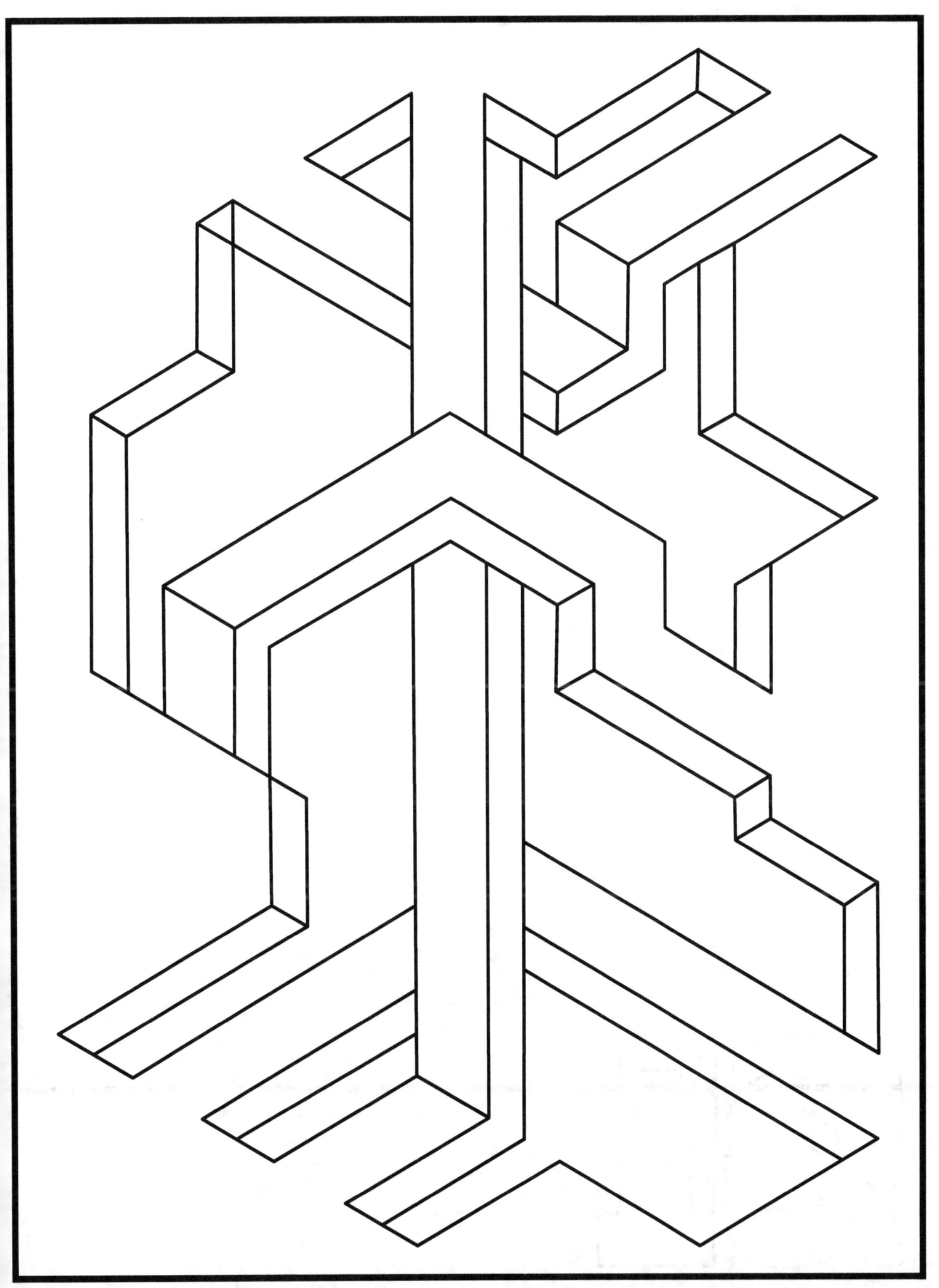

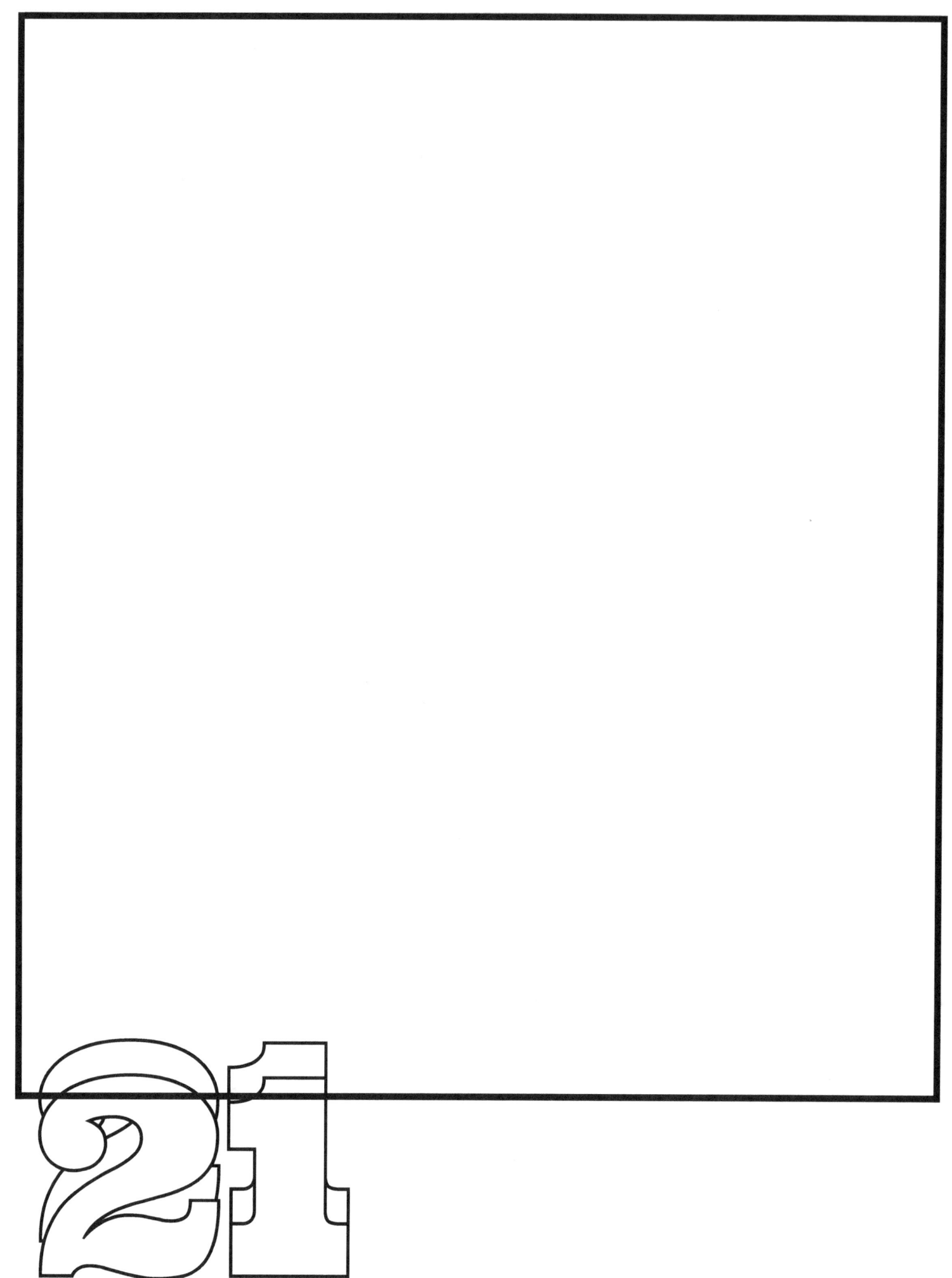

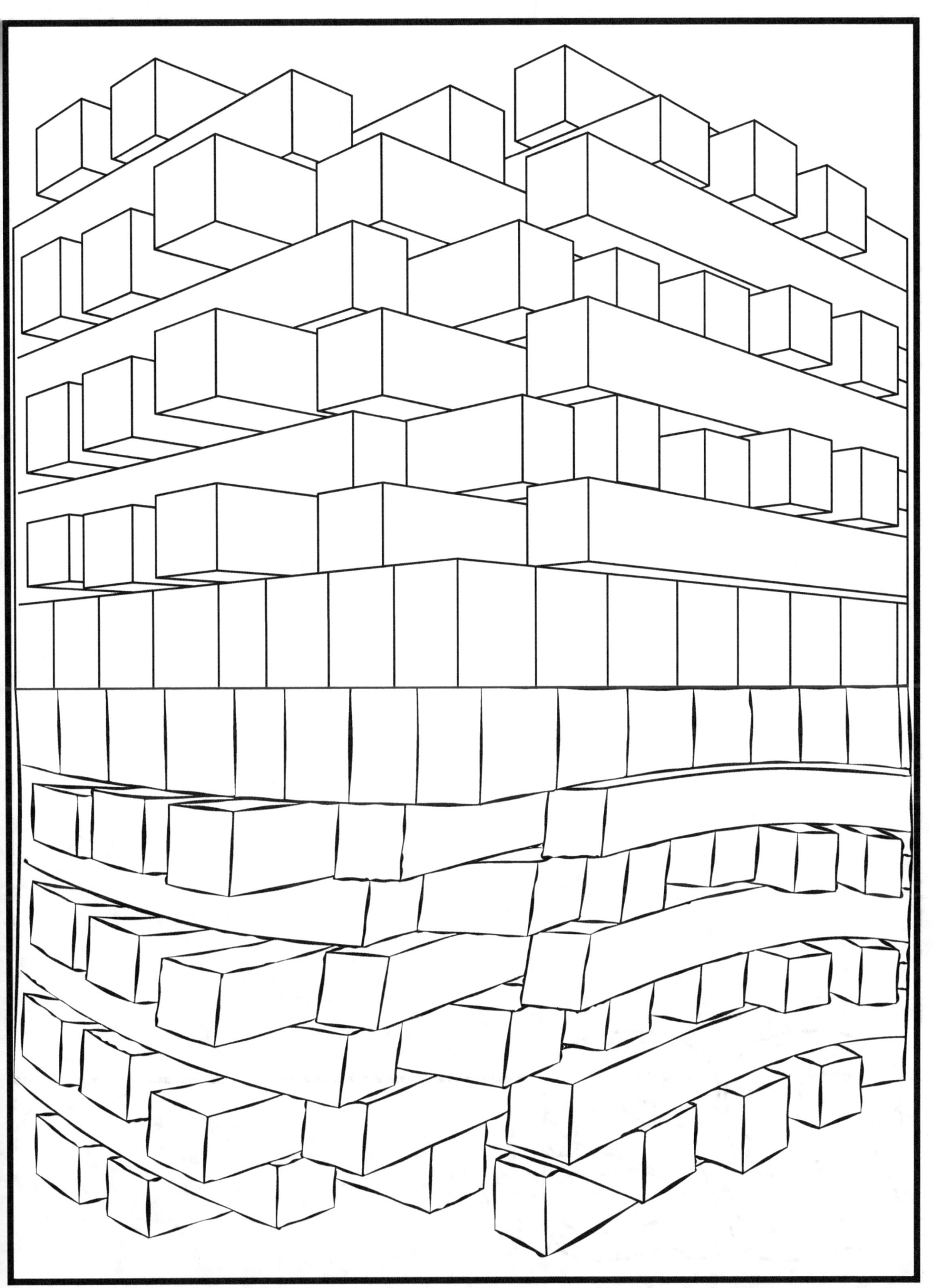

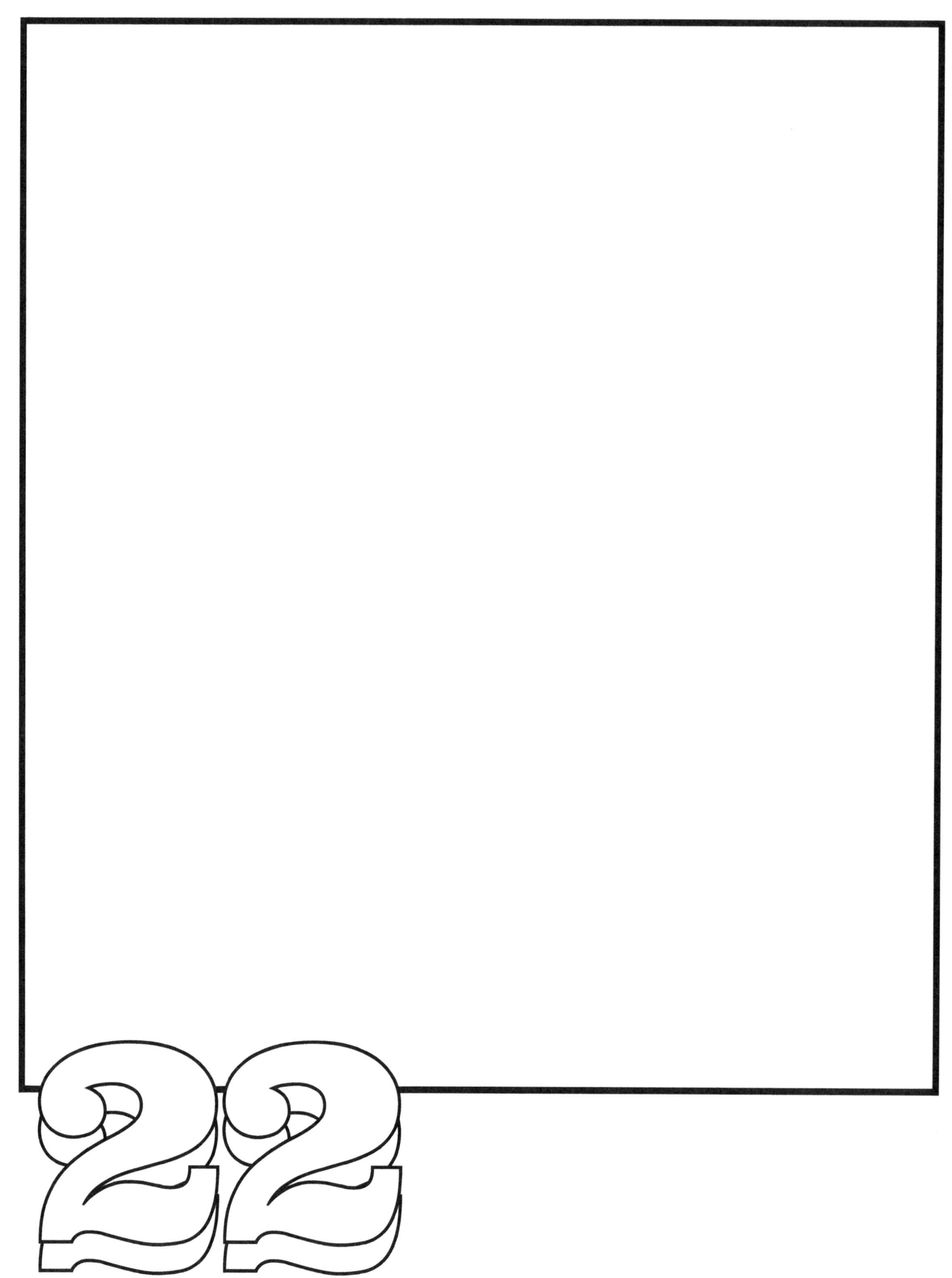

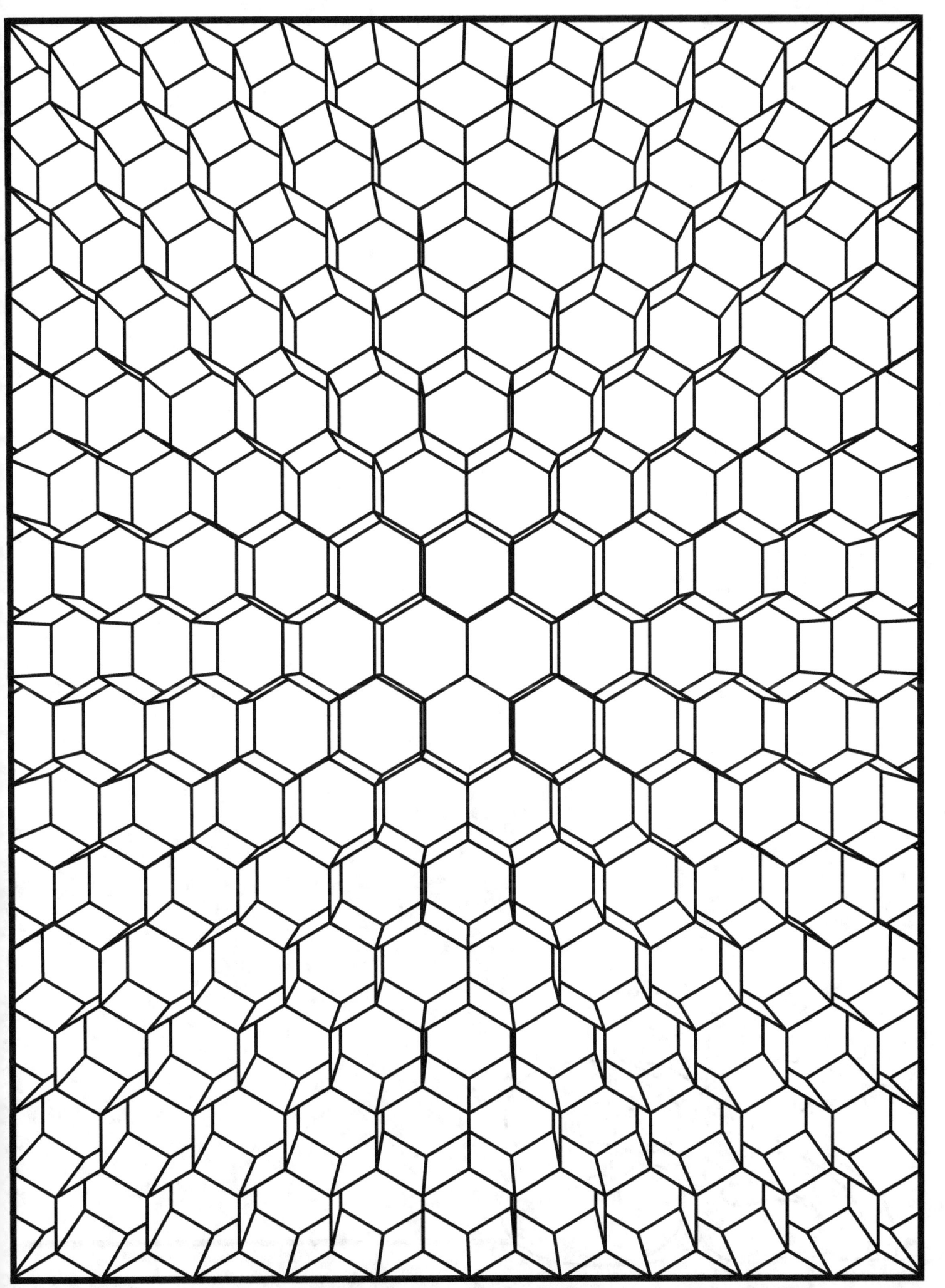

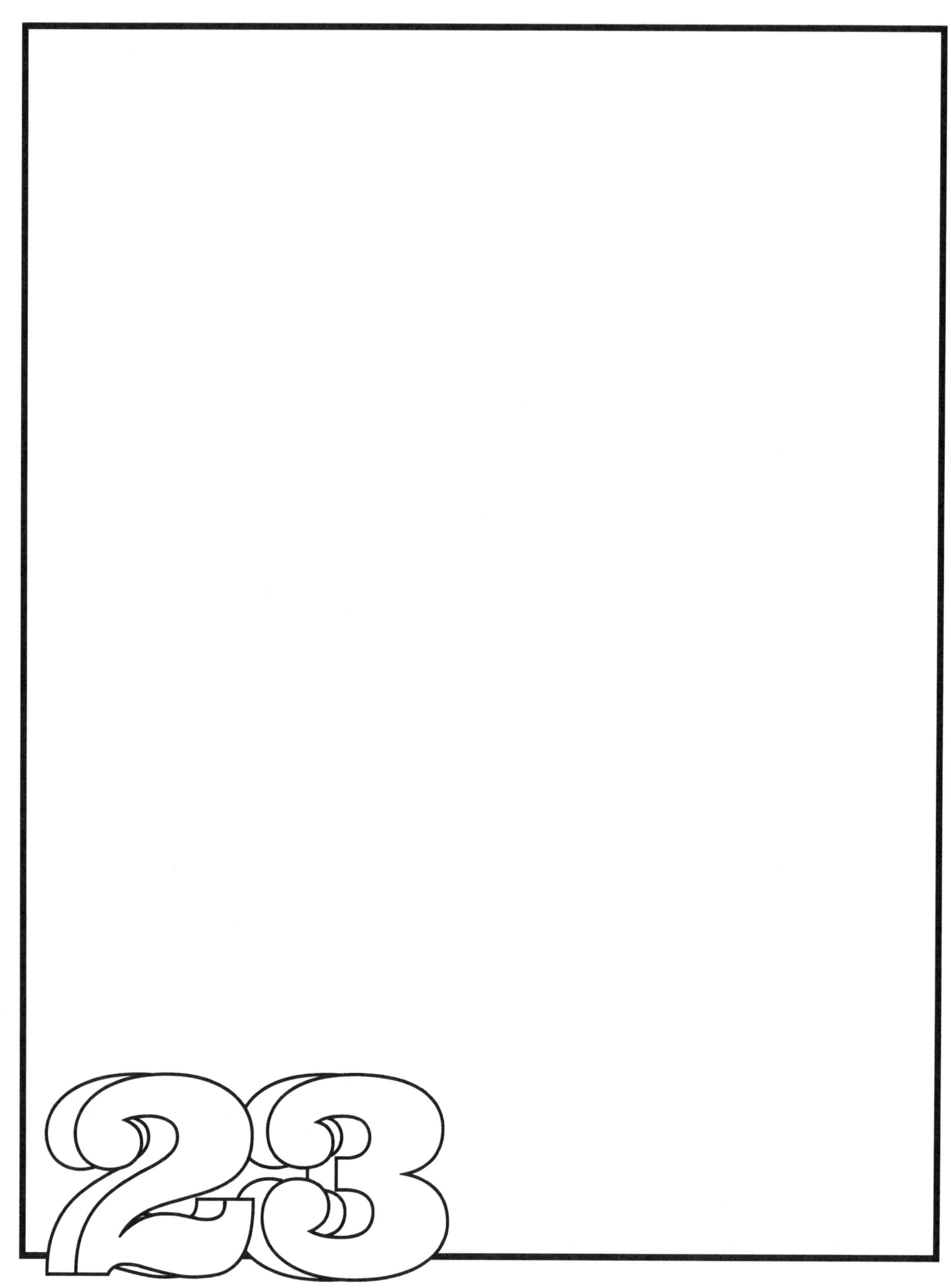

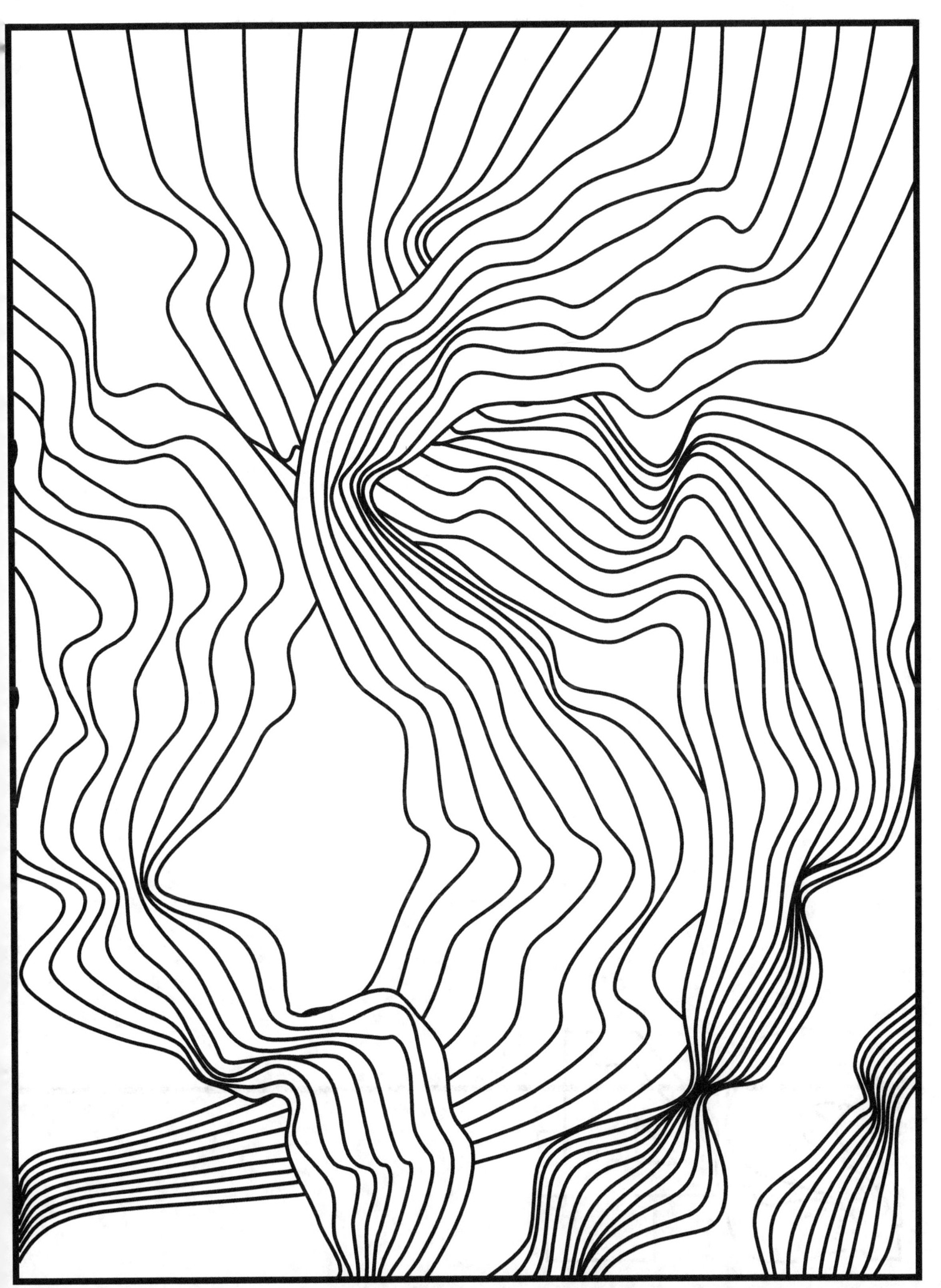

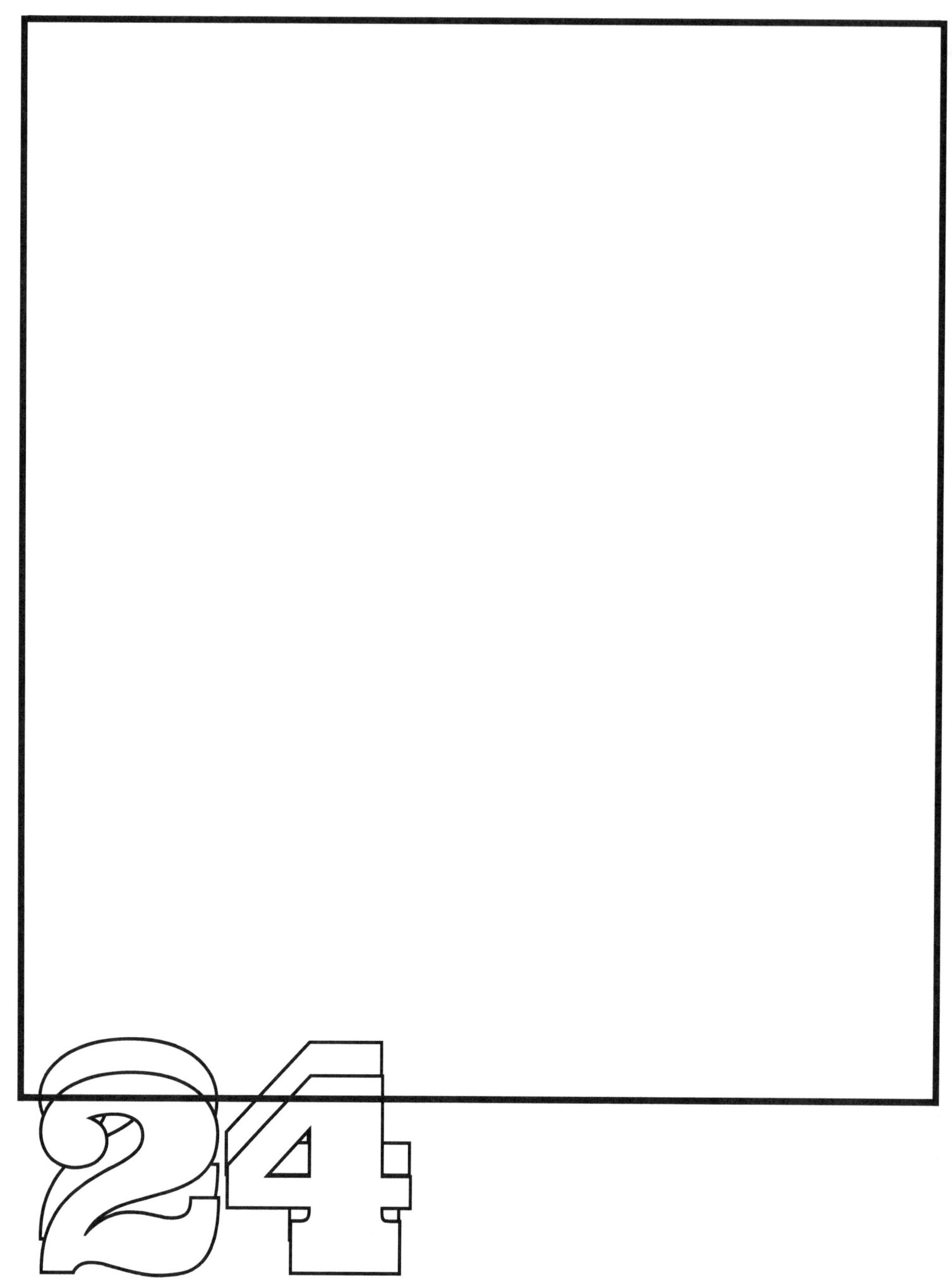

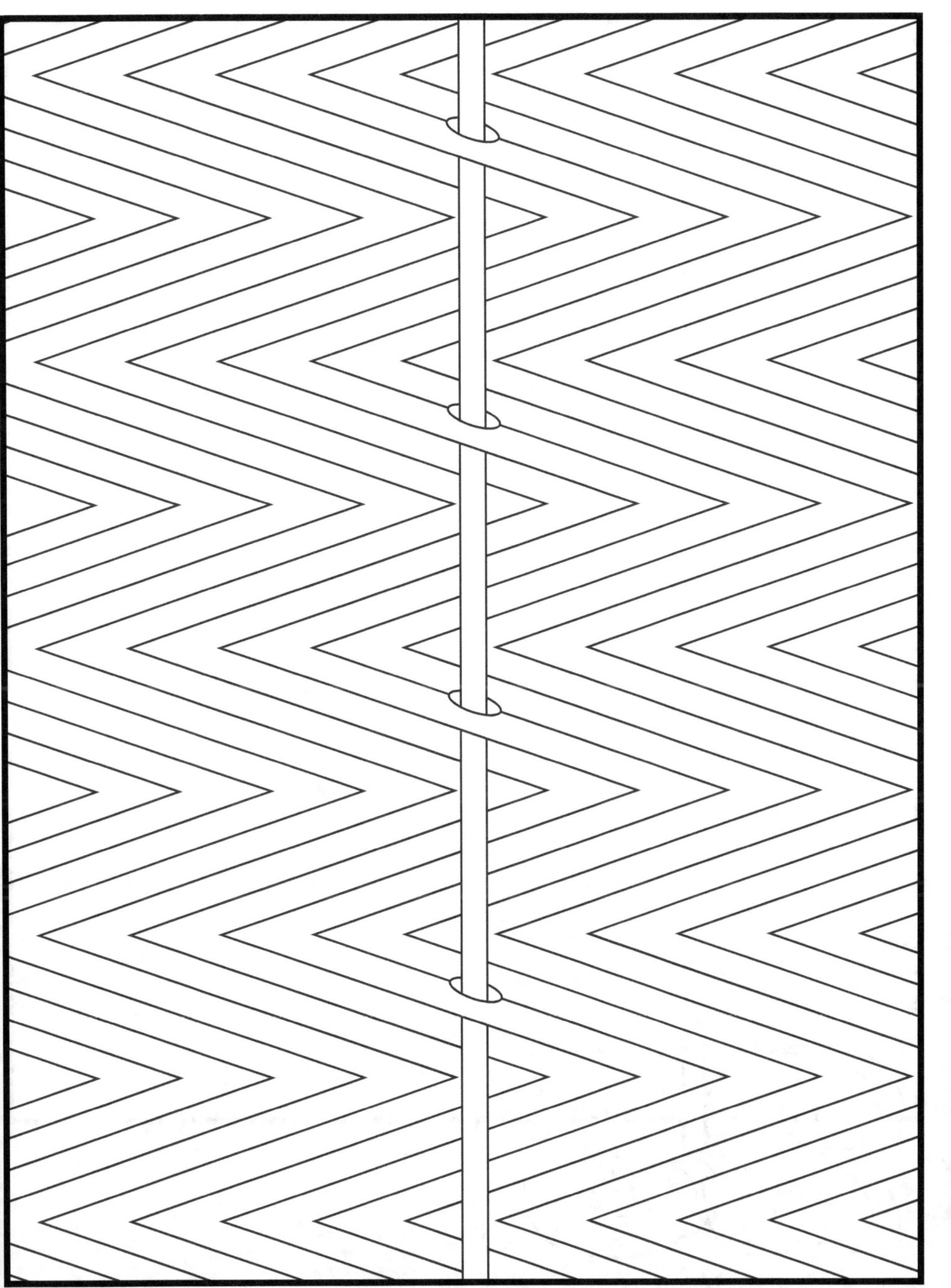

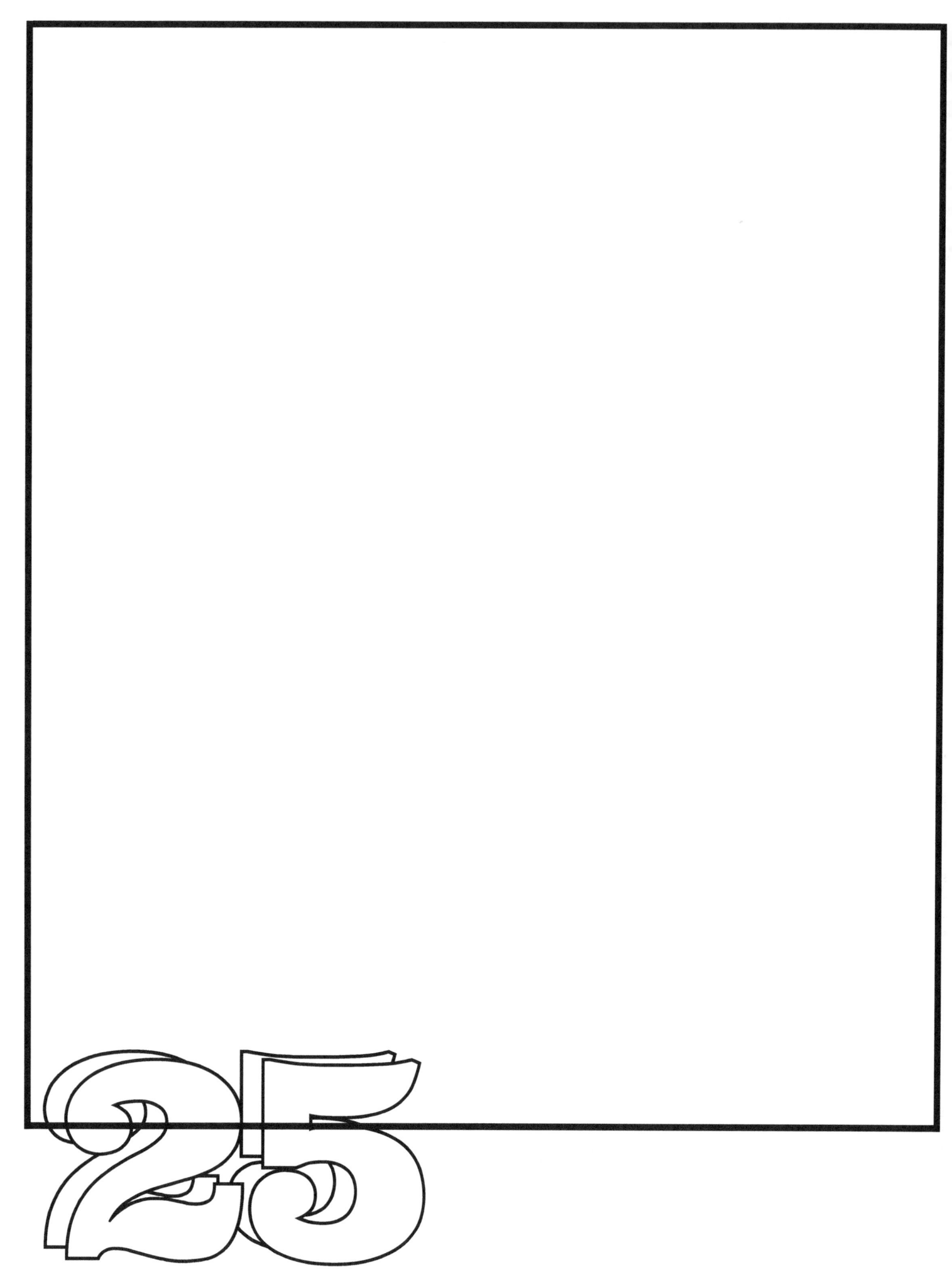

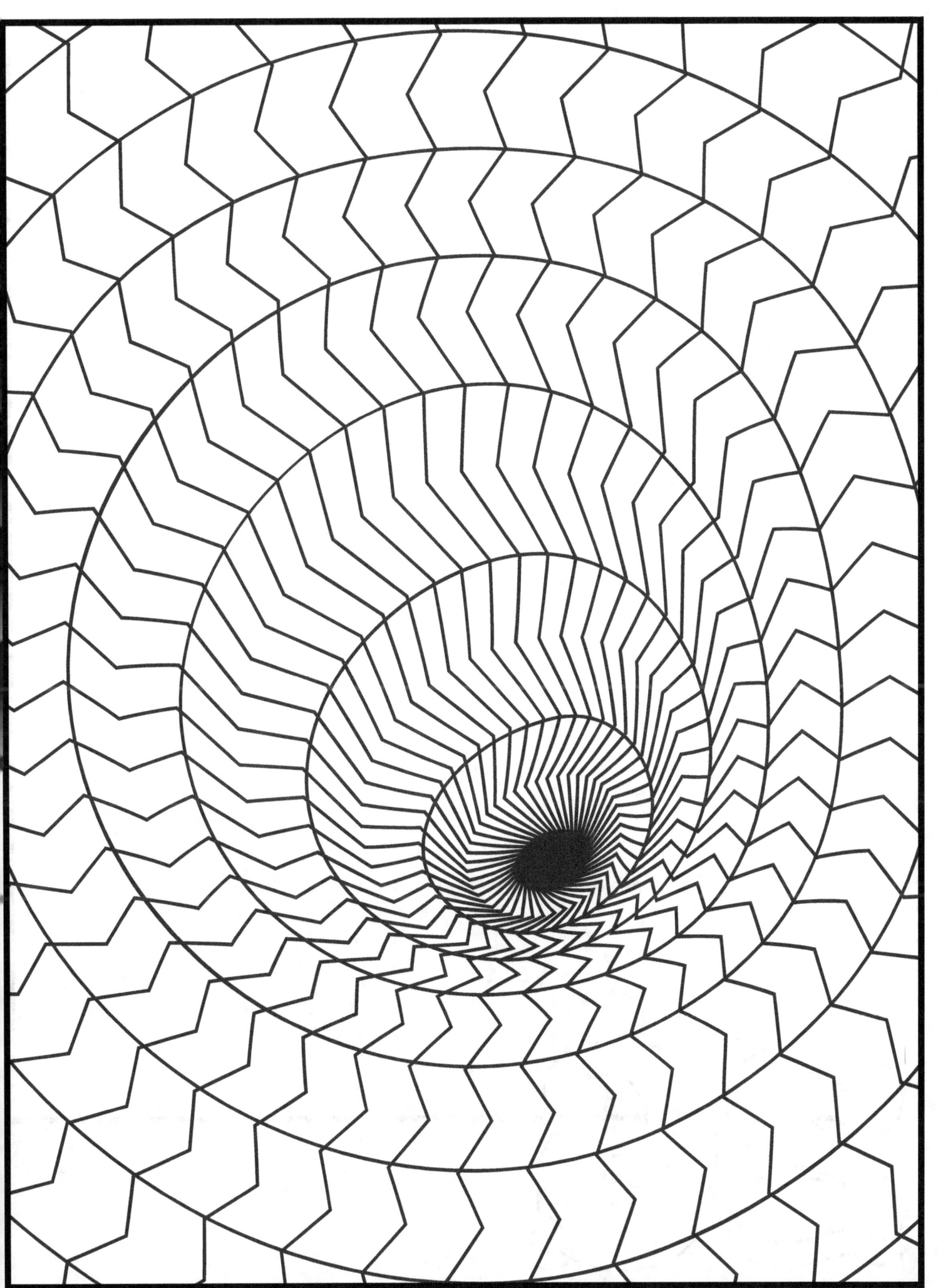

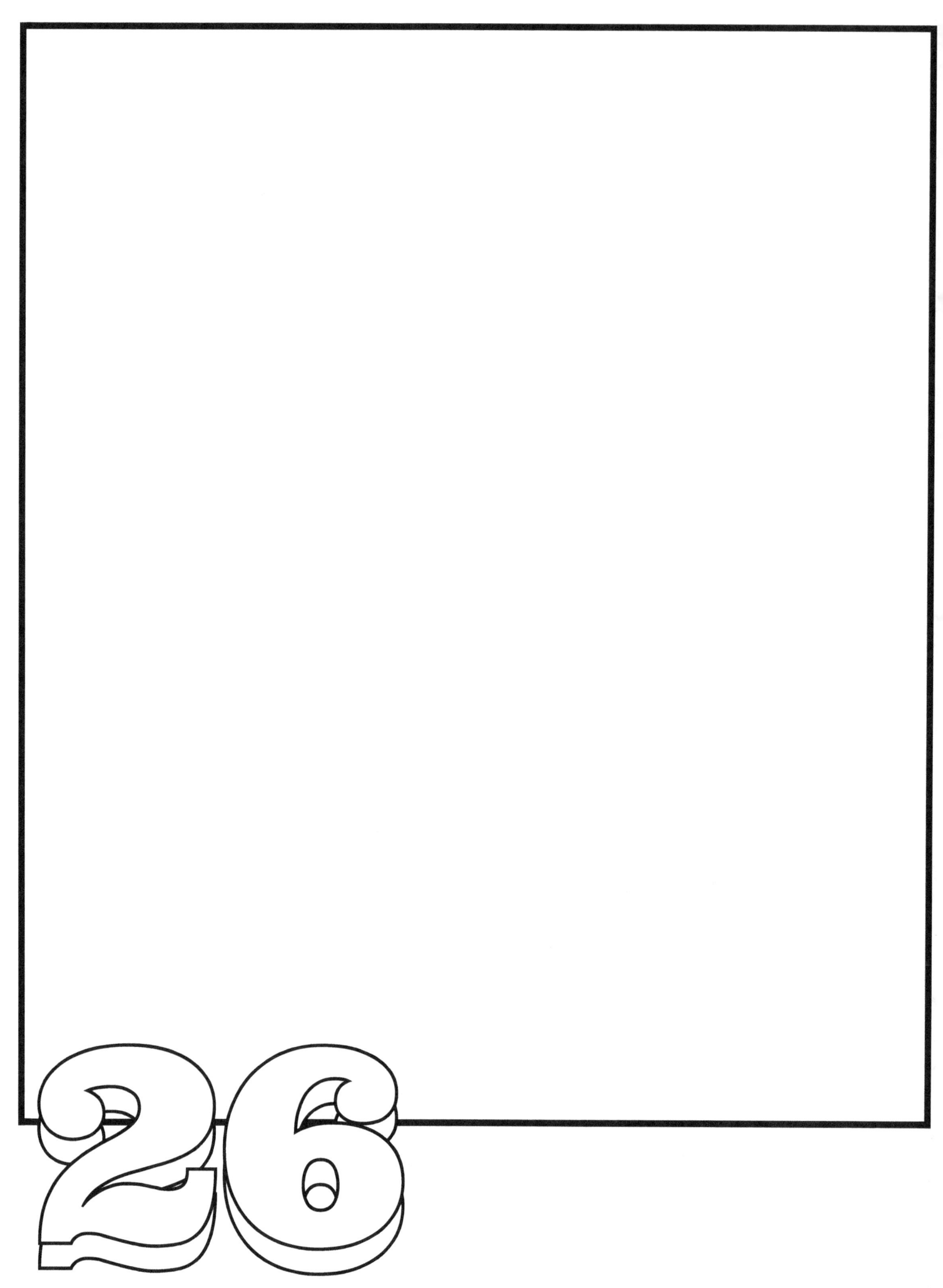

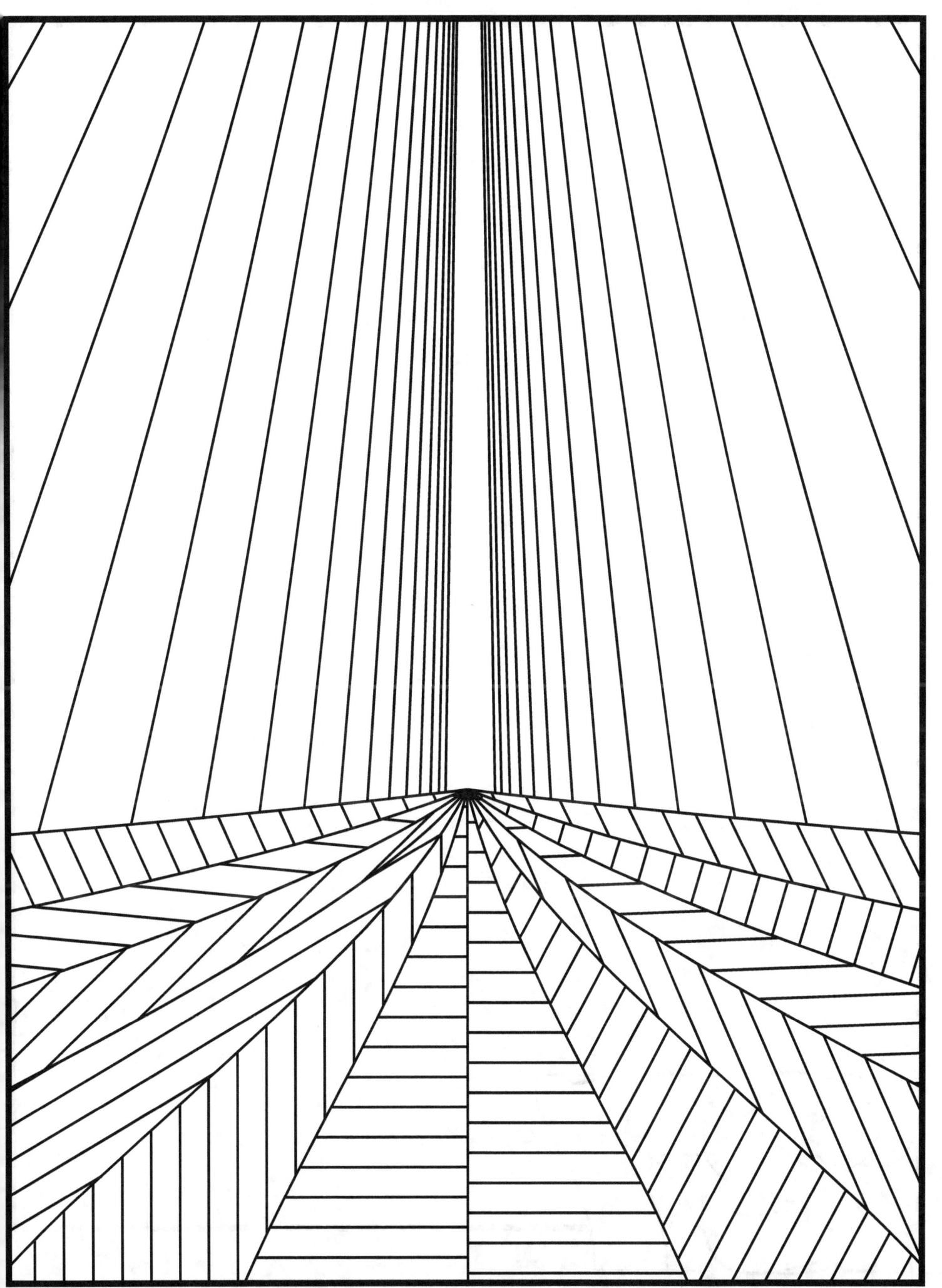

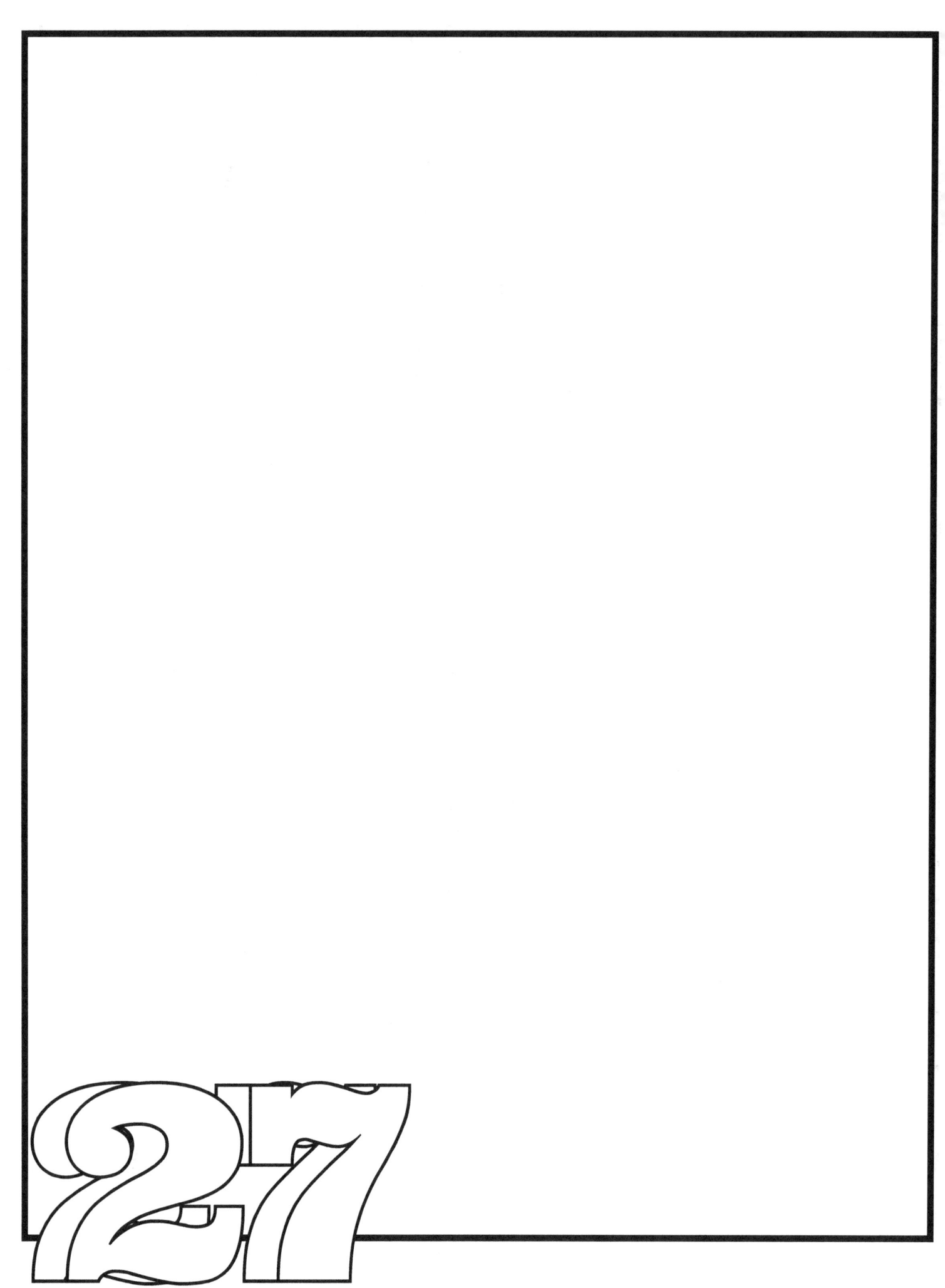

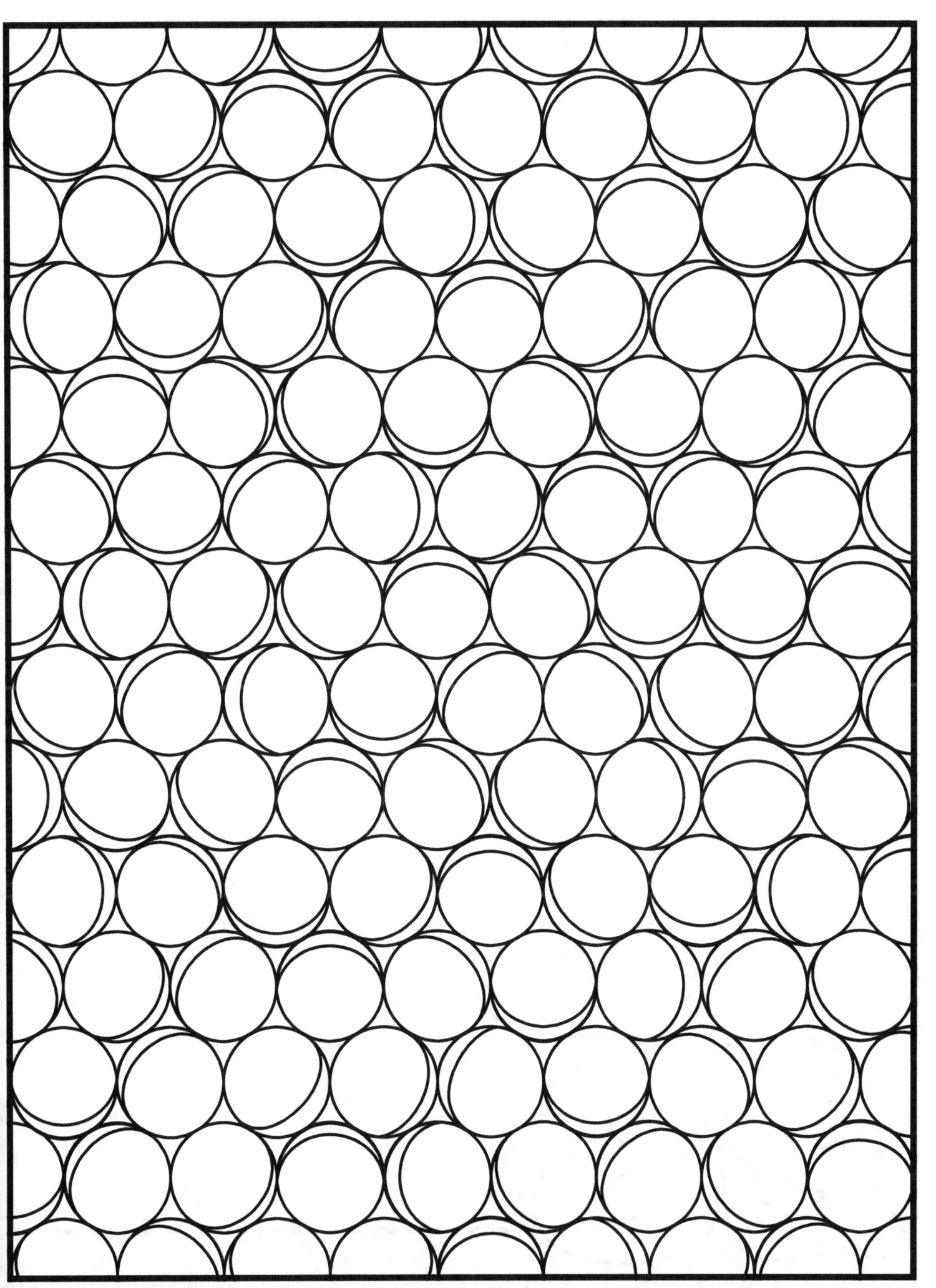

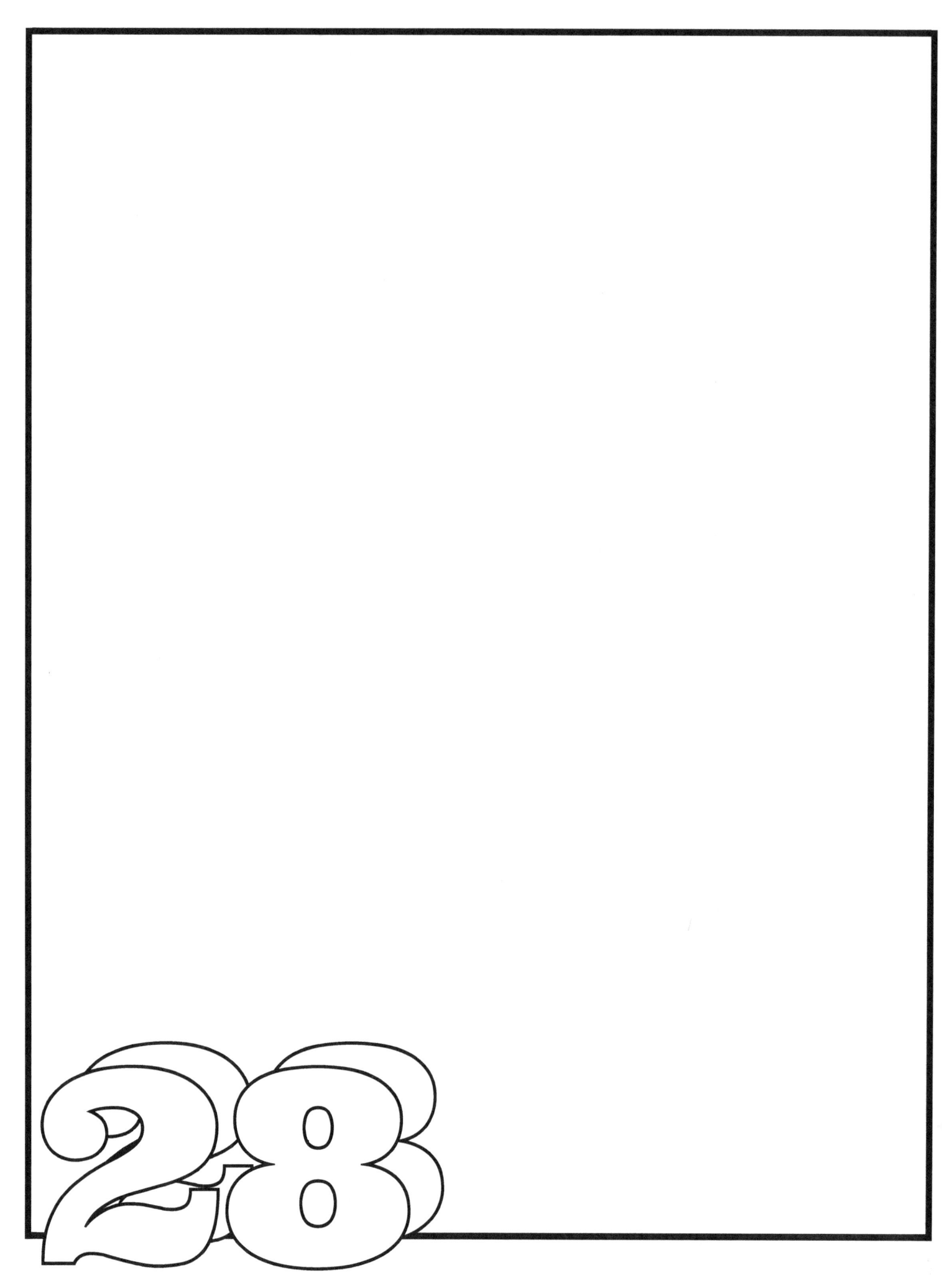

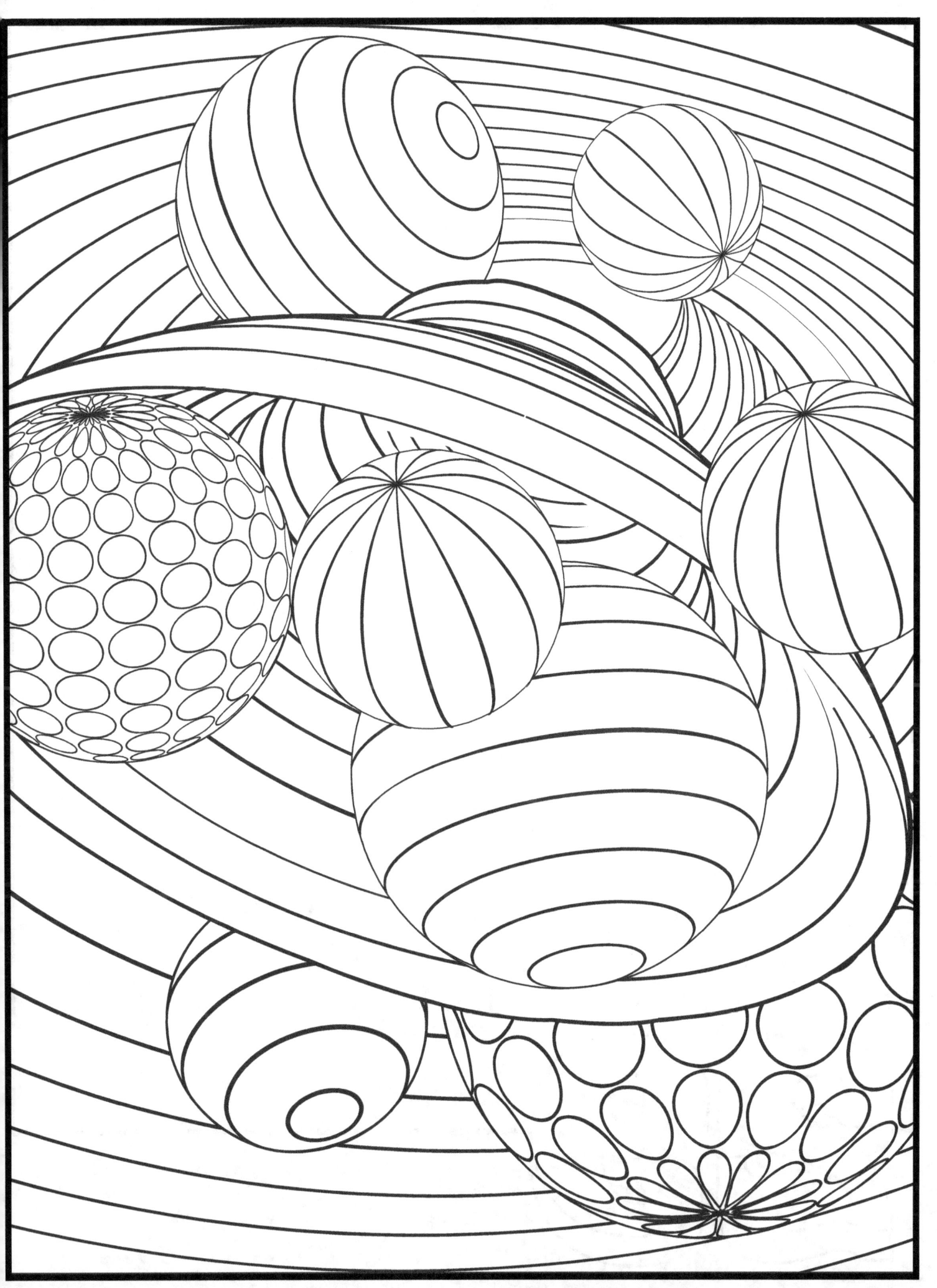

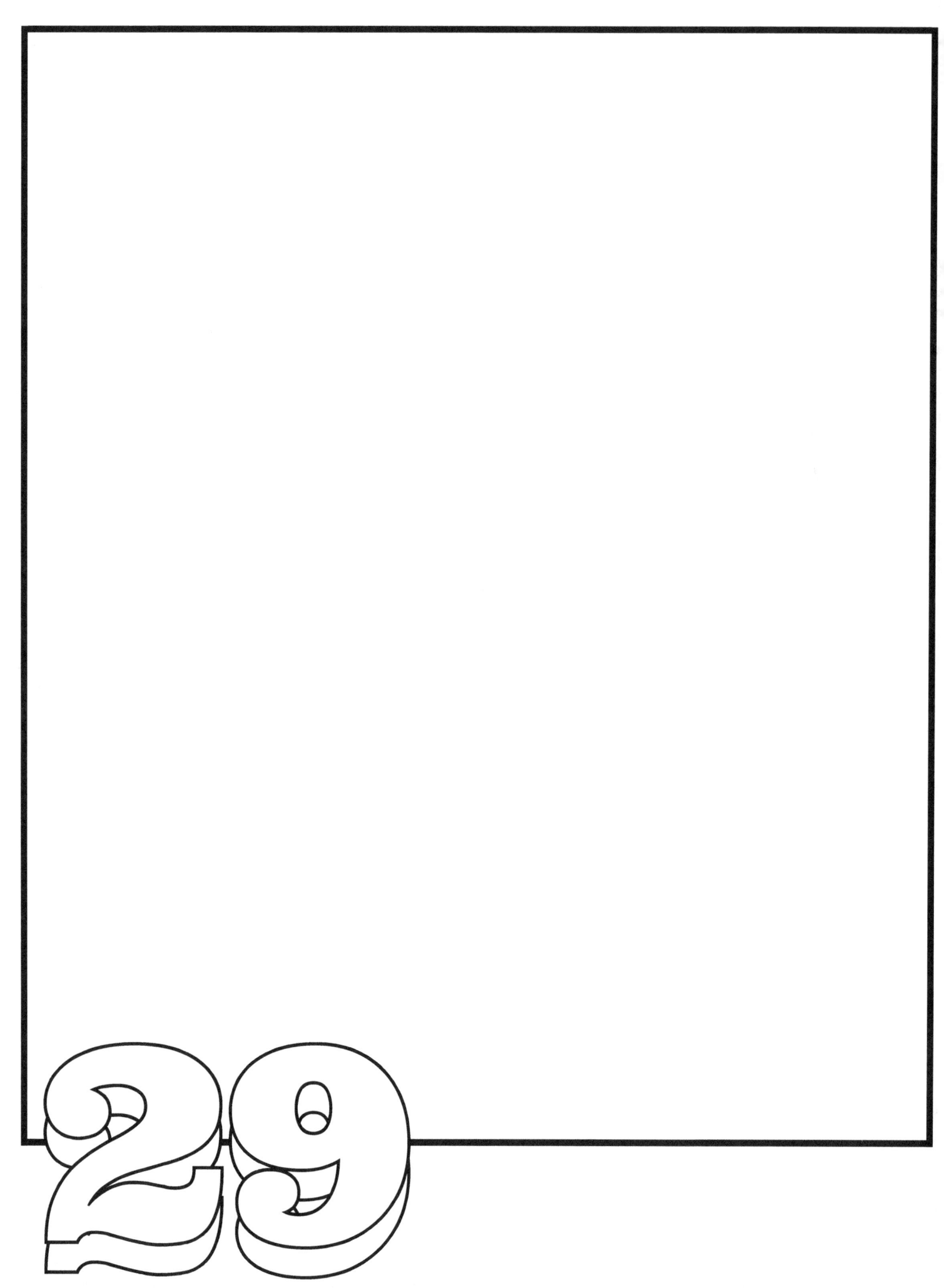

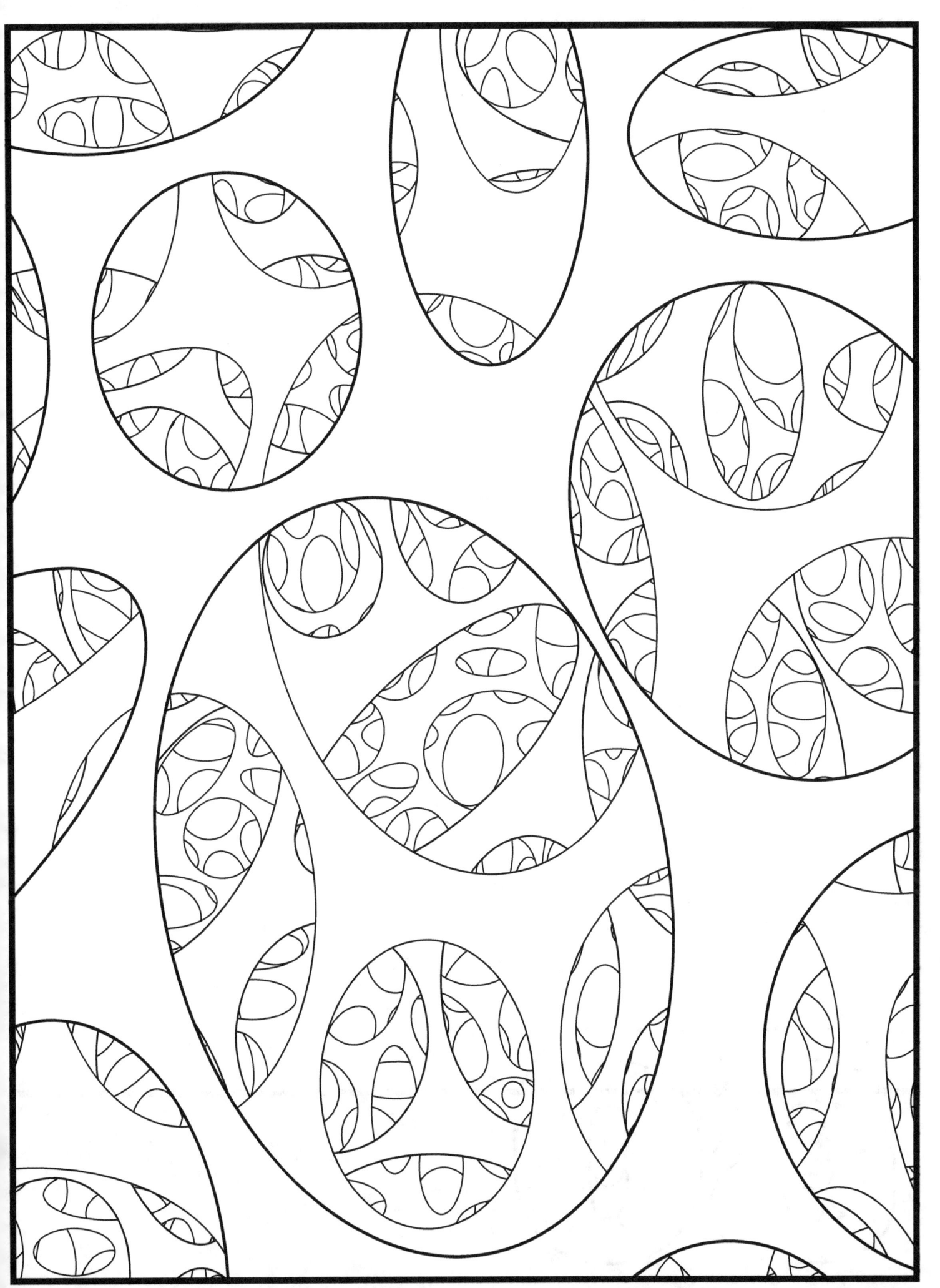

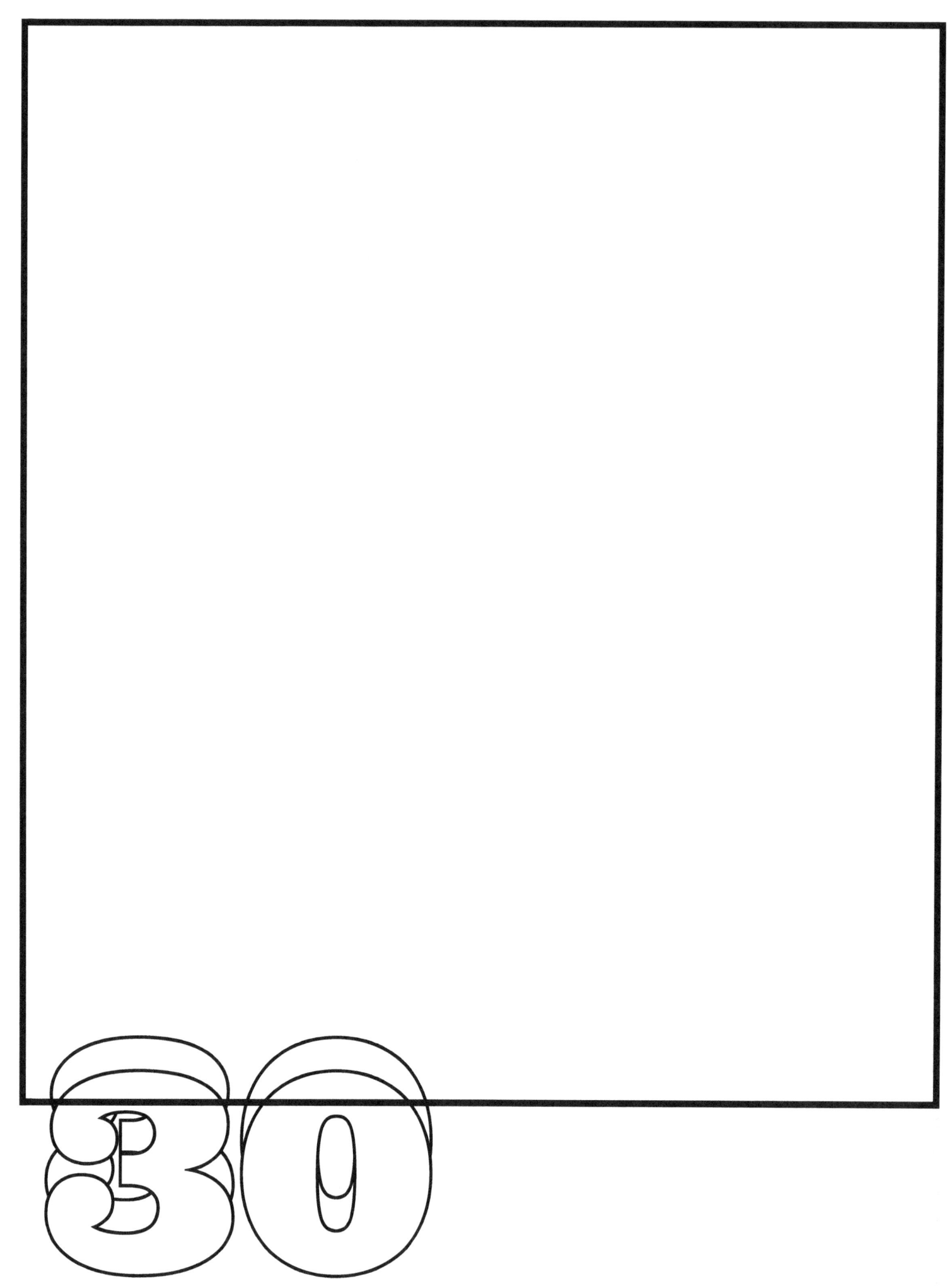

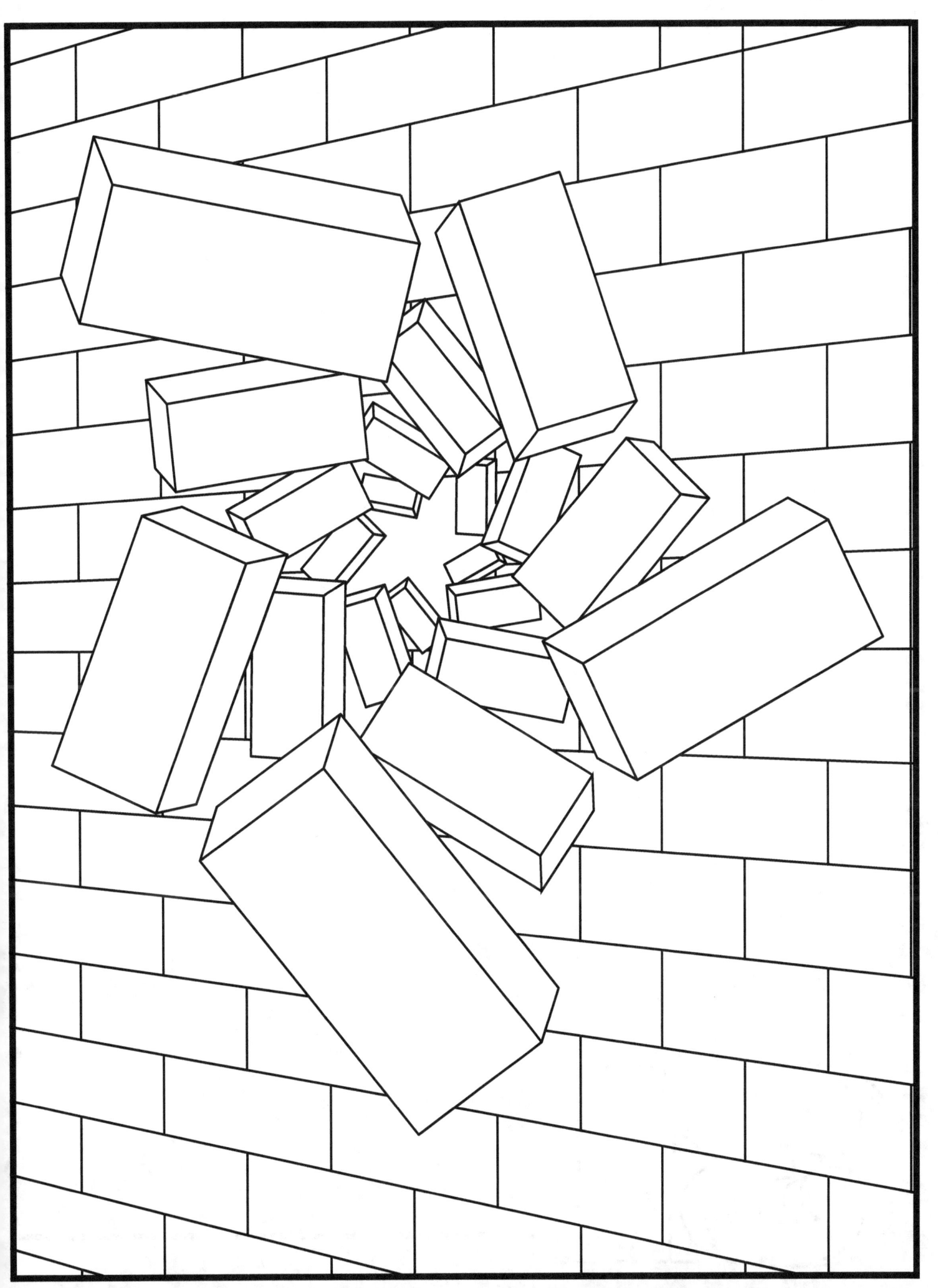

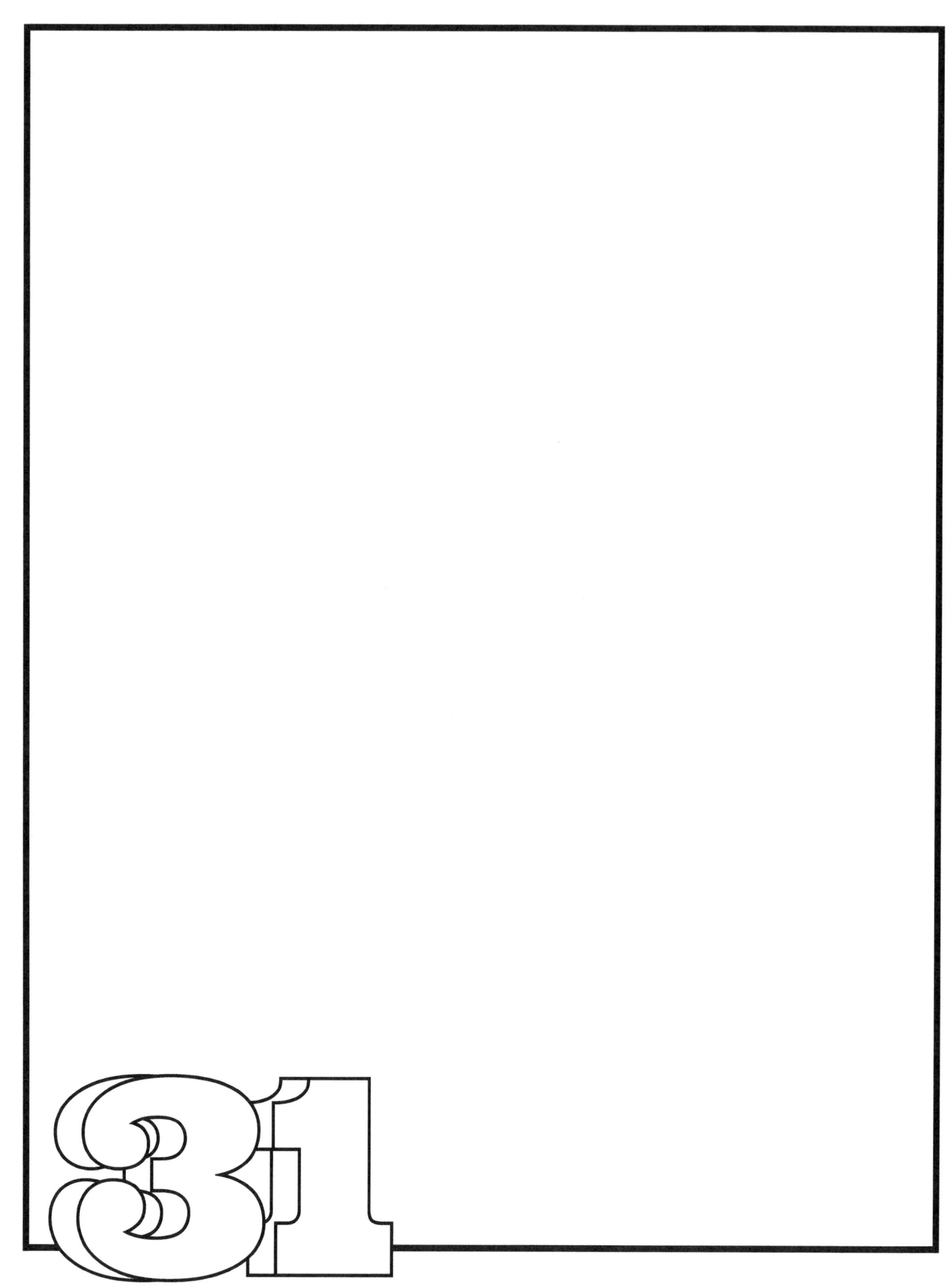

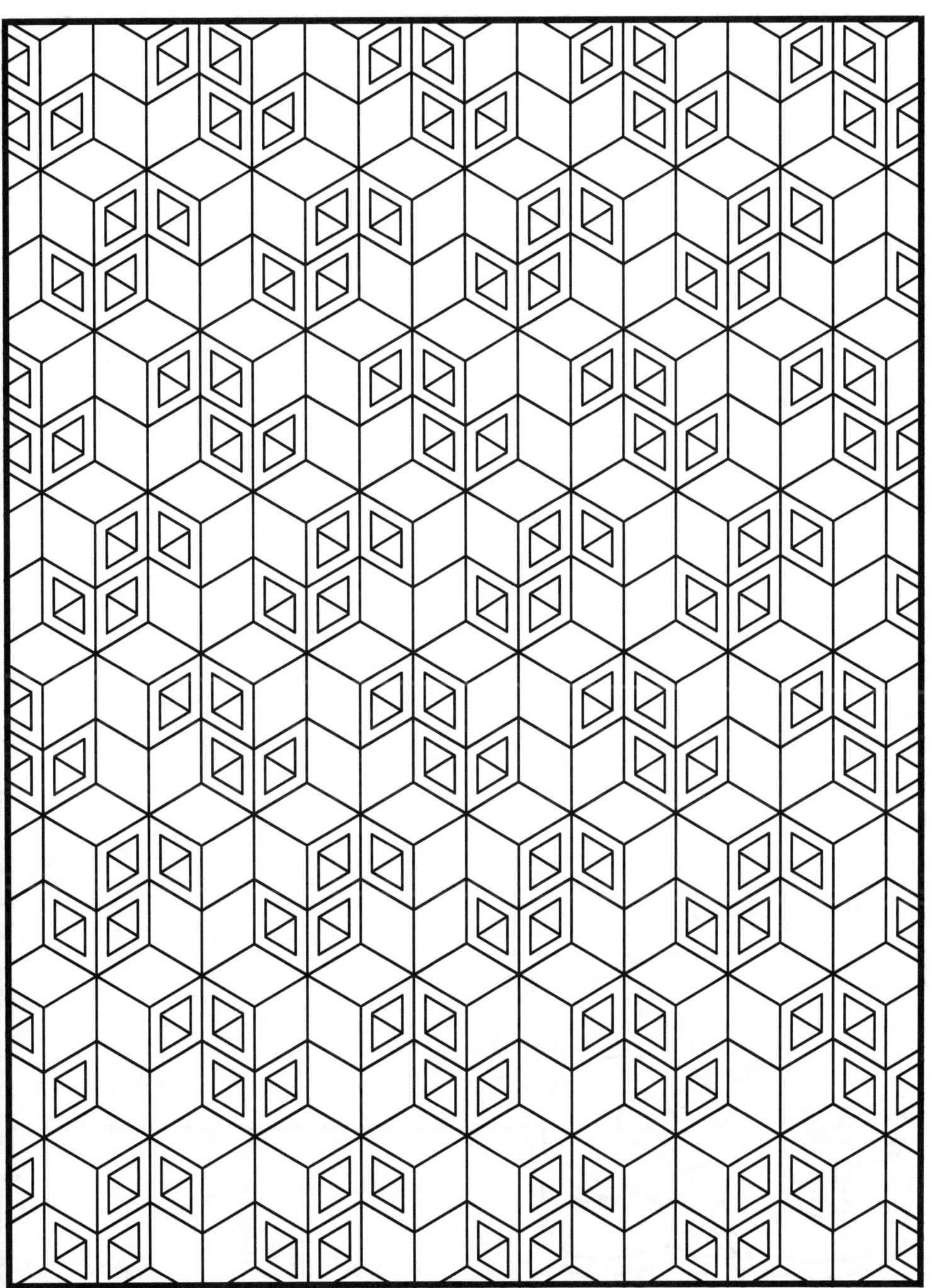

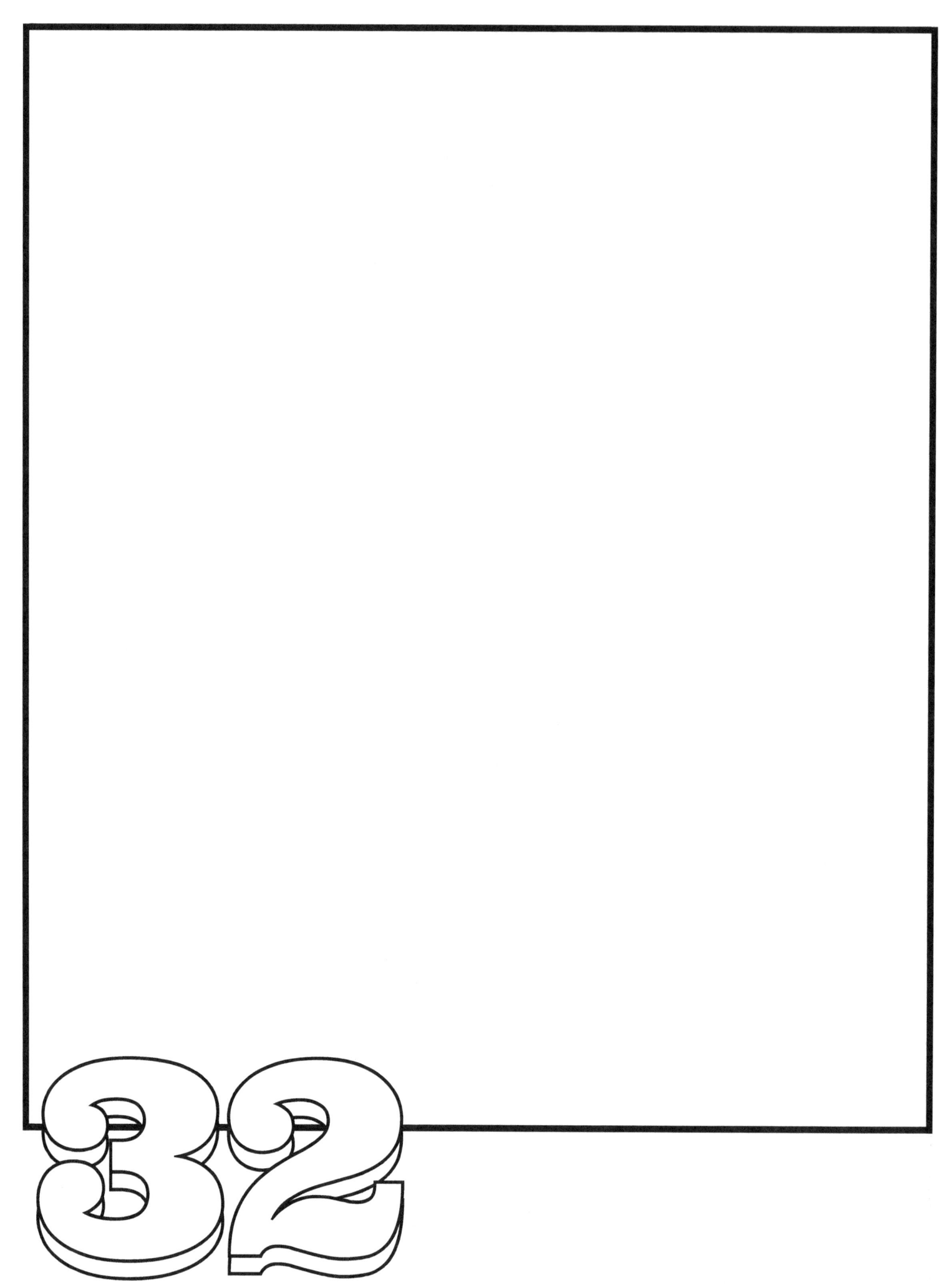

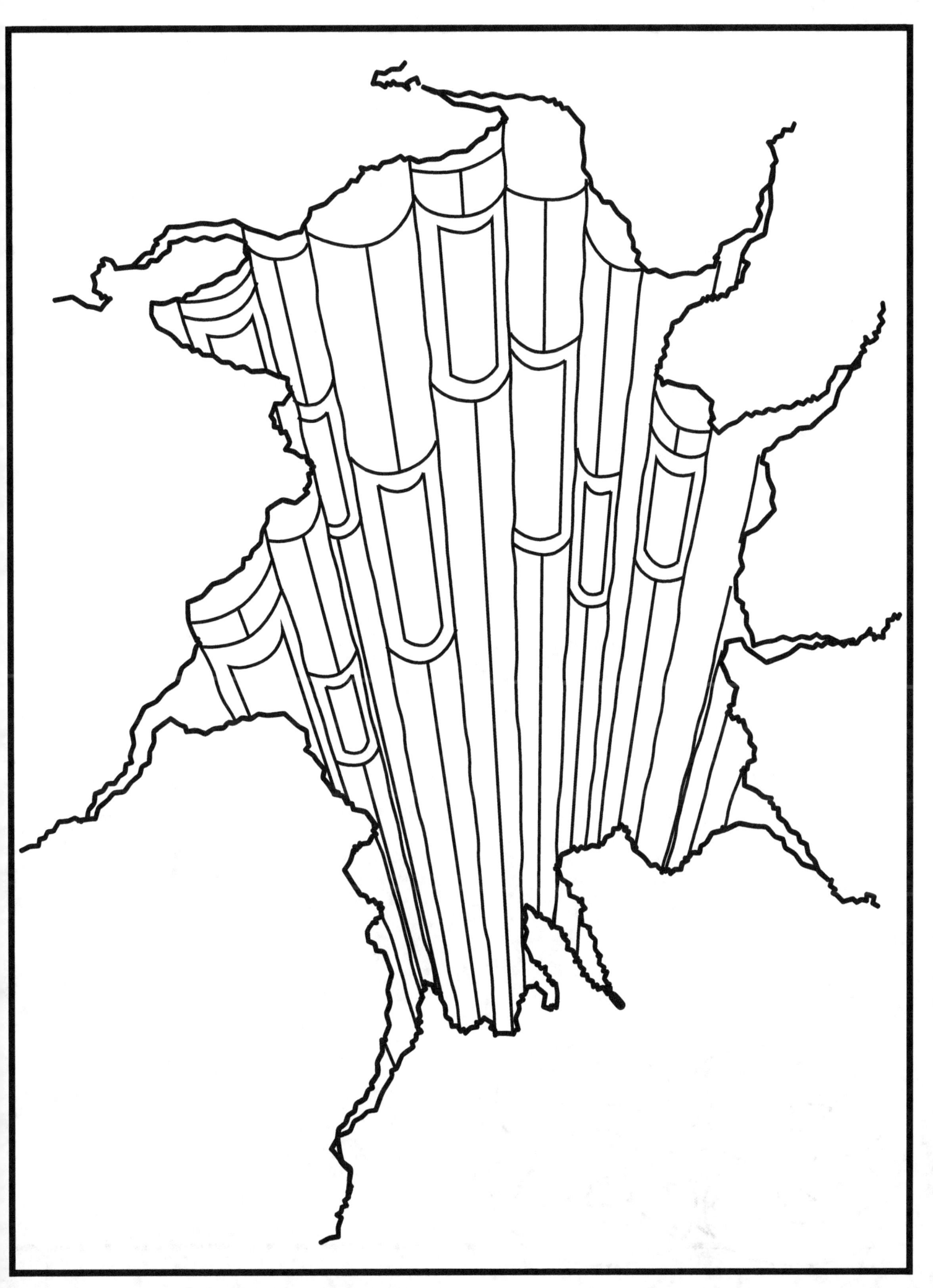

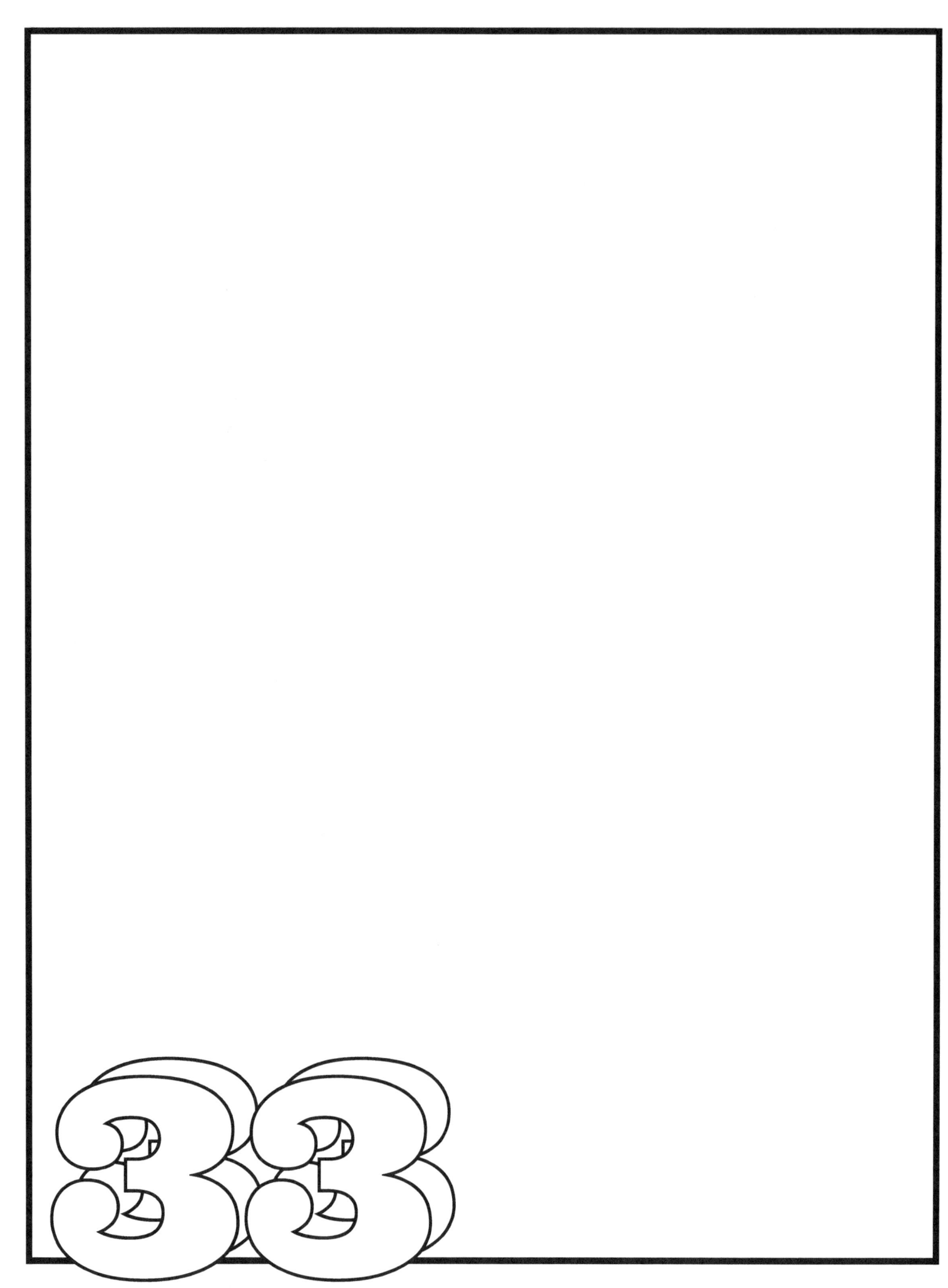

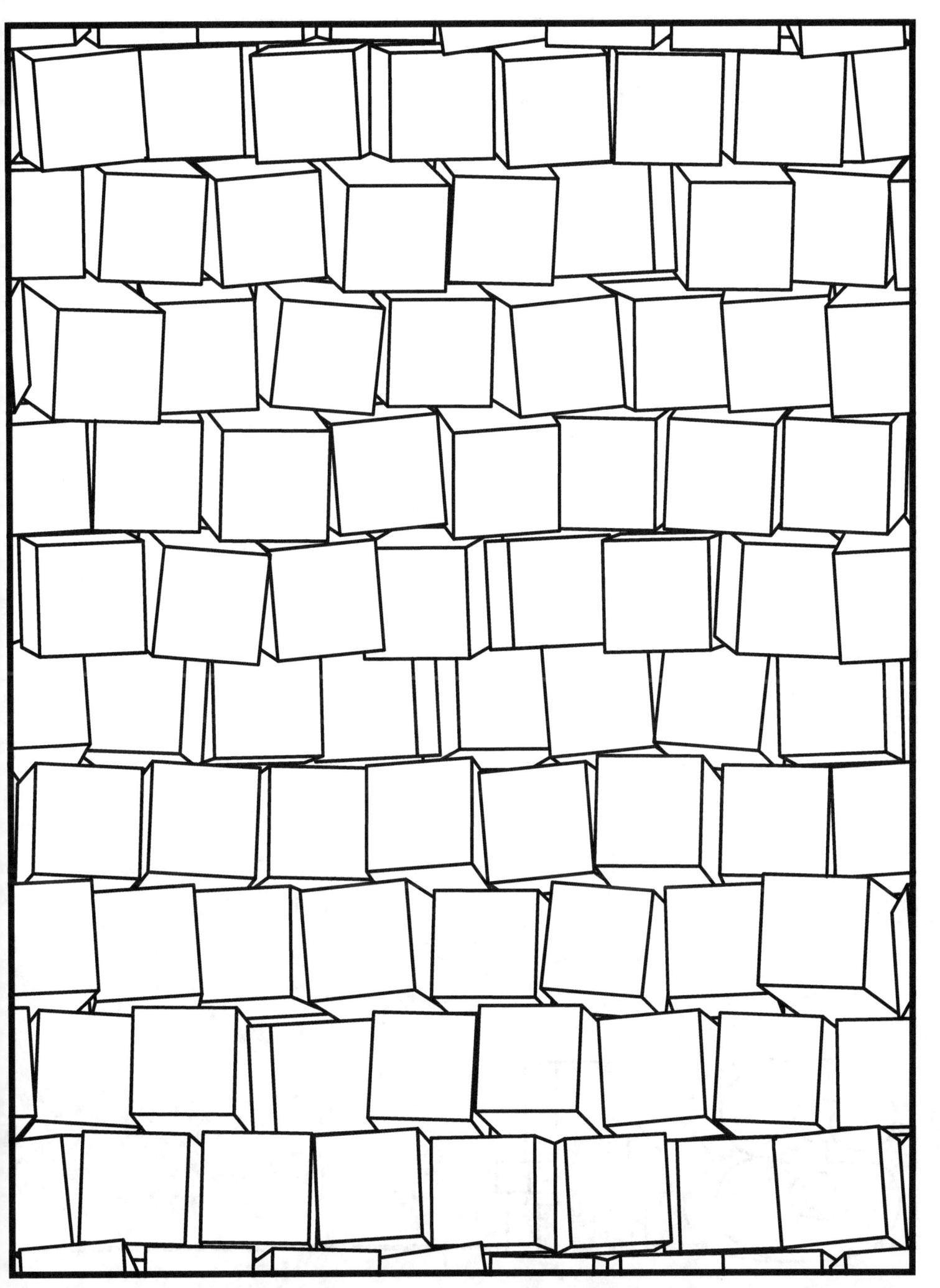

34

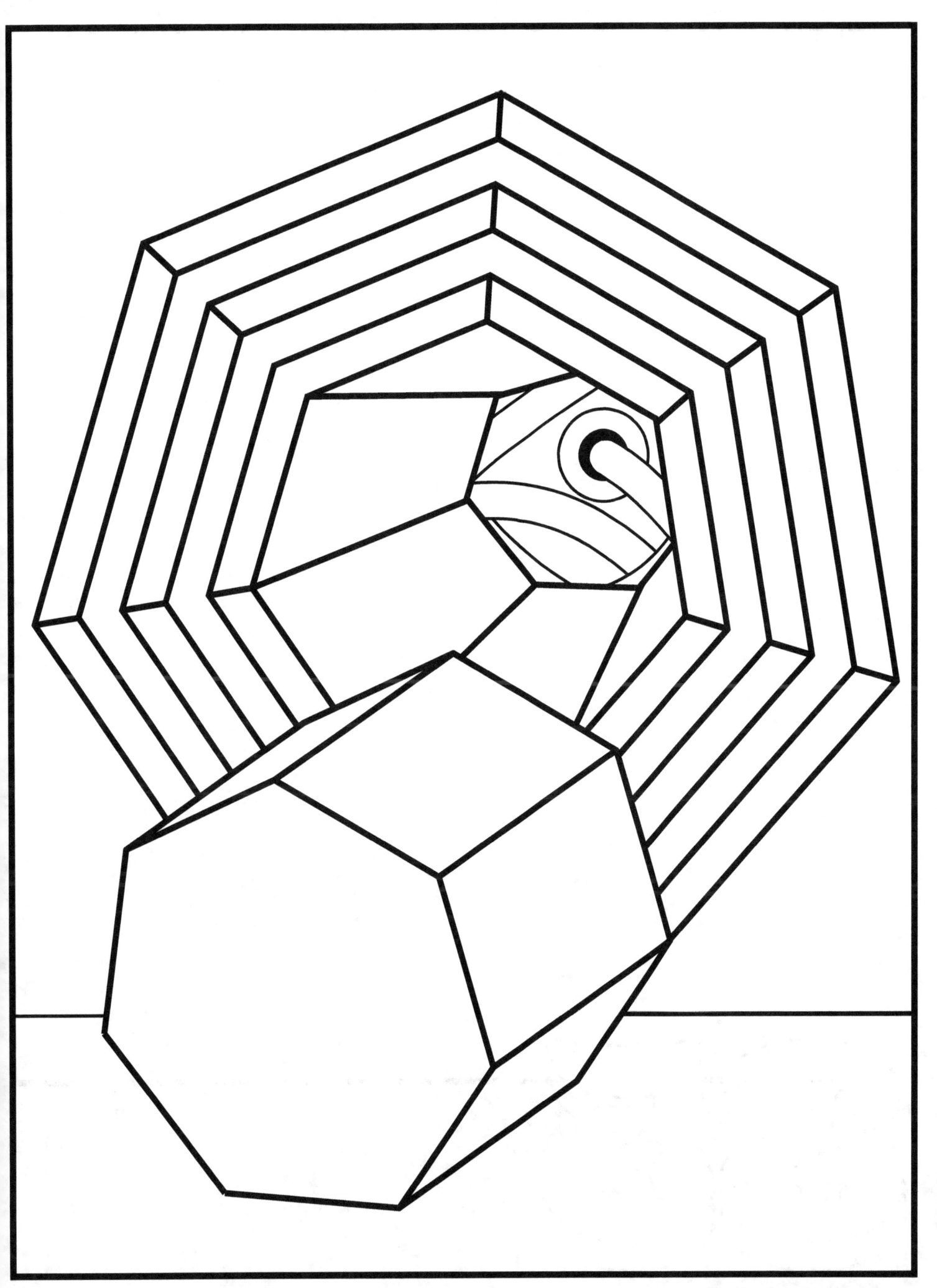

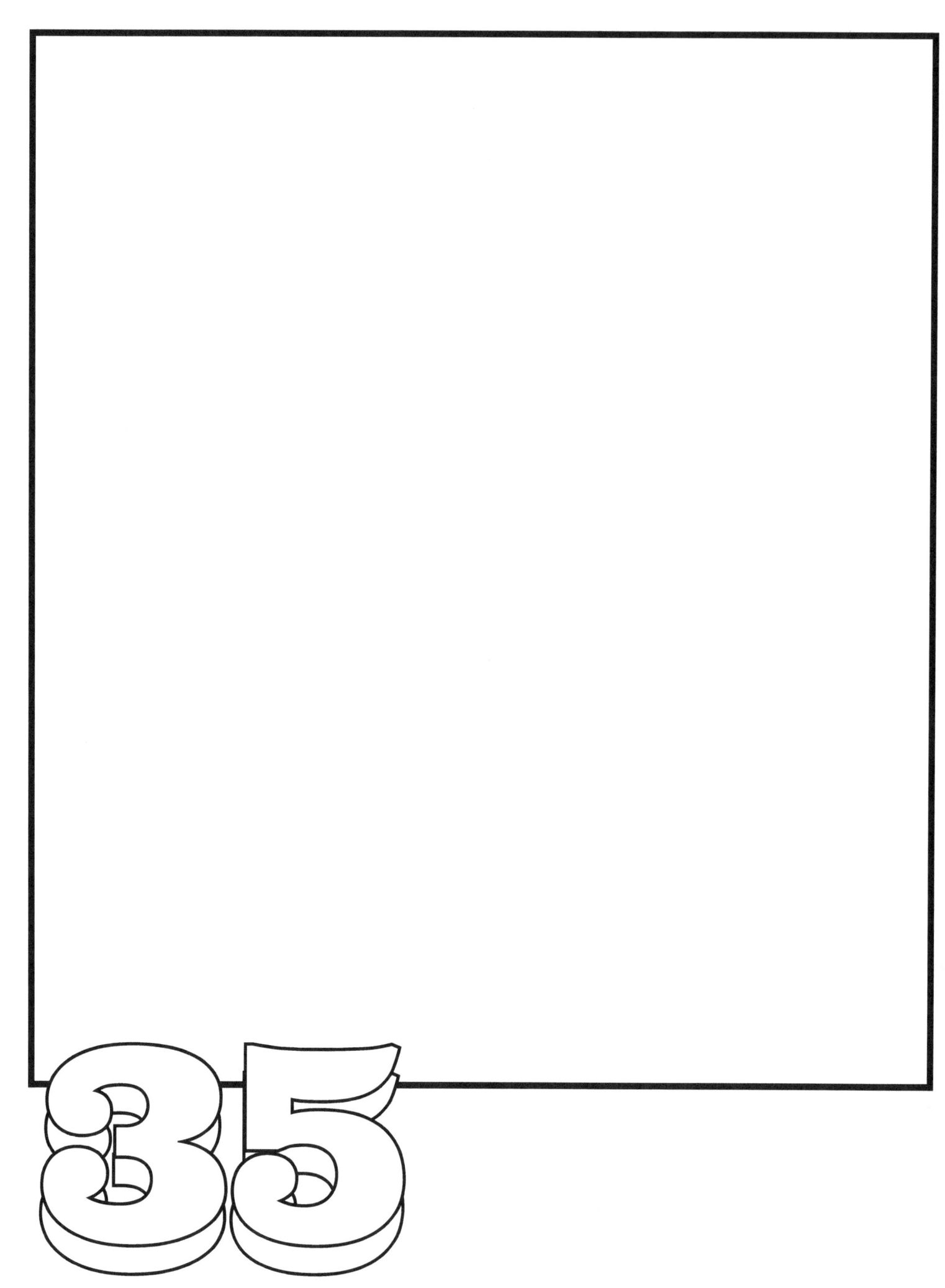

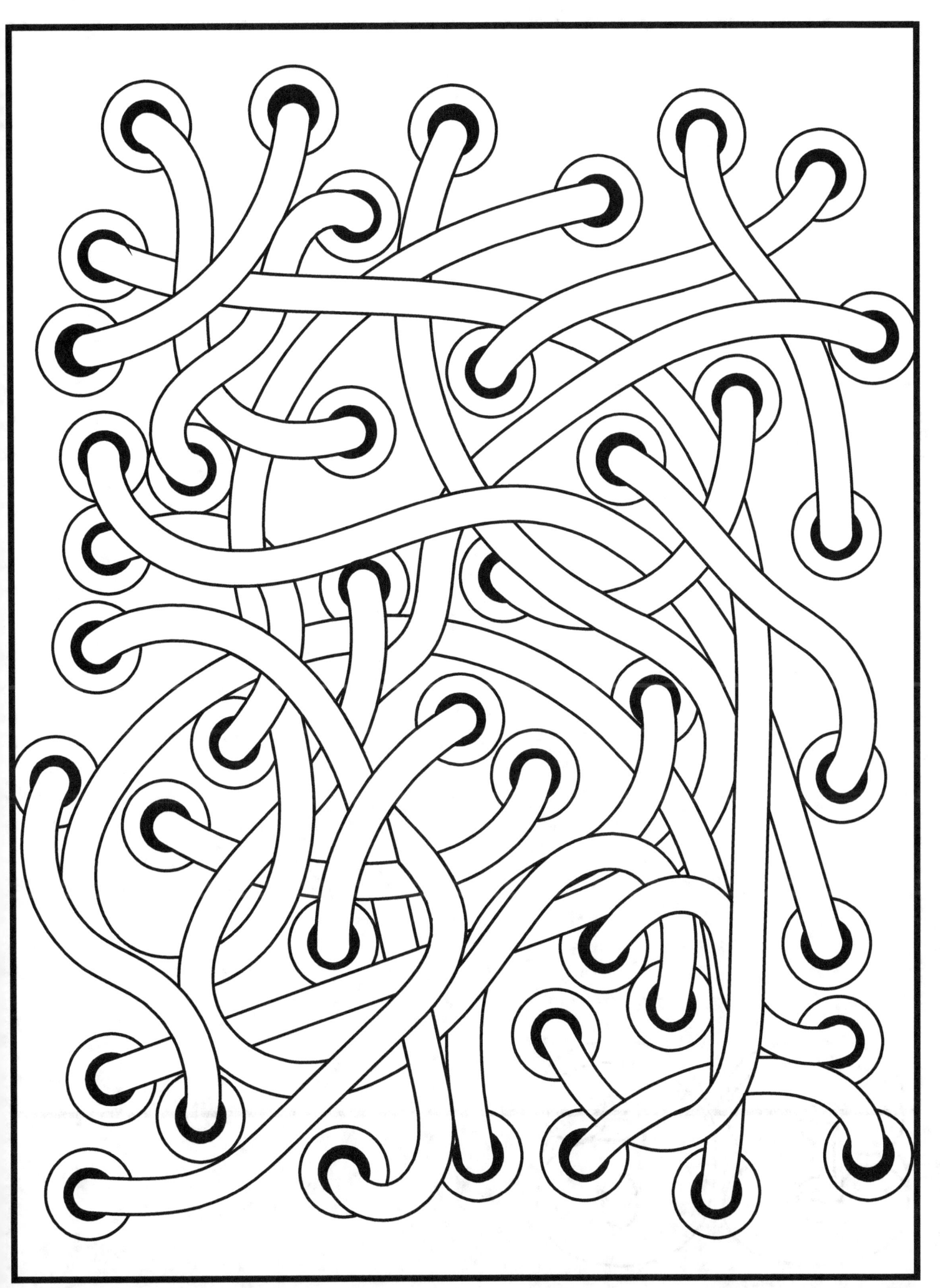

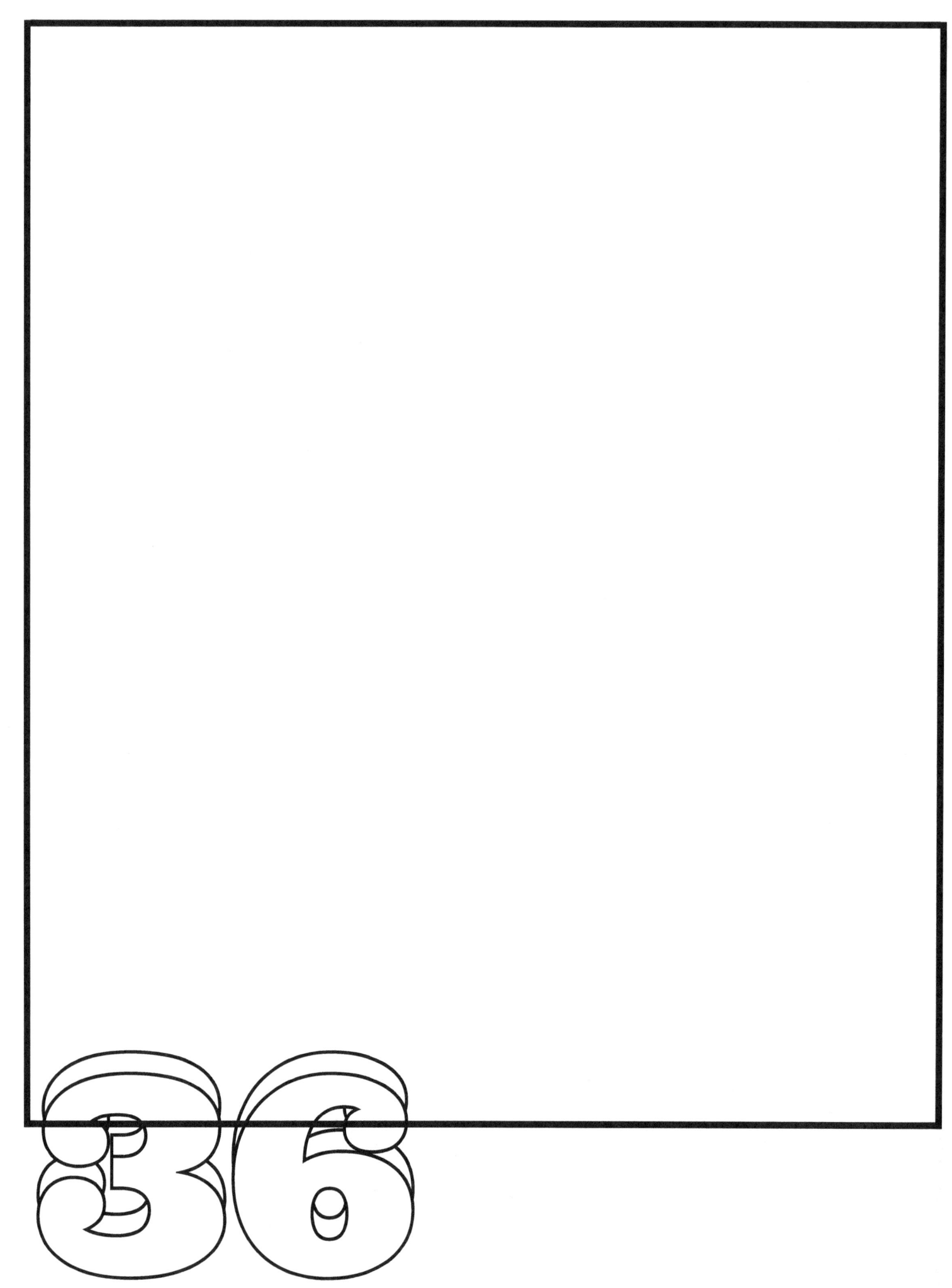

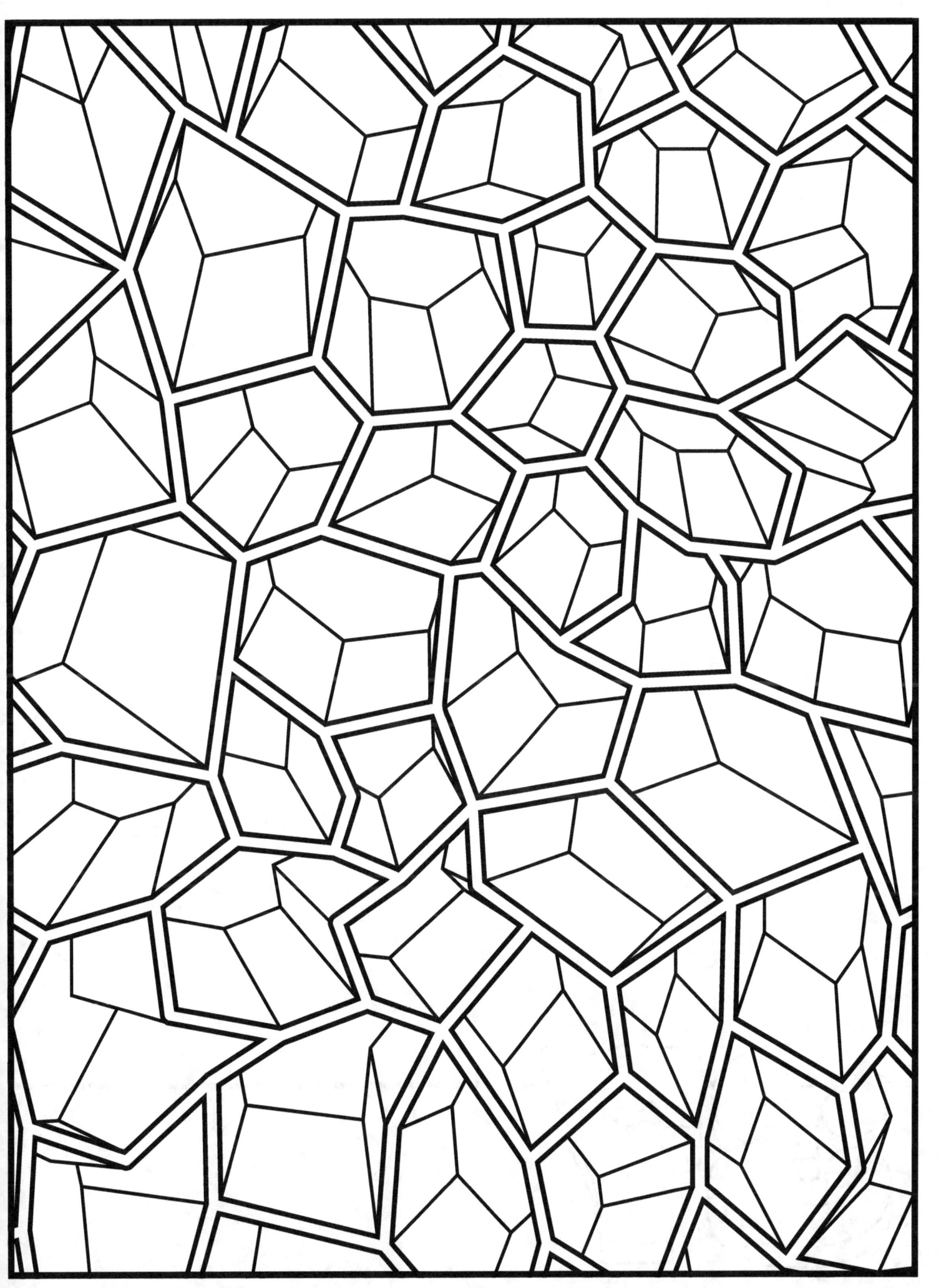

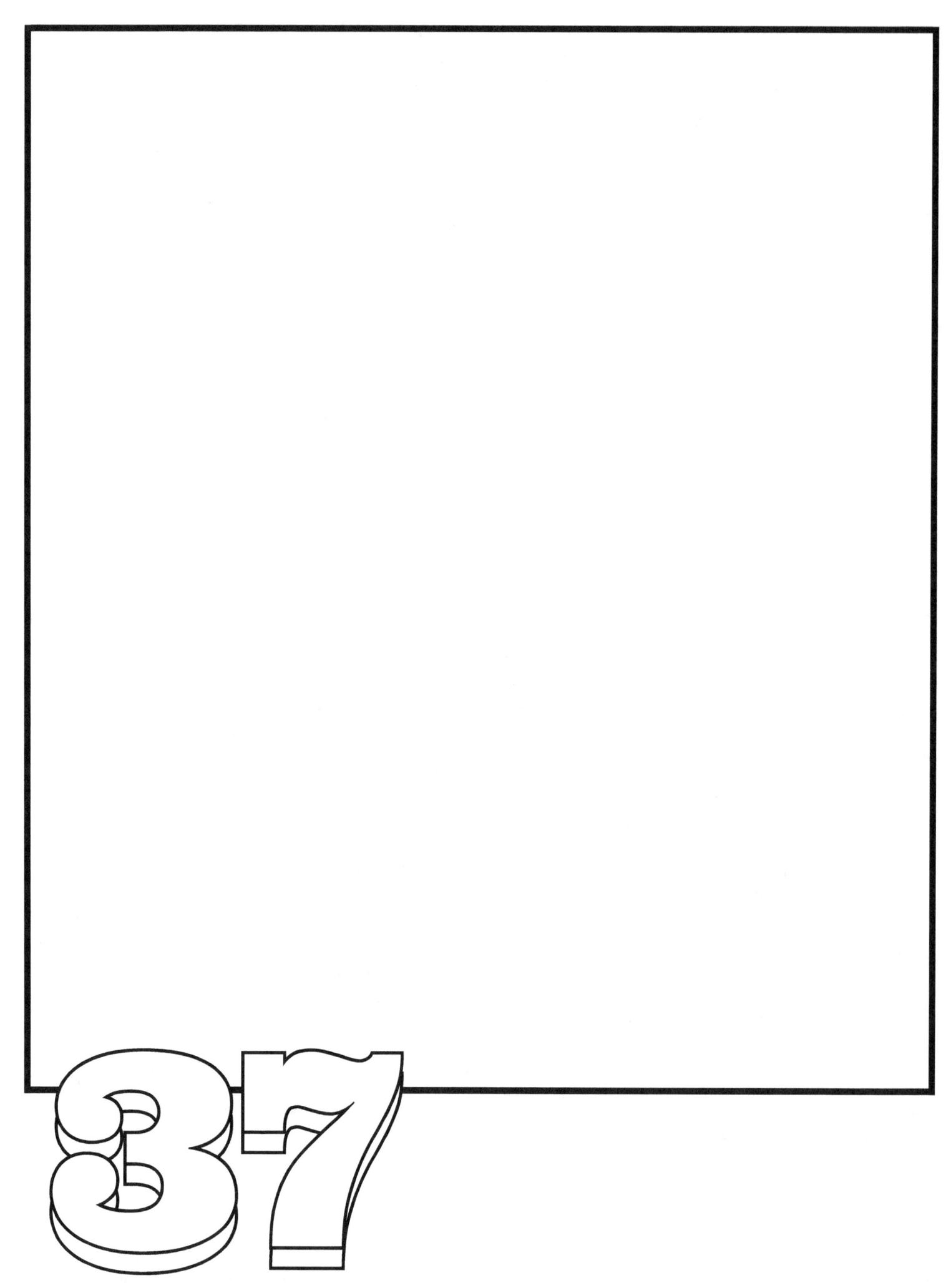

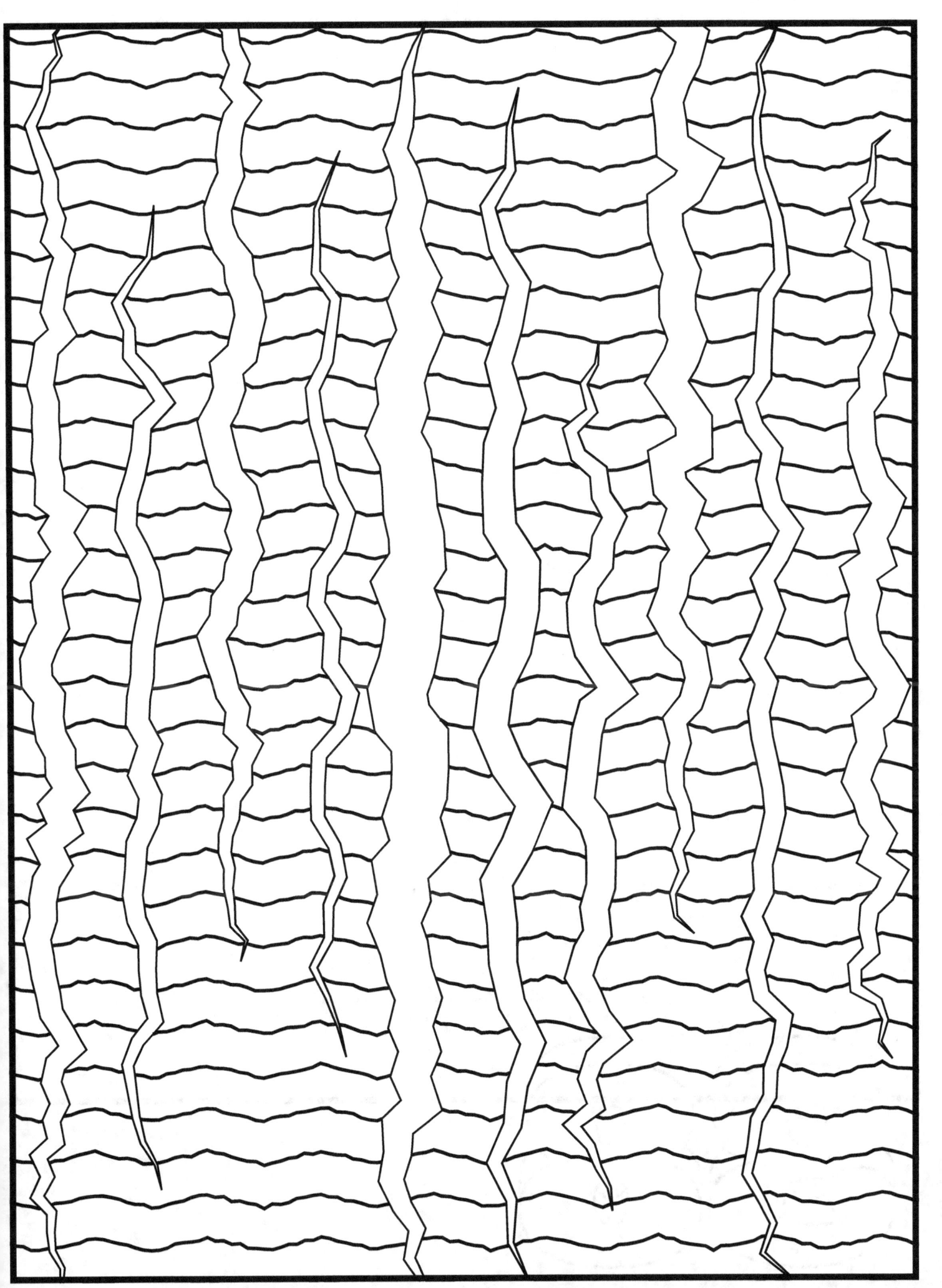

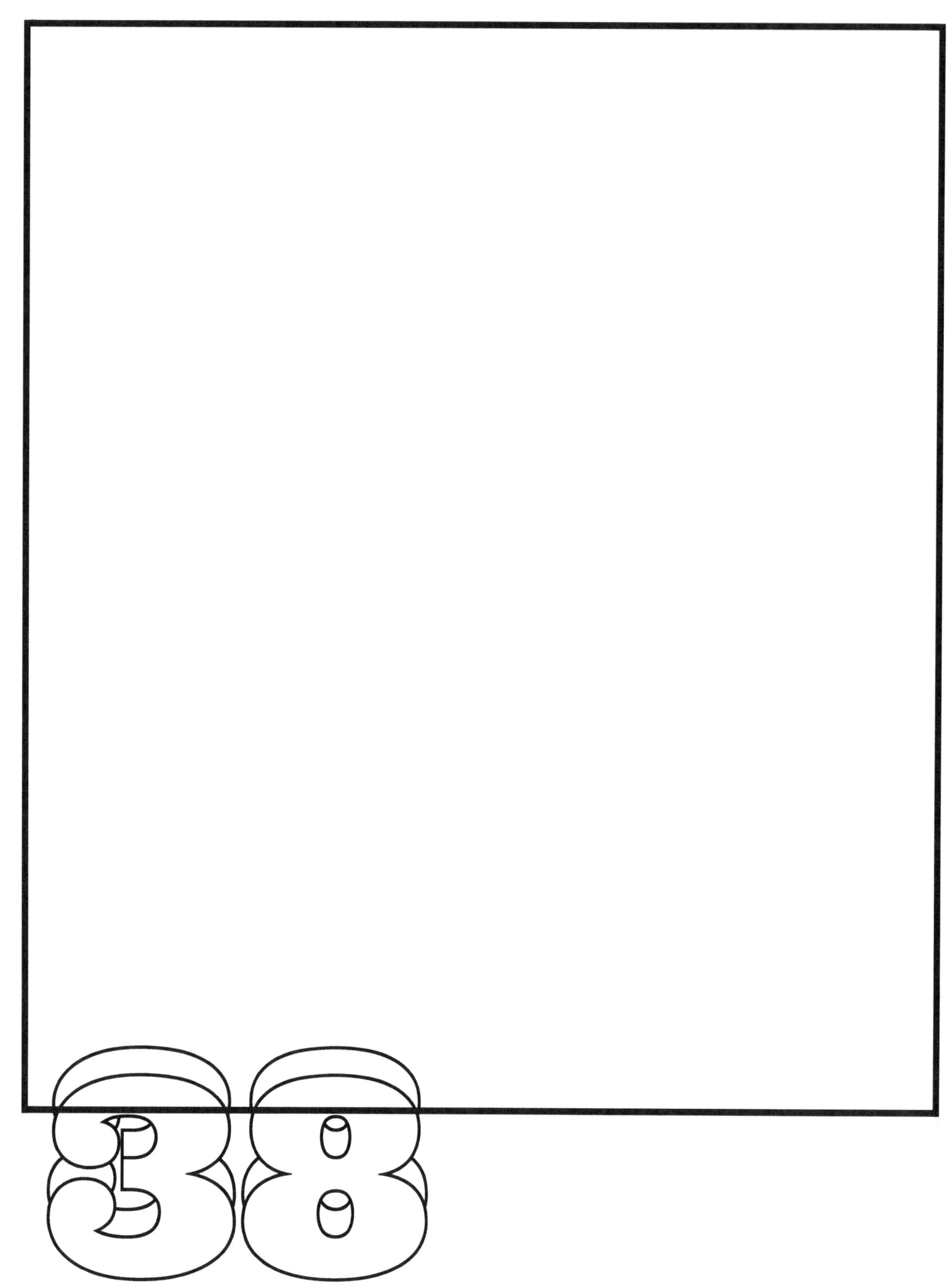

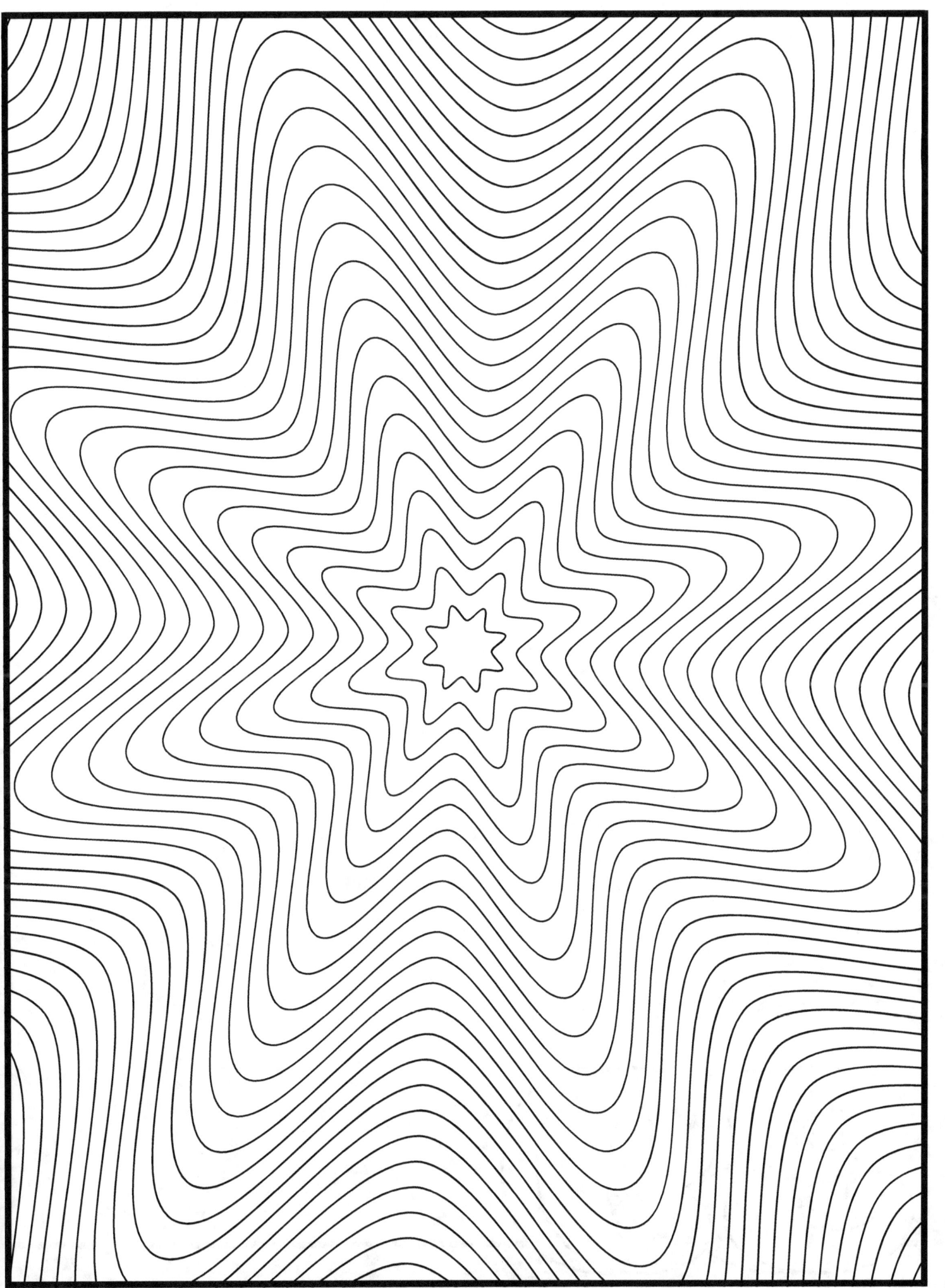

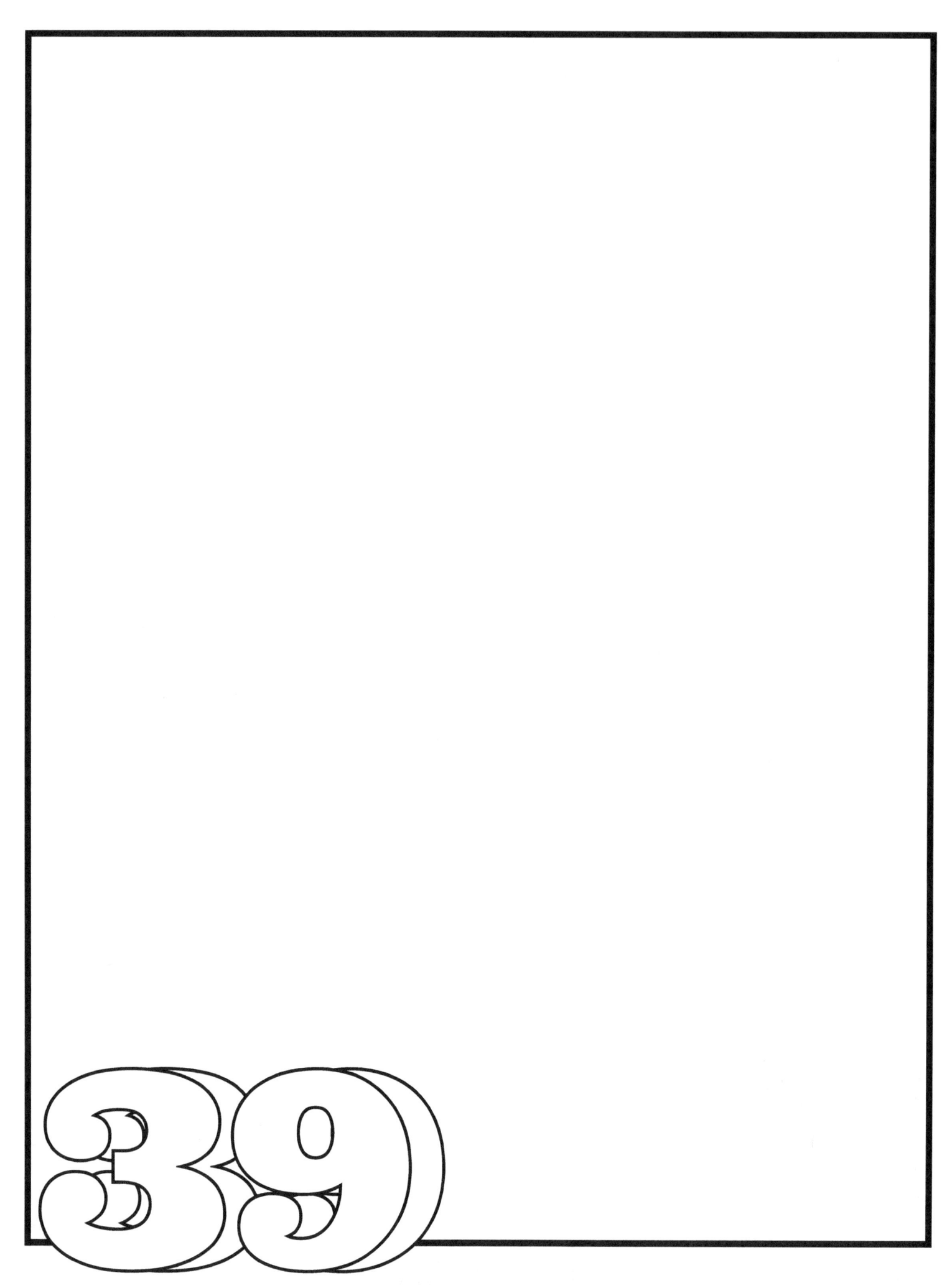

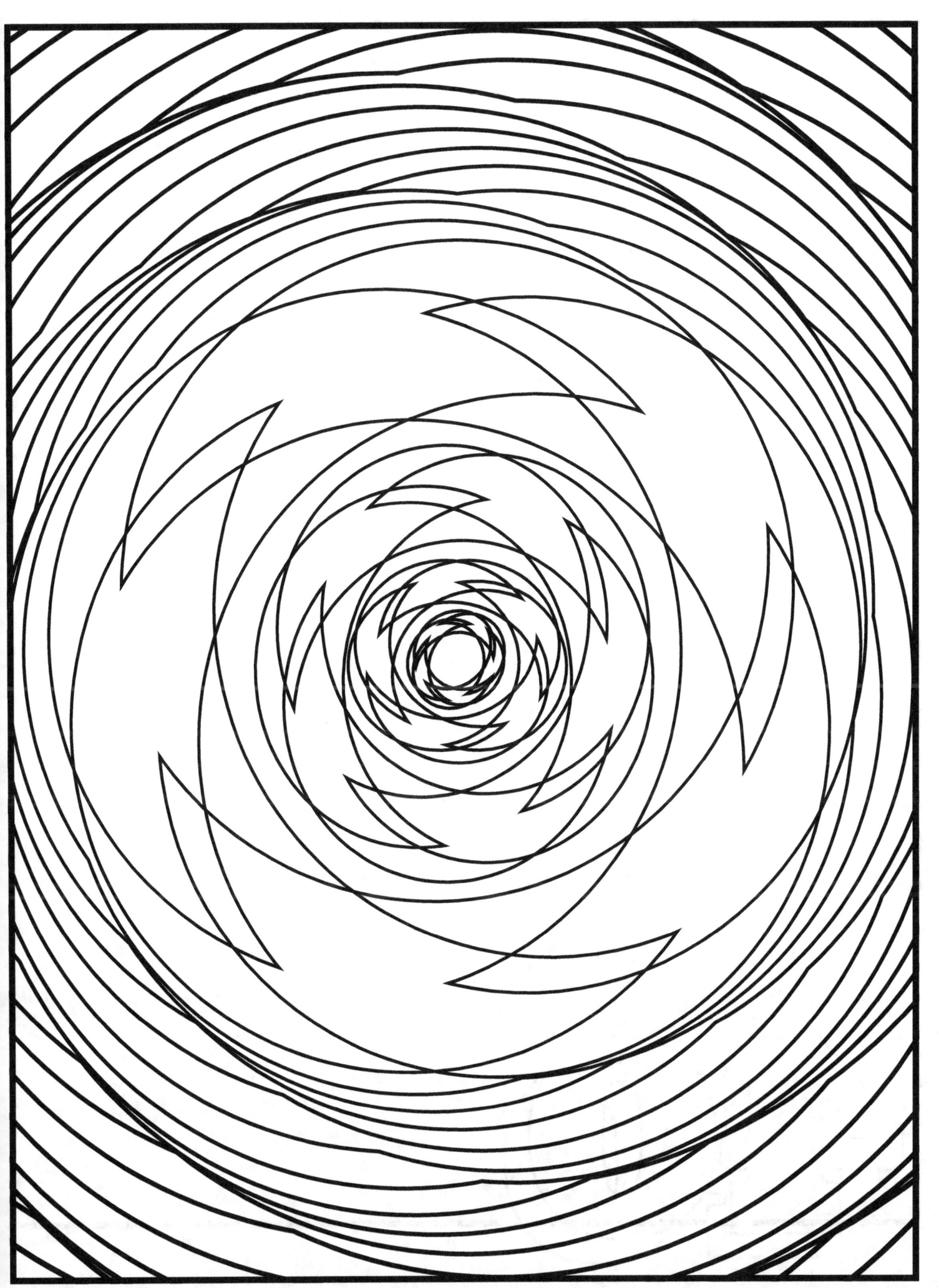

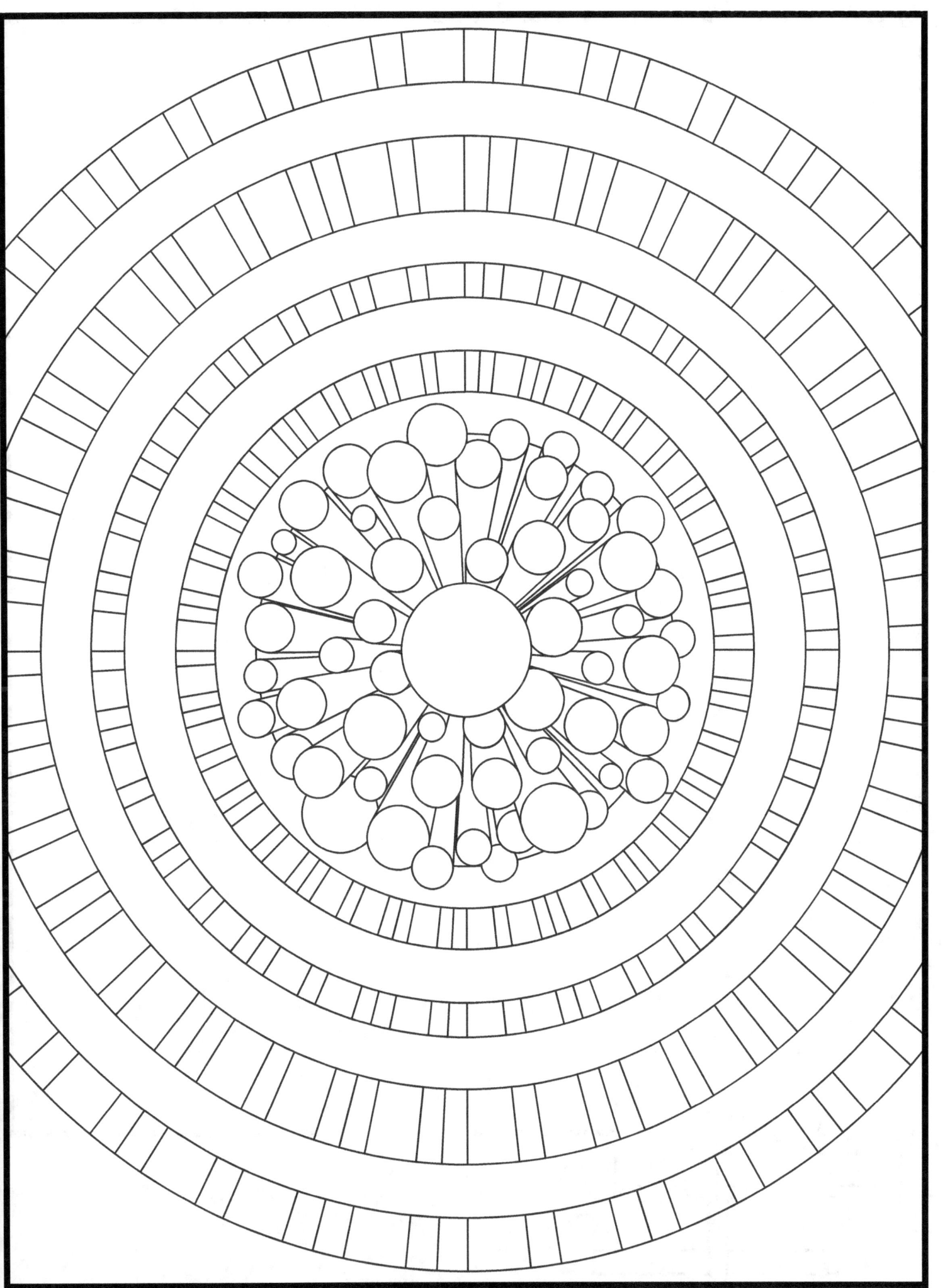

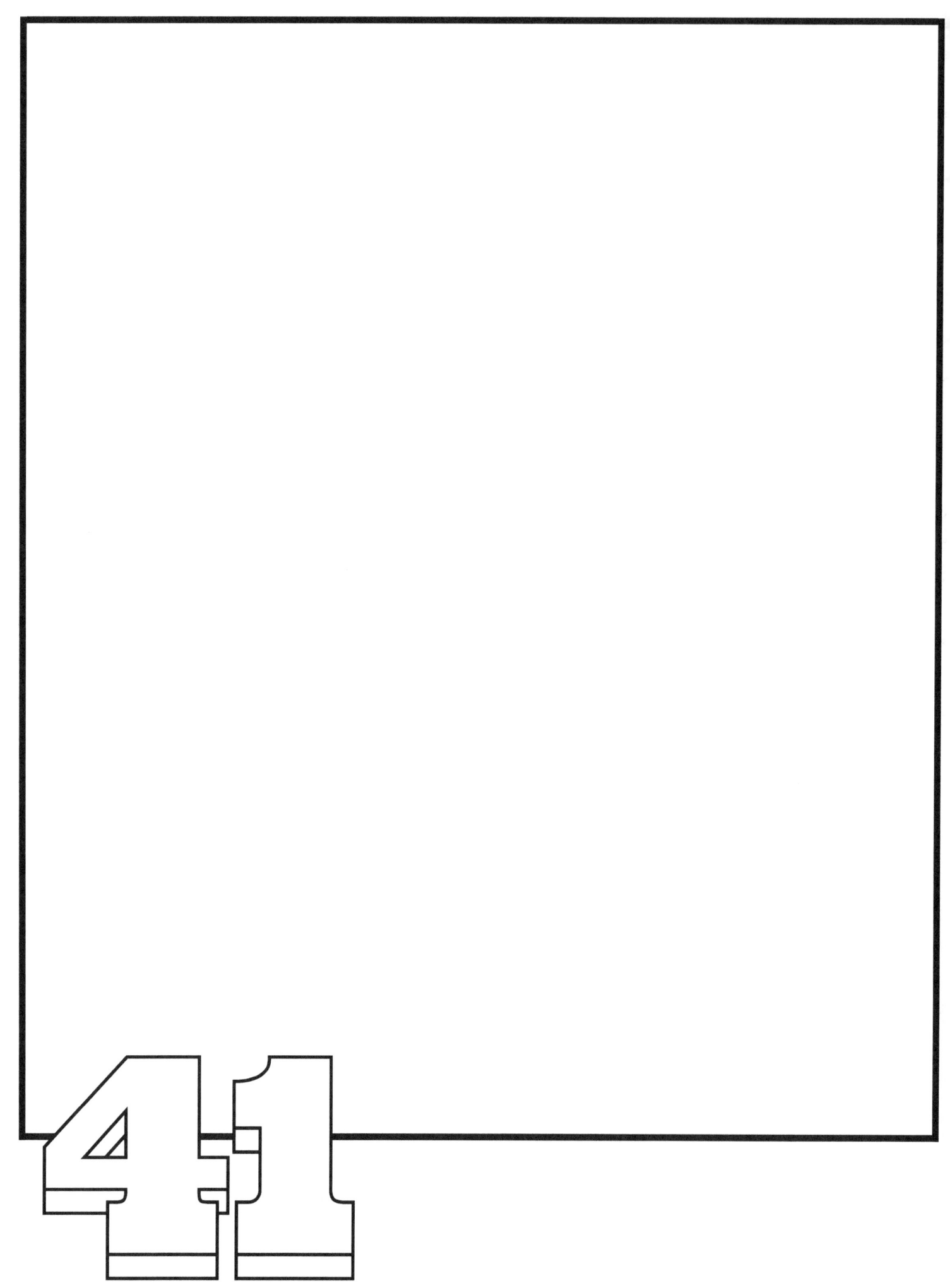

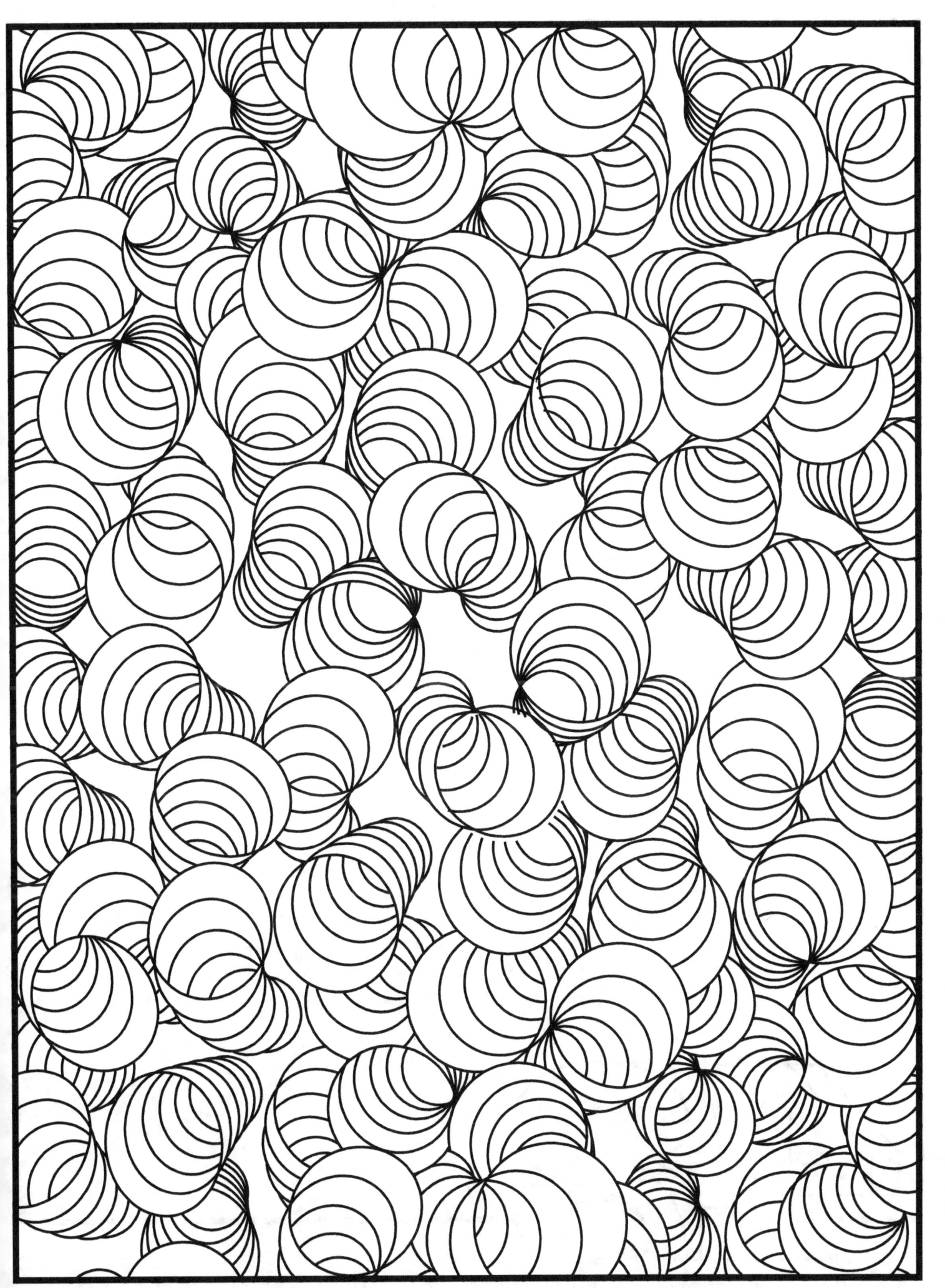

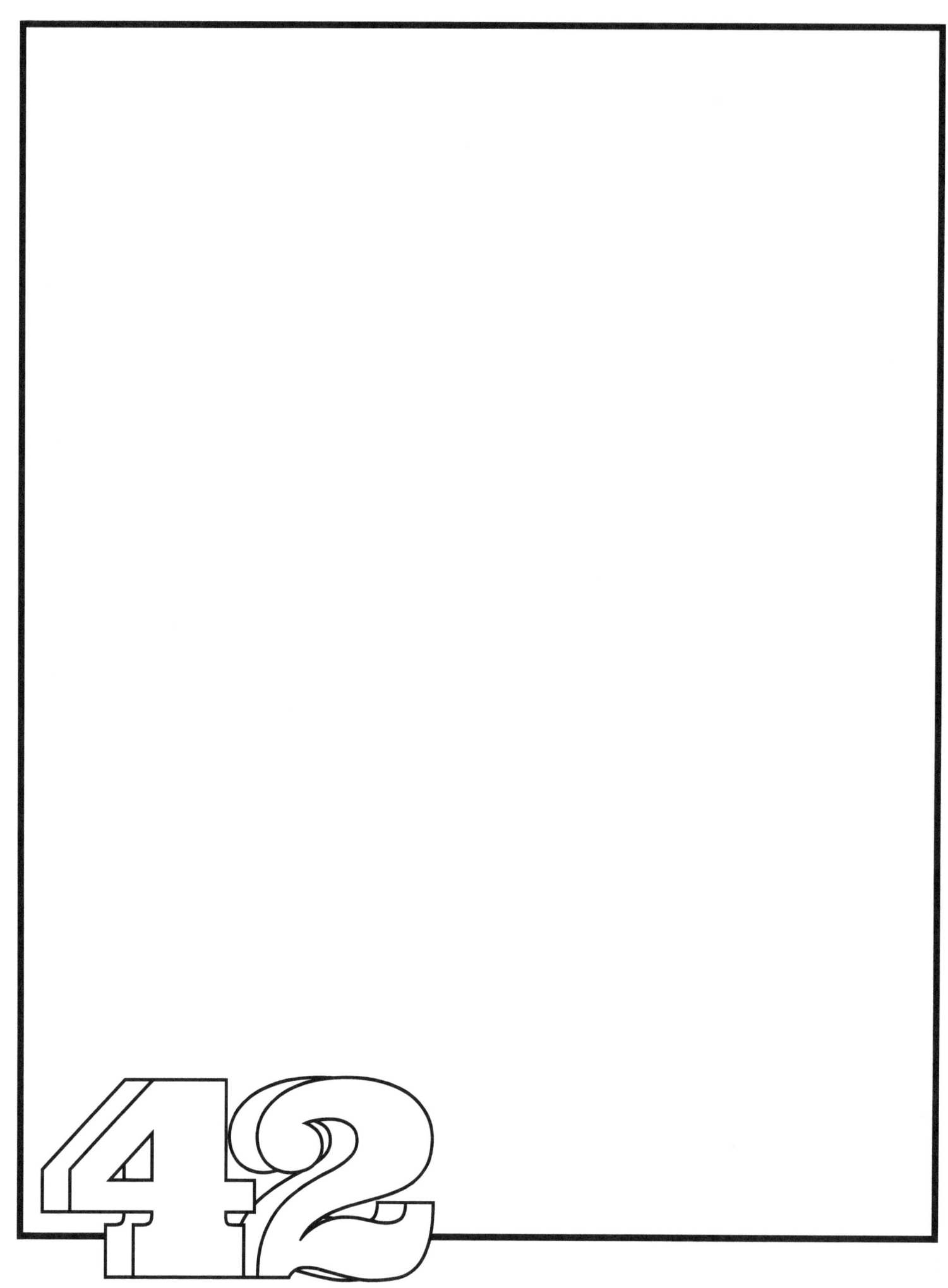

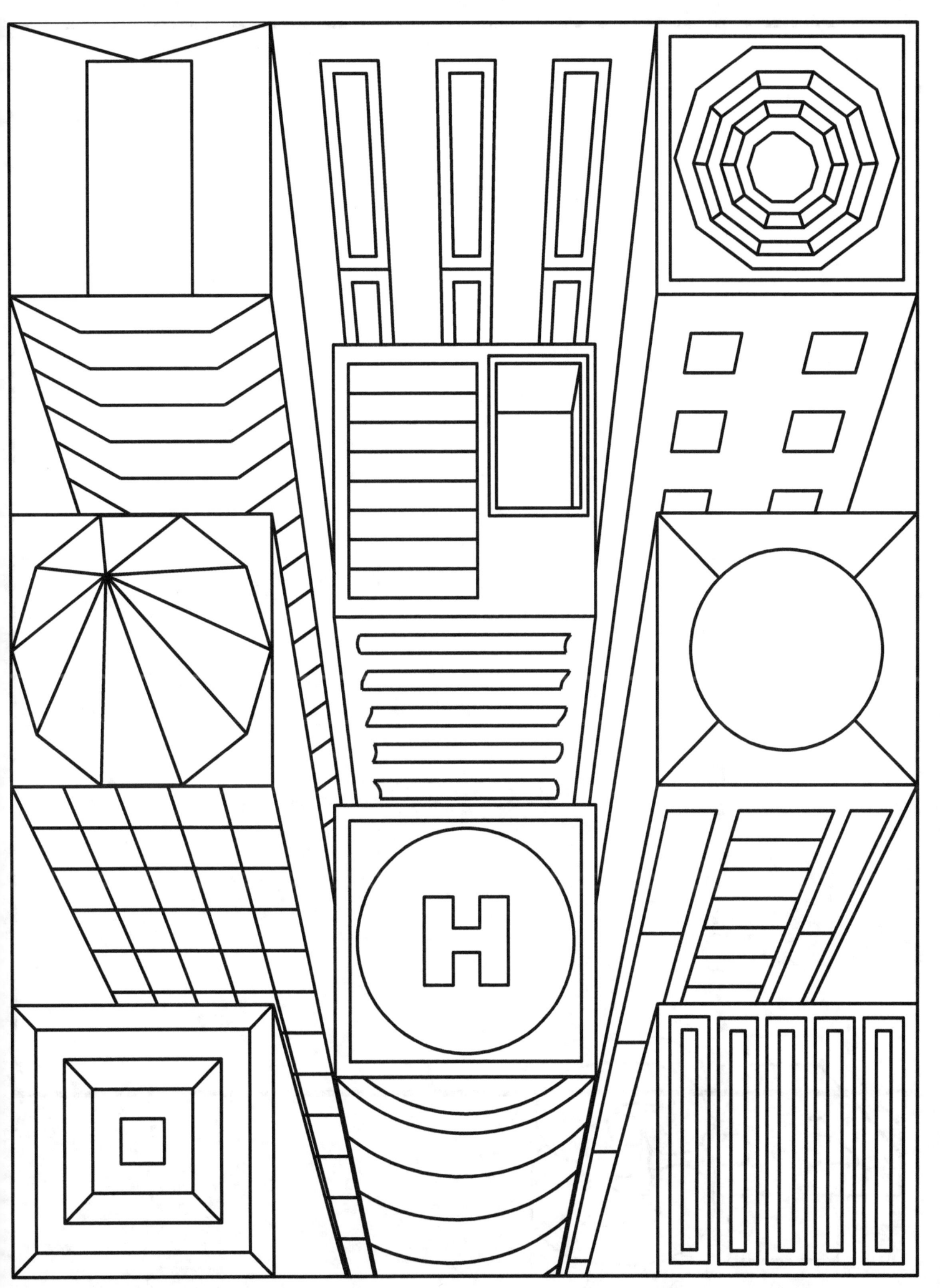

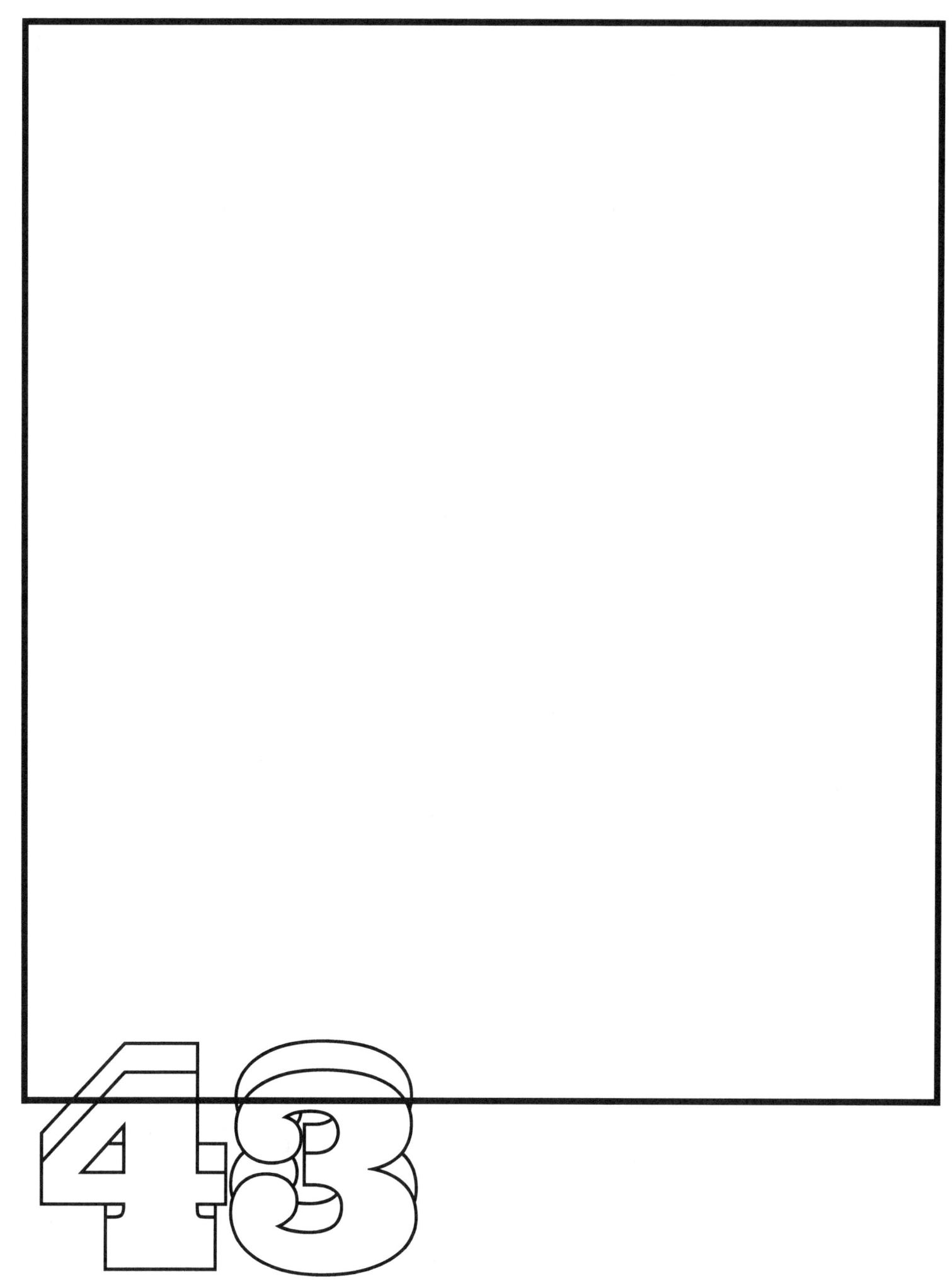

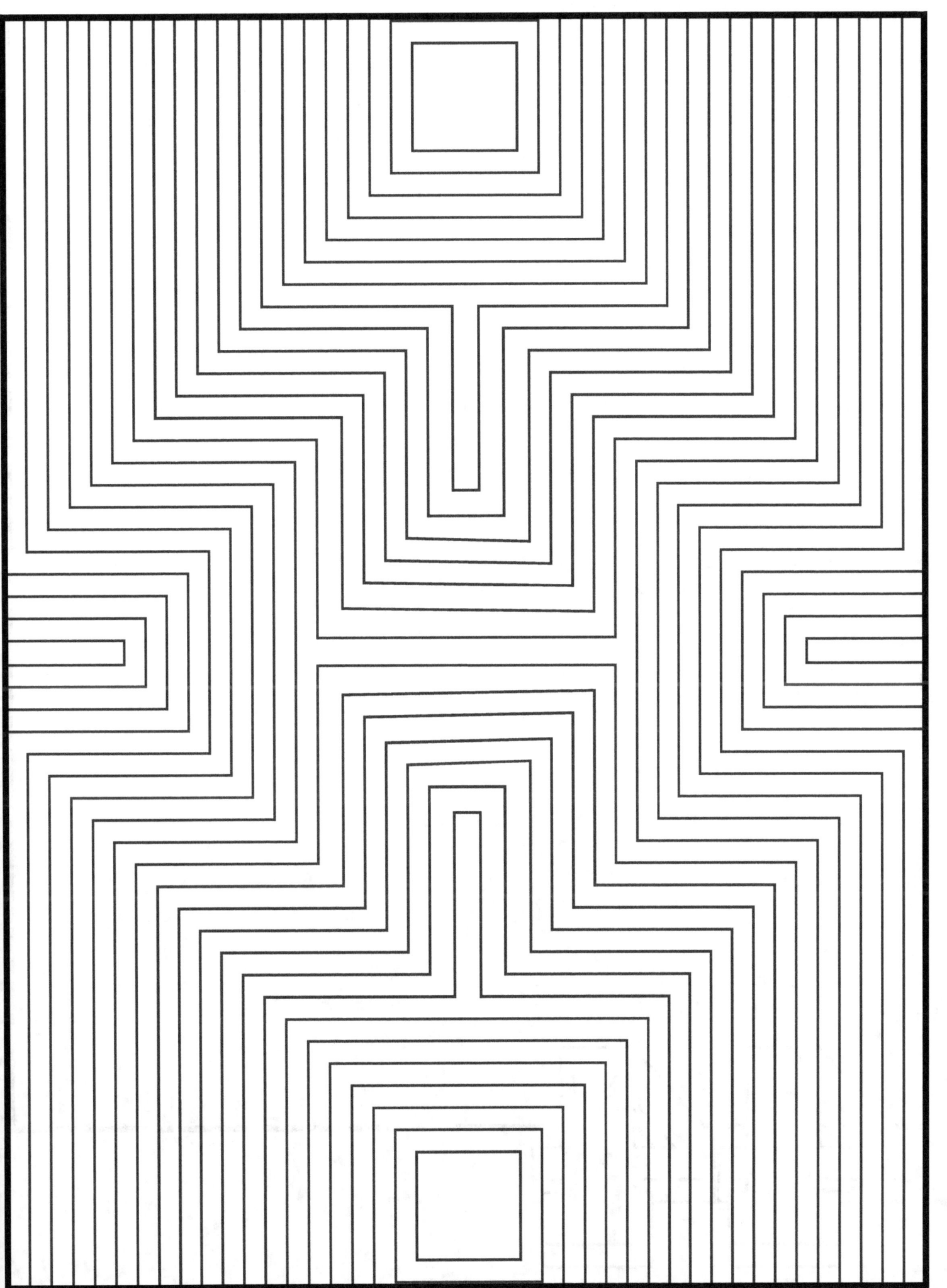

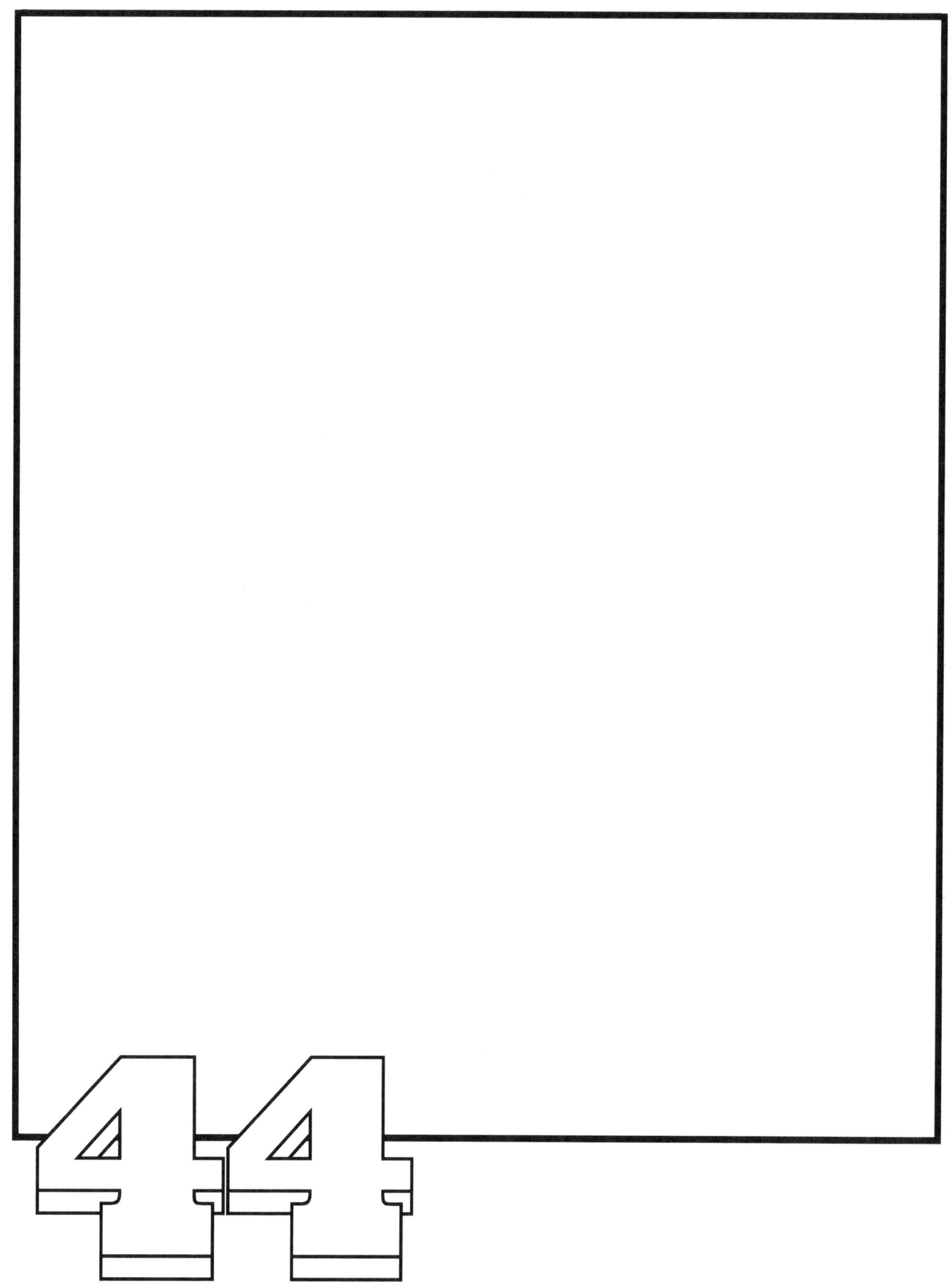

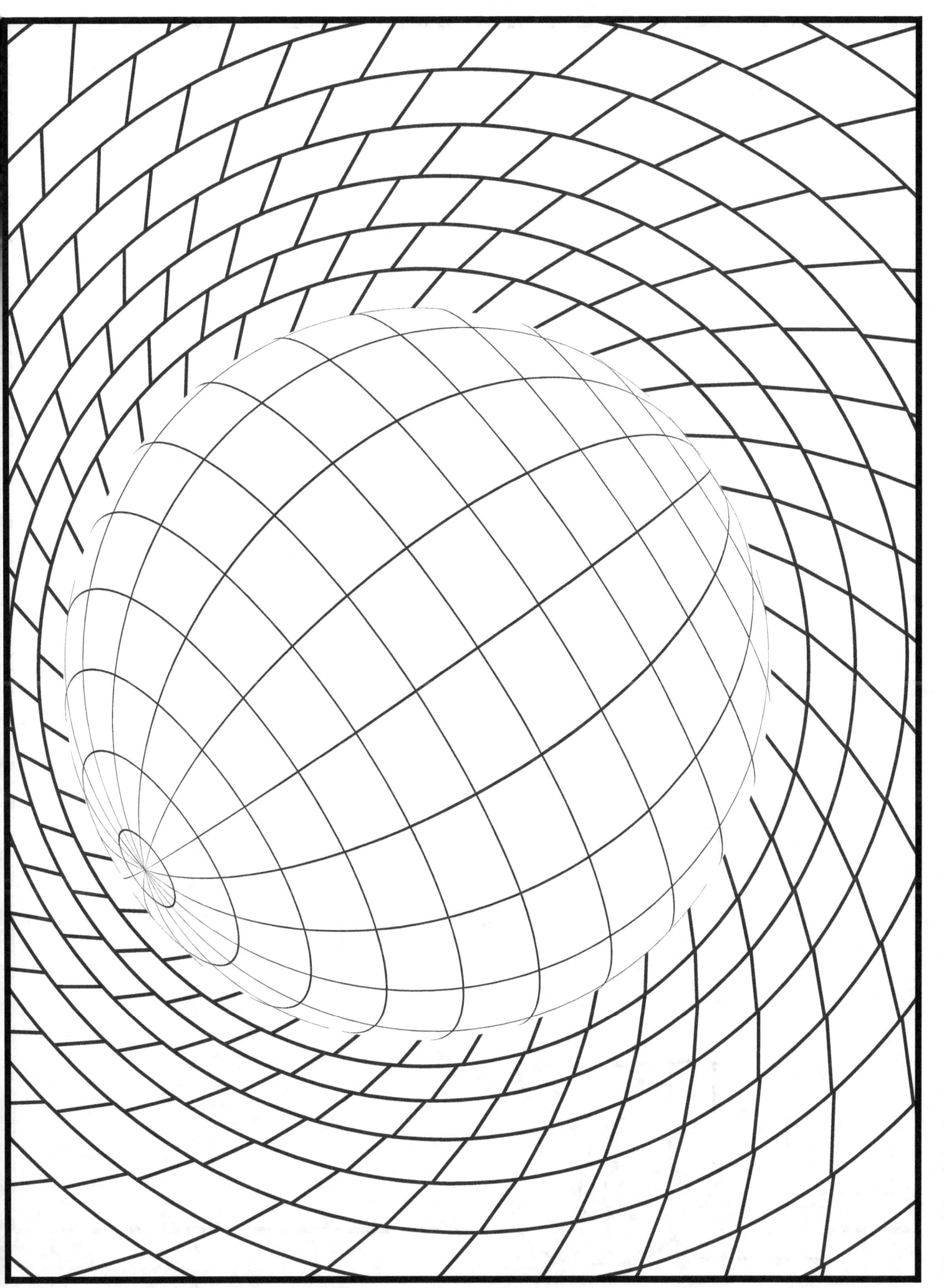

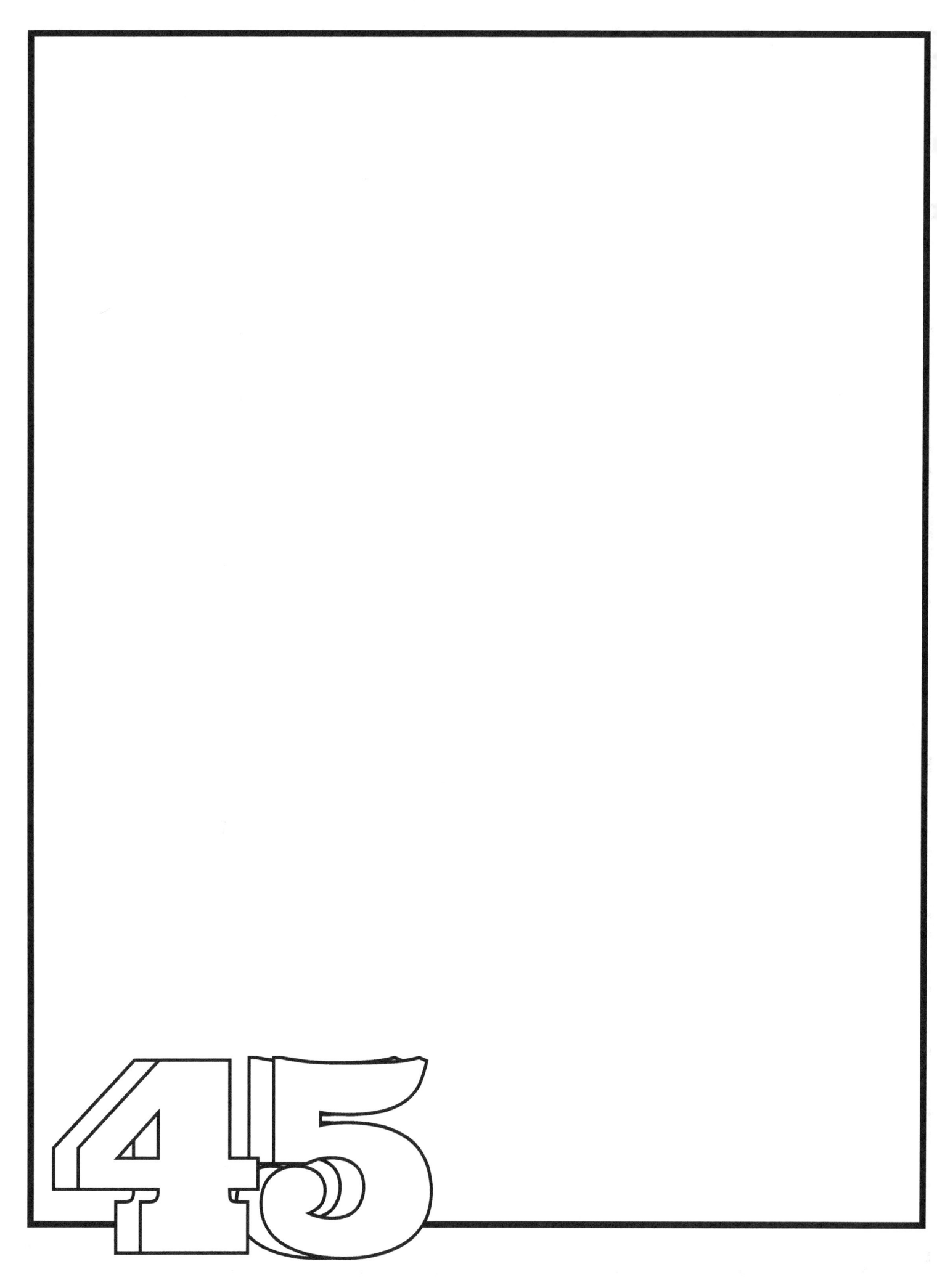

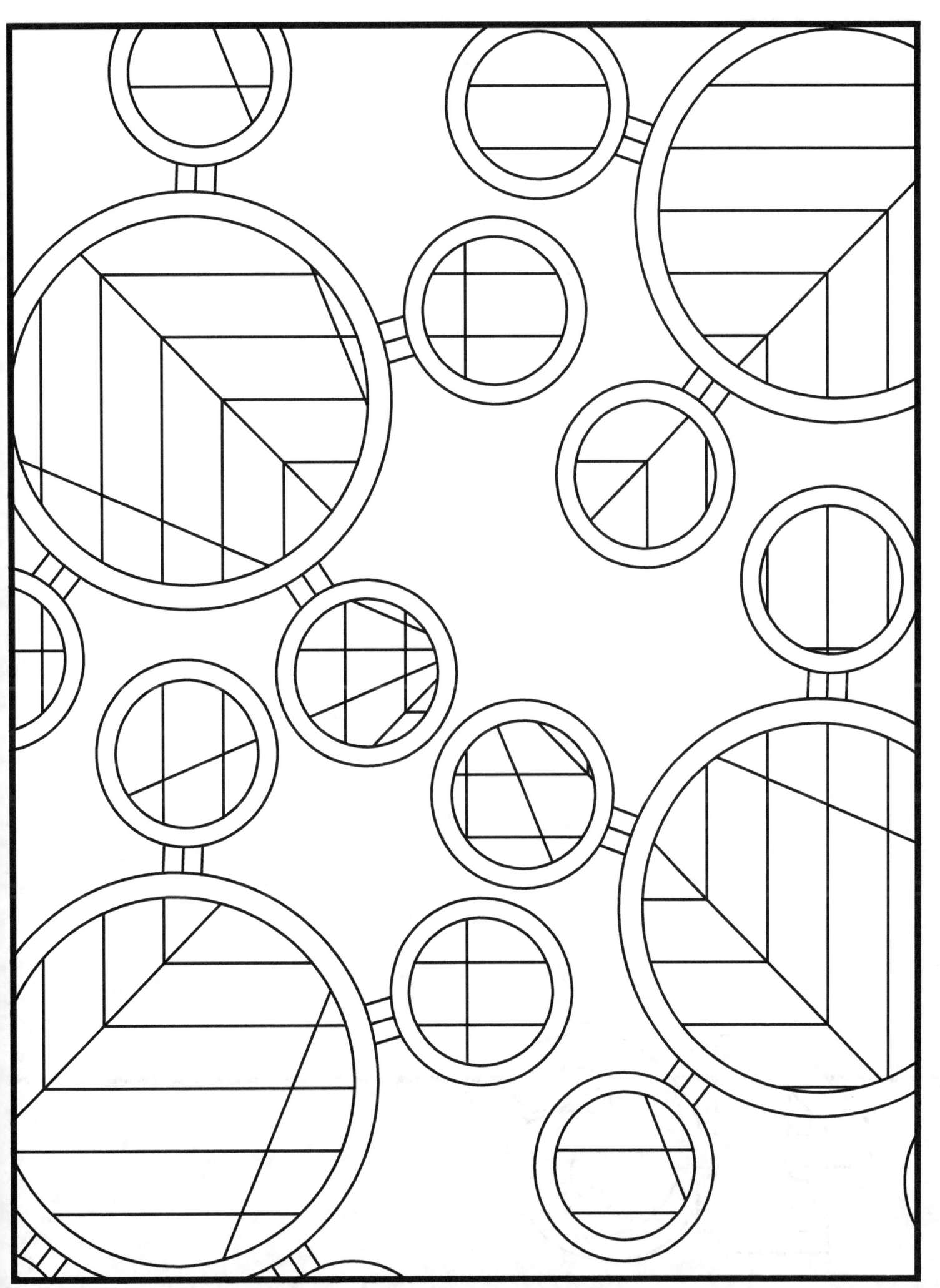

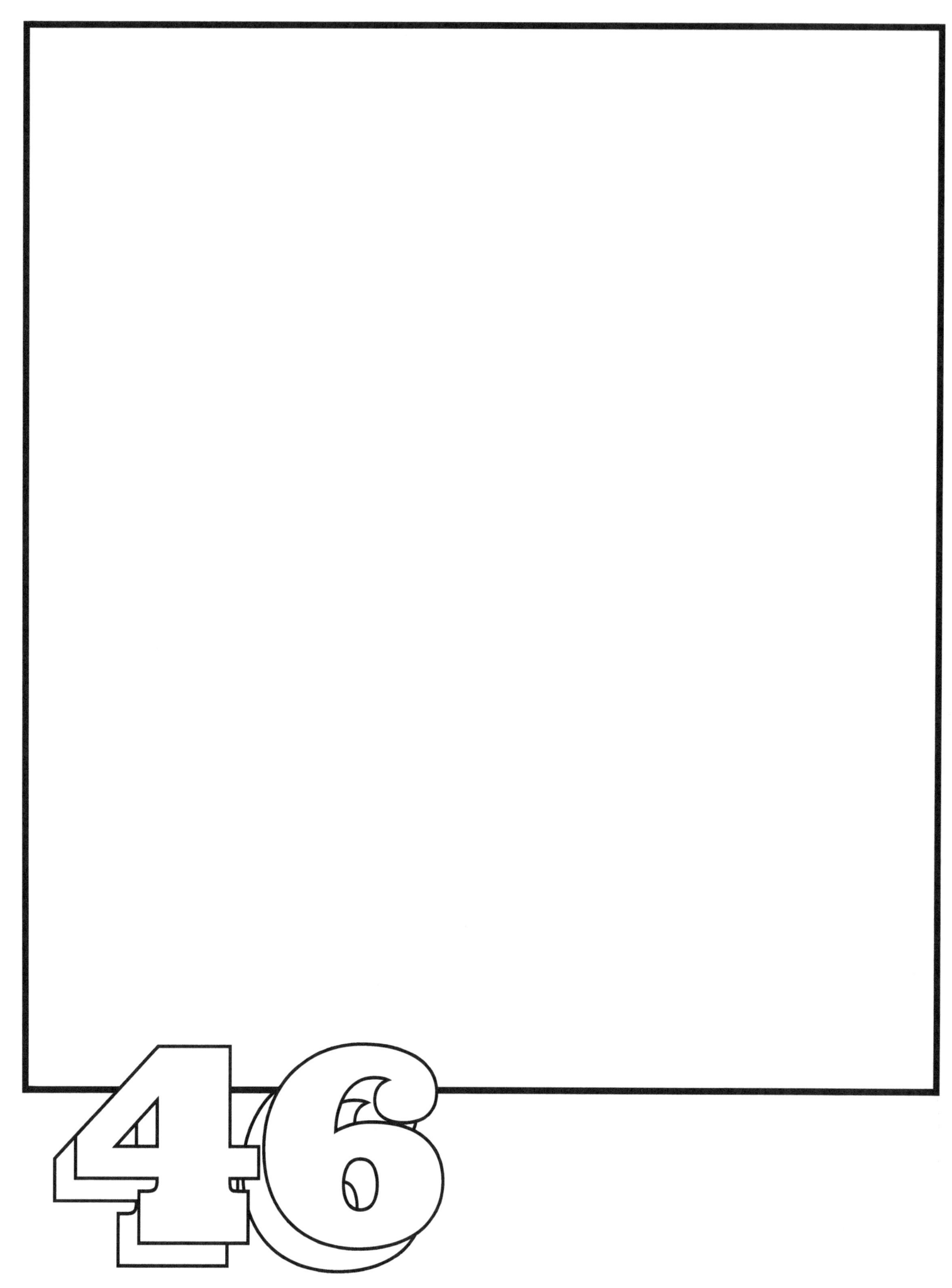

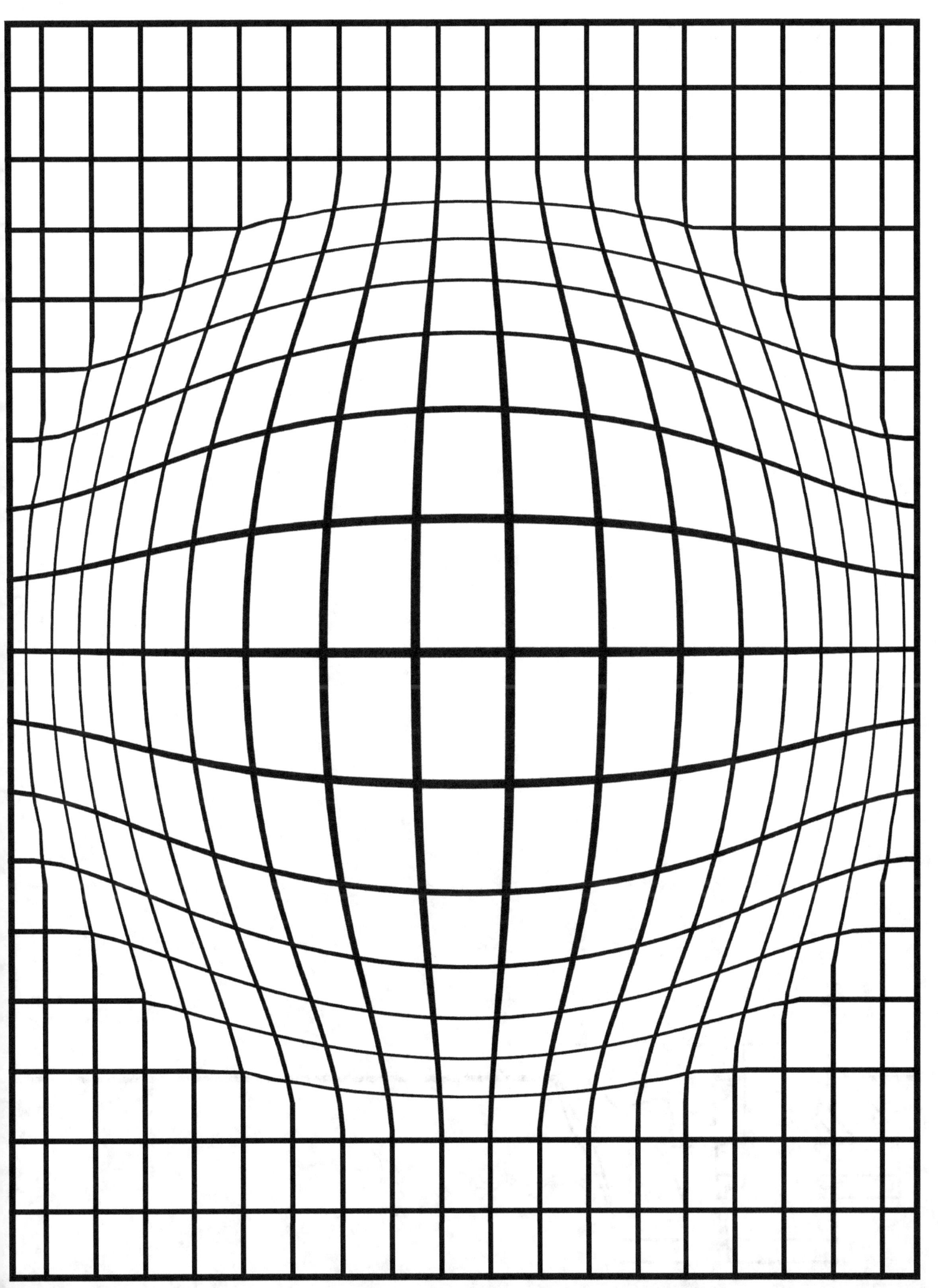

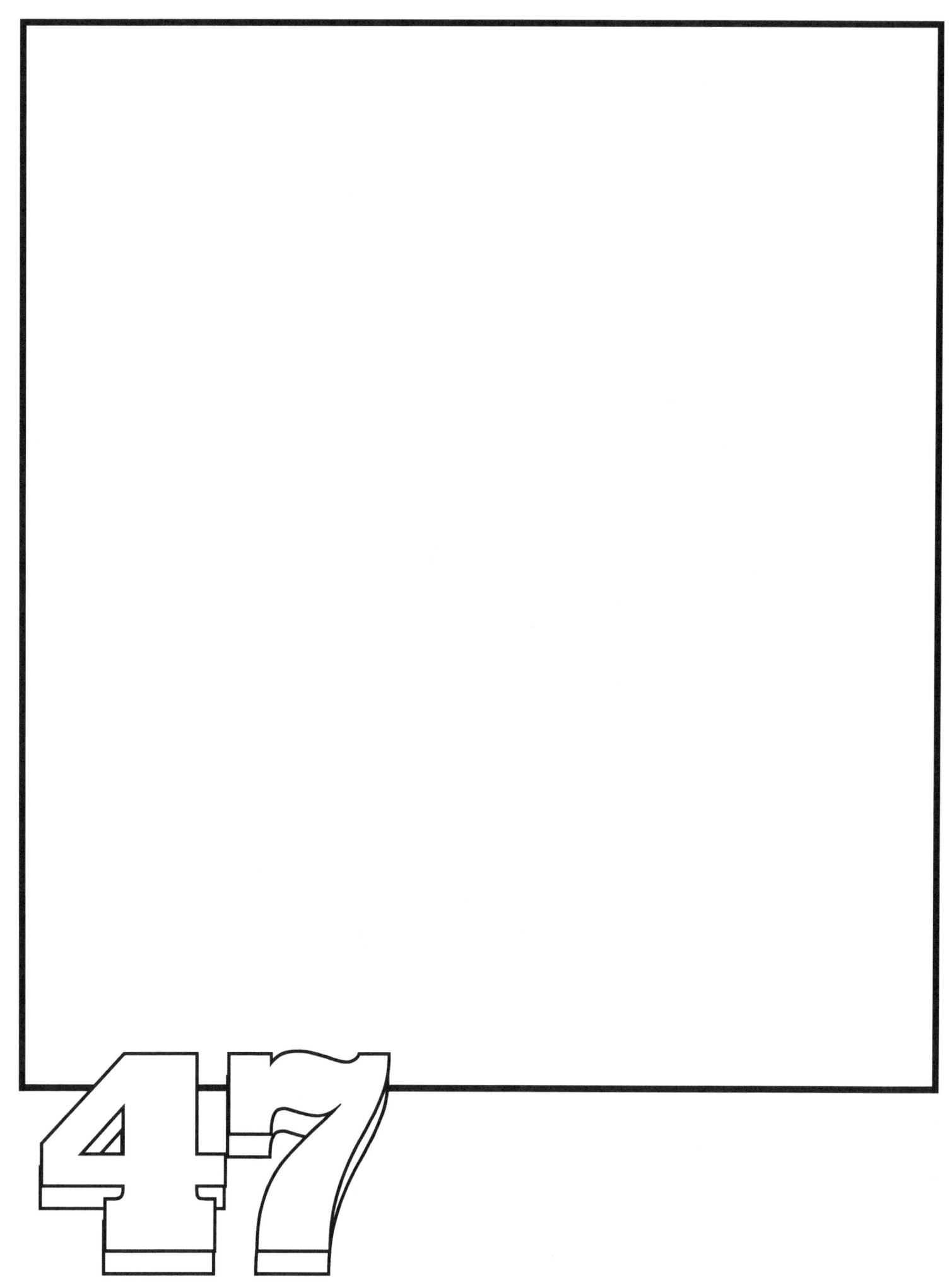

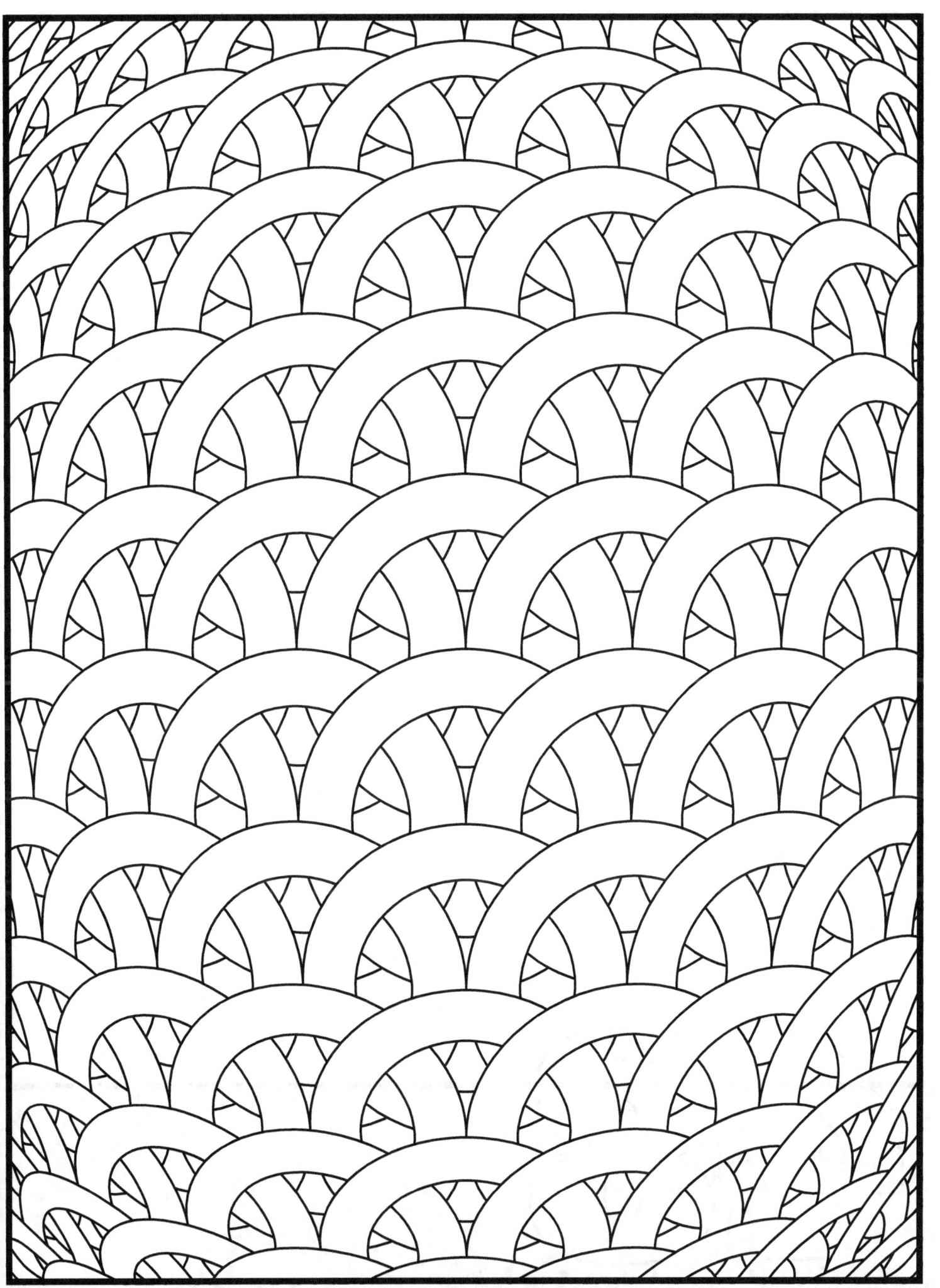

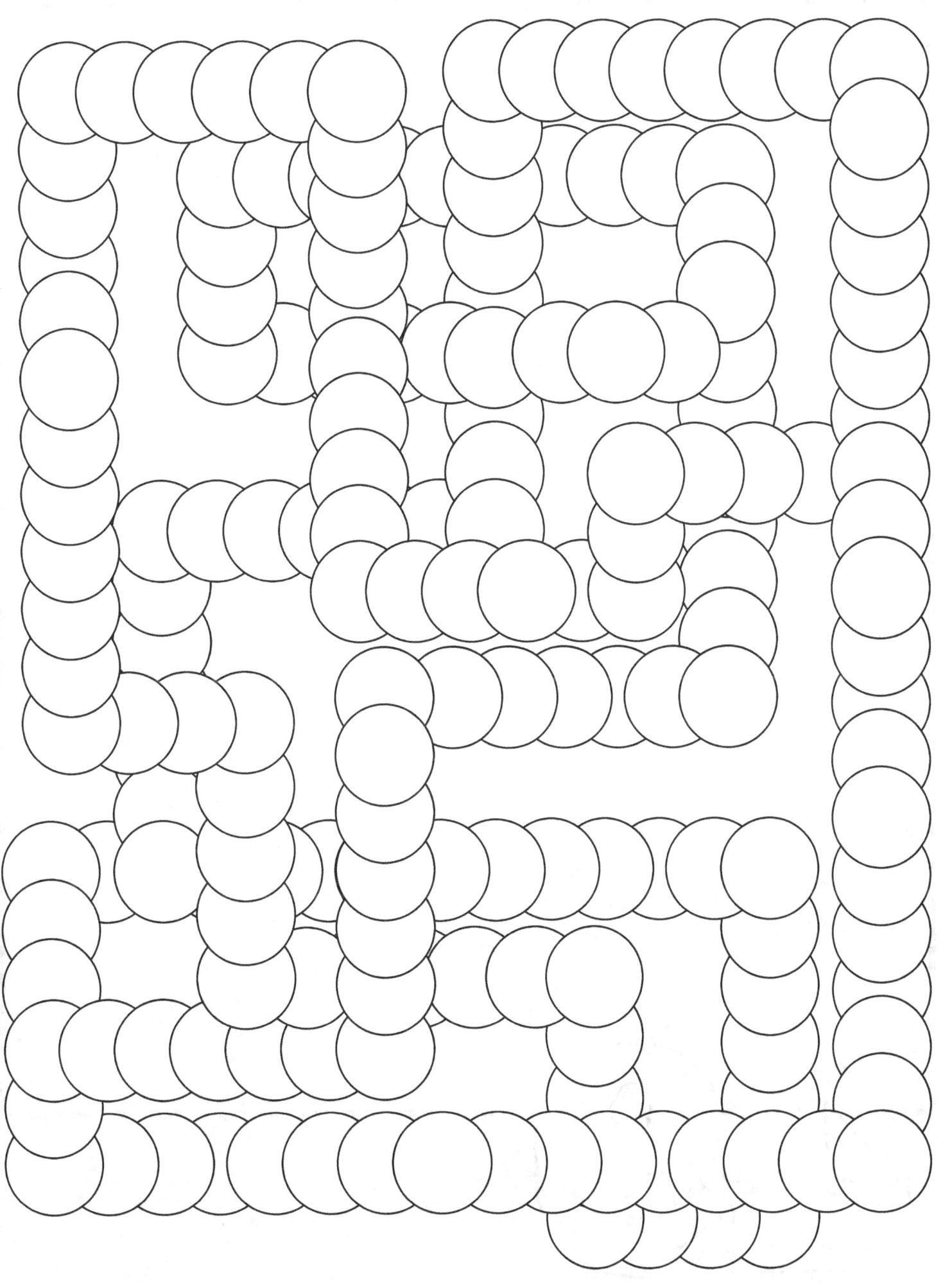

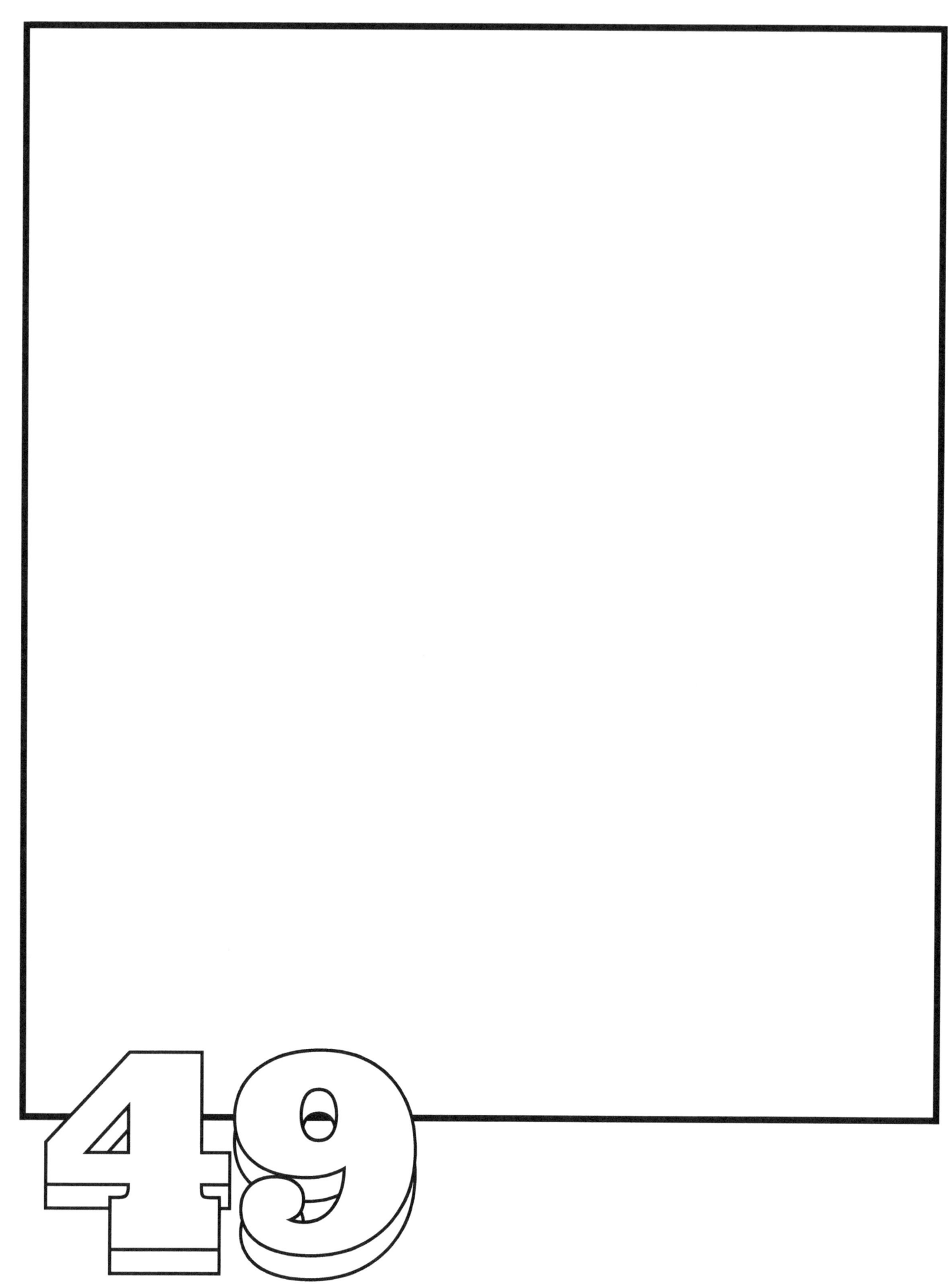

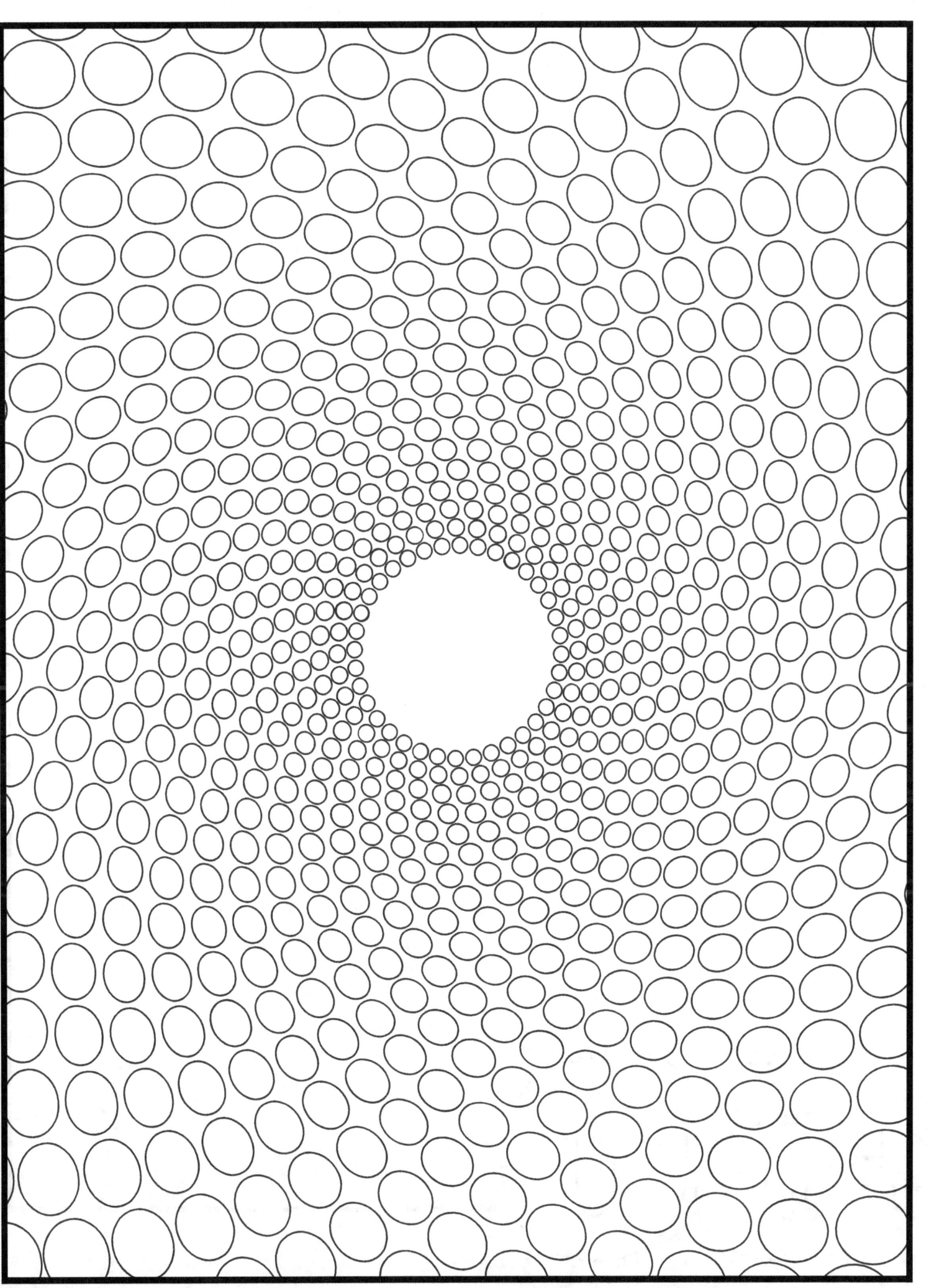

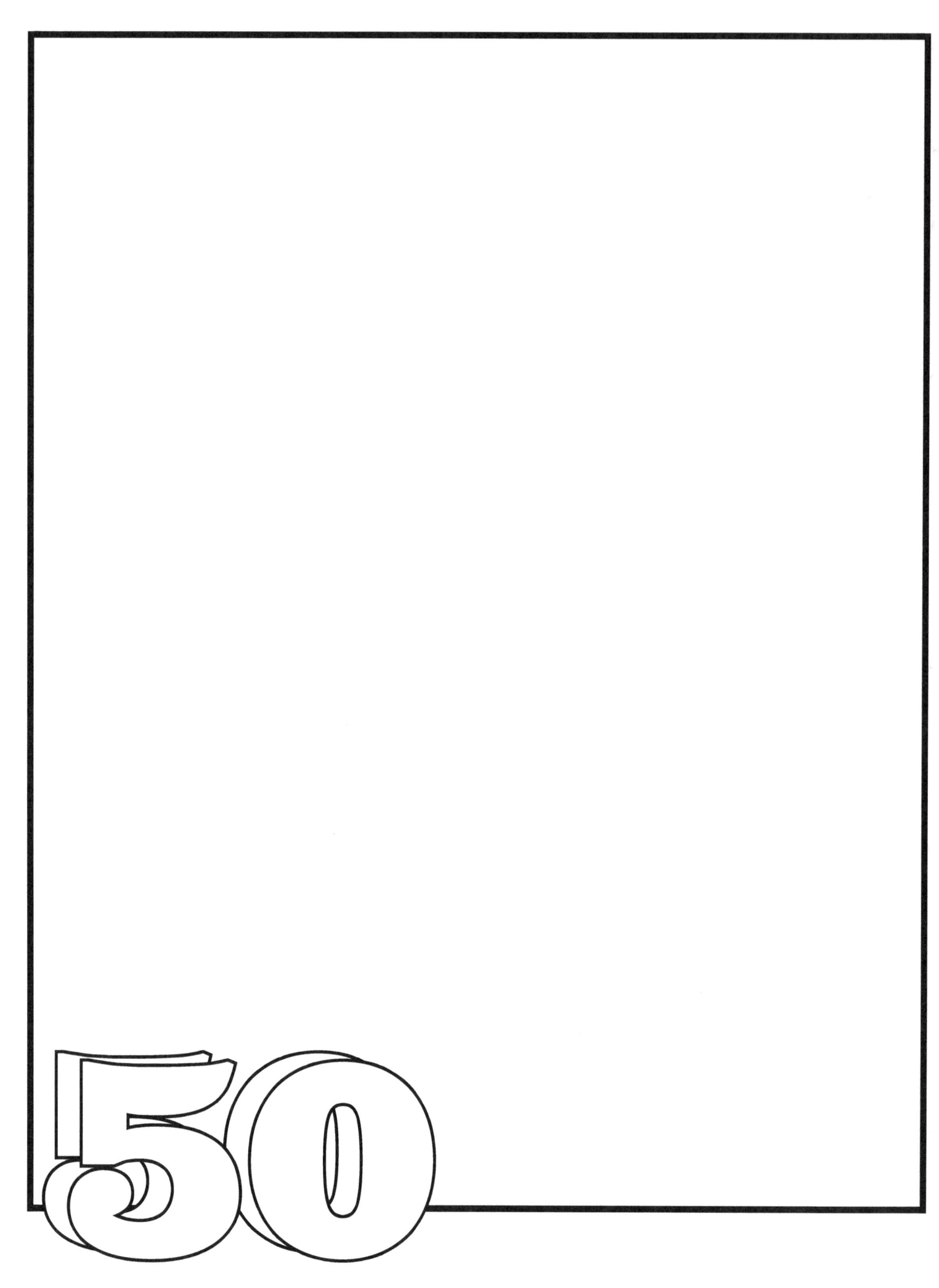

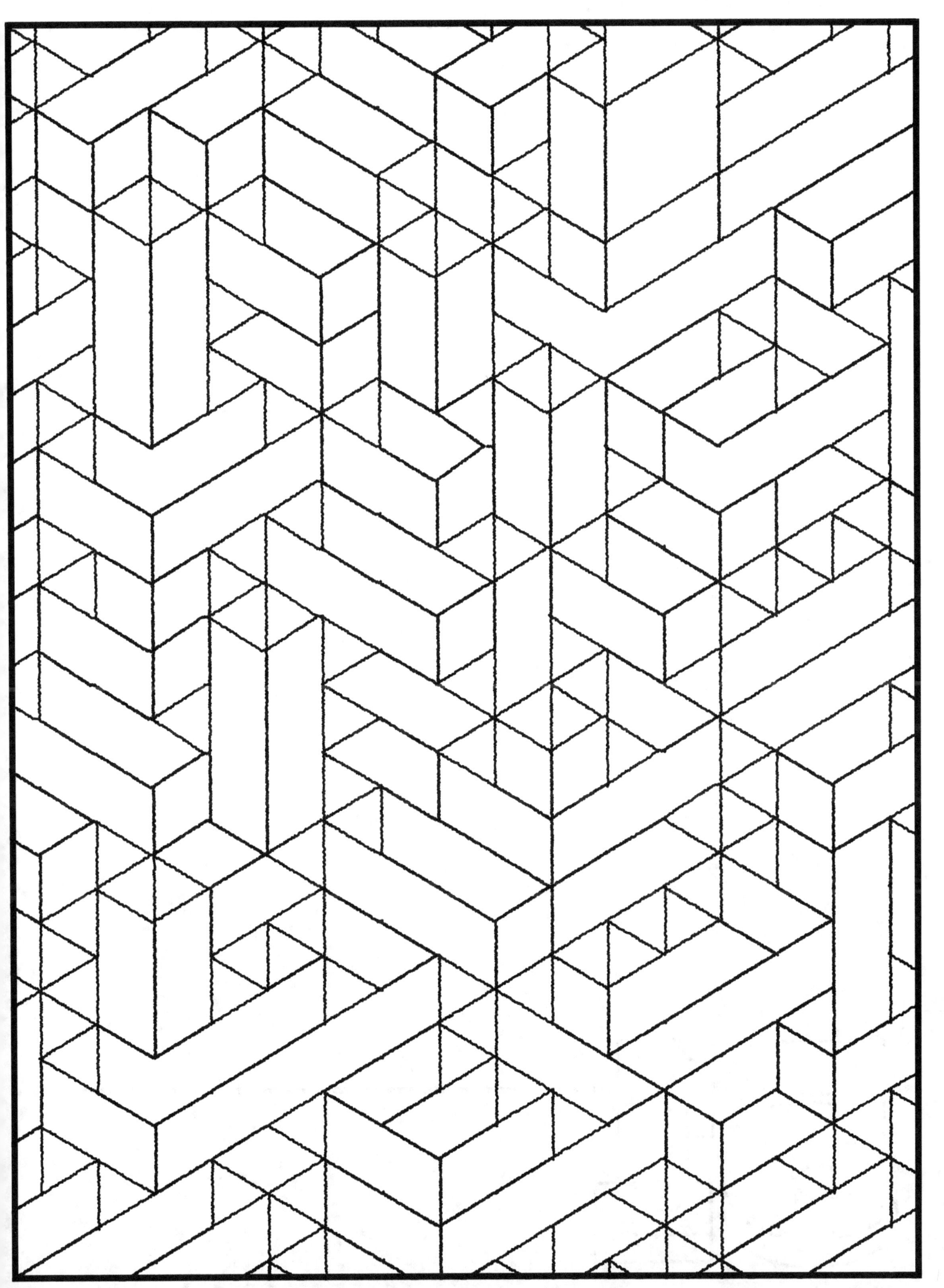

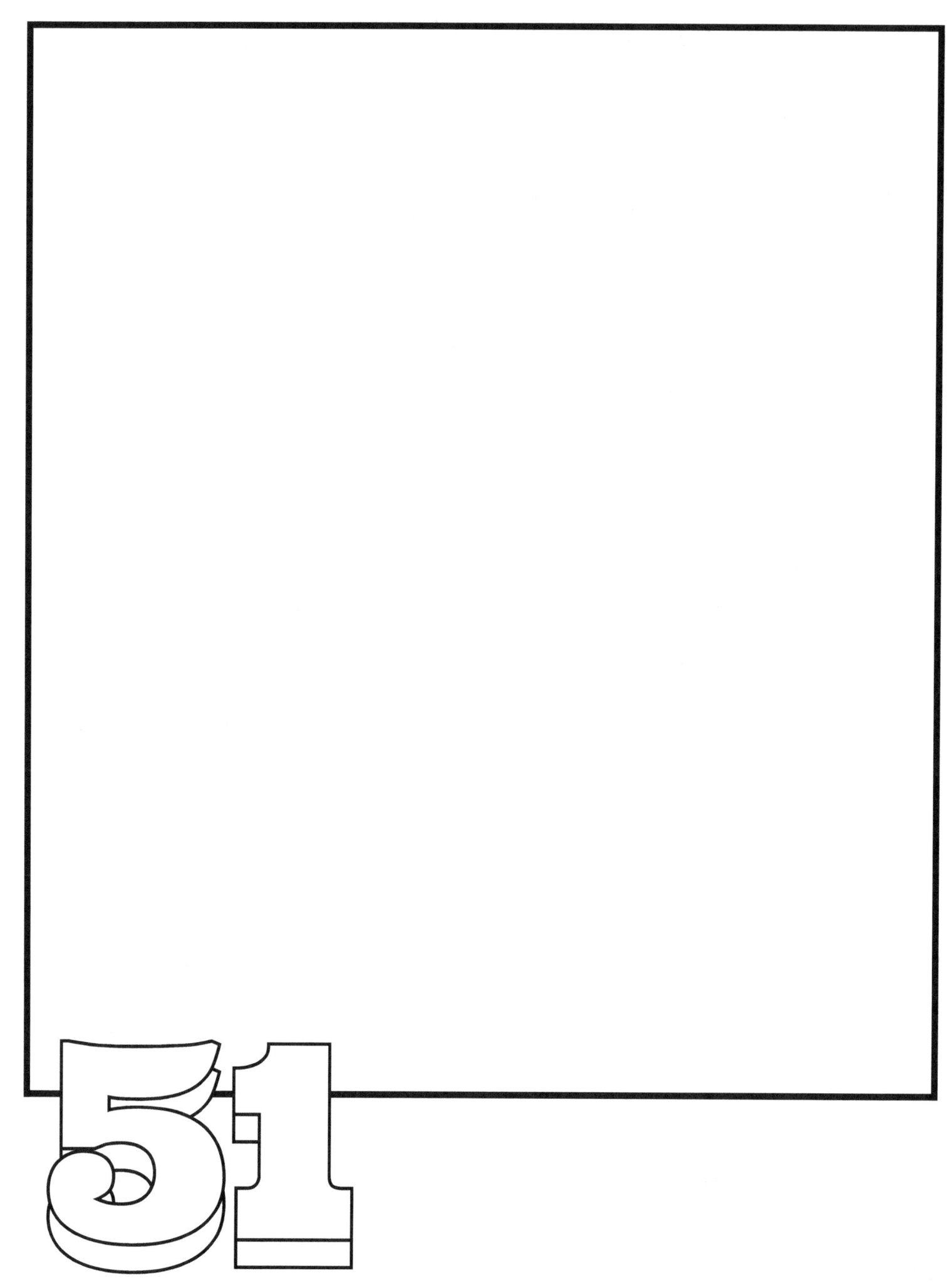

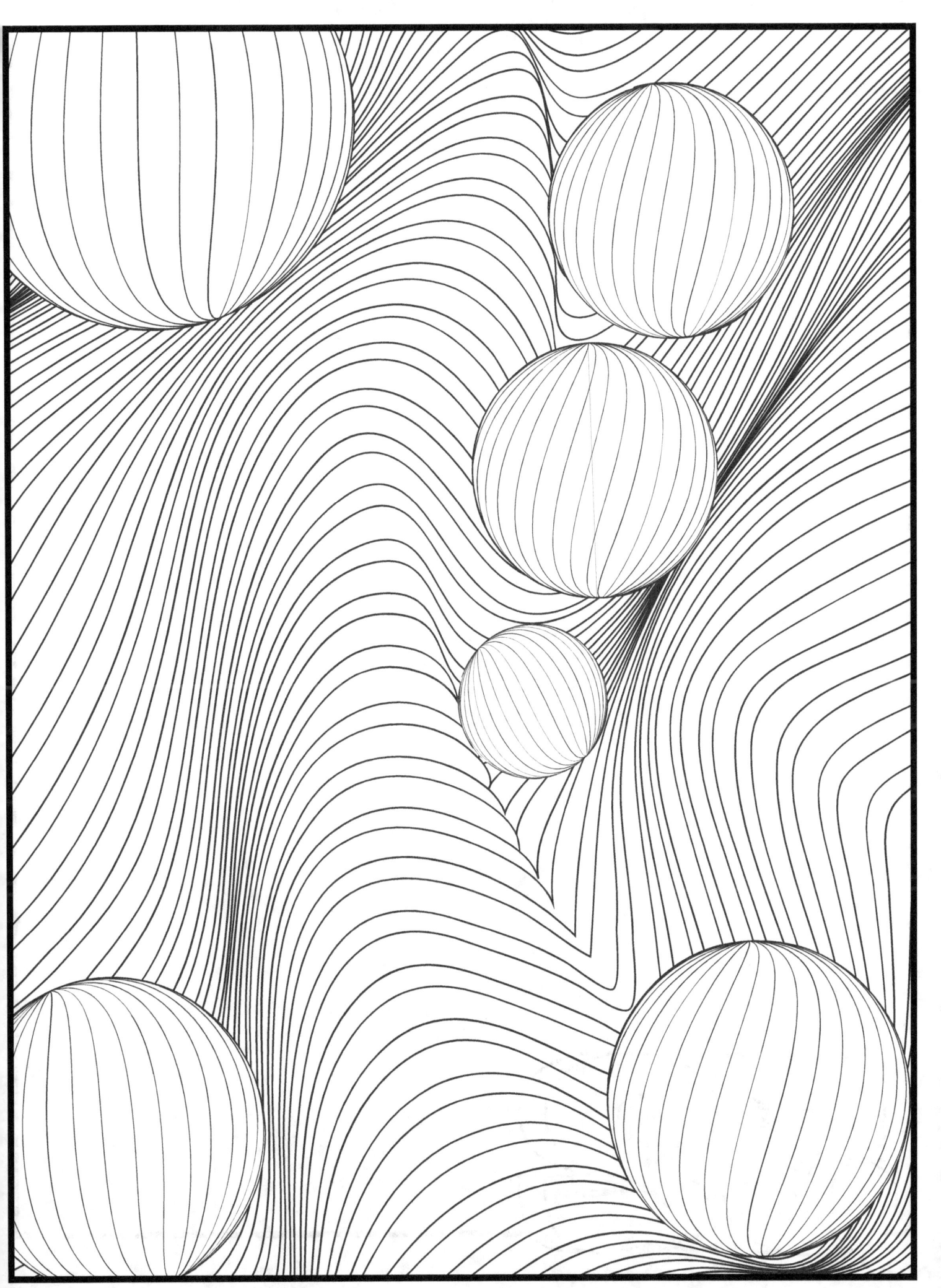

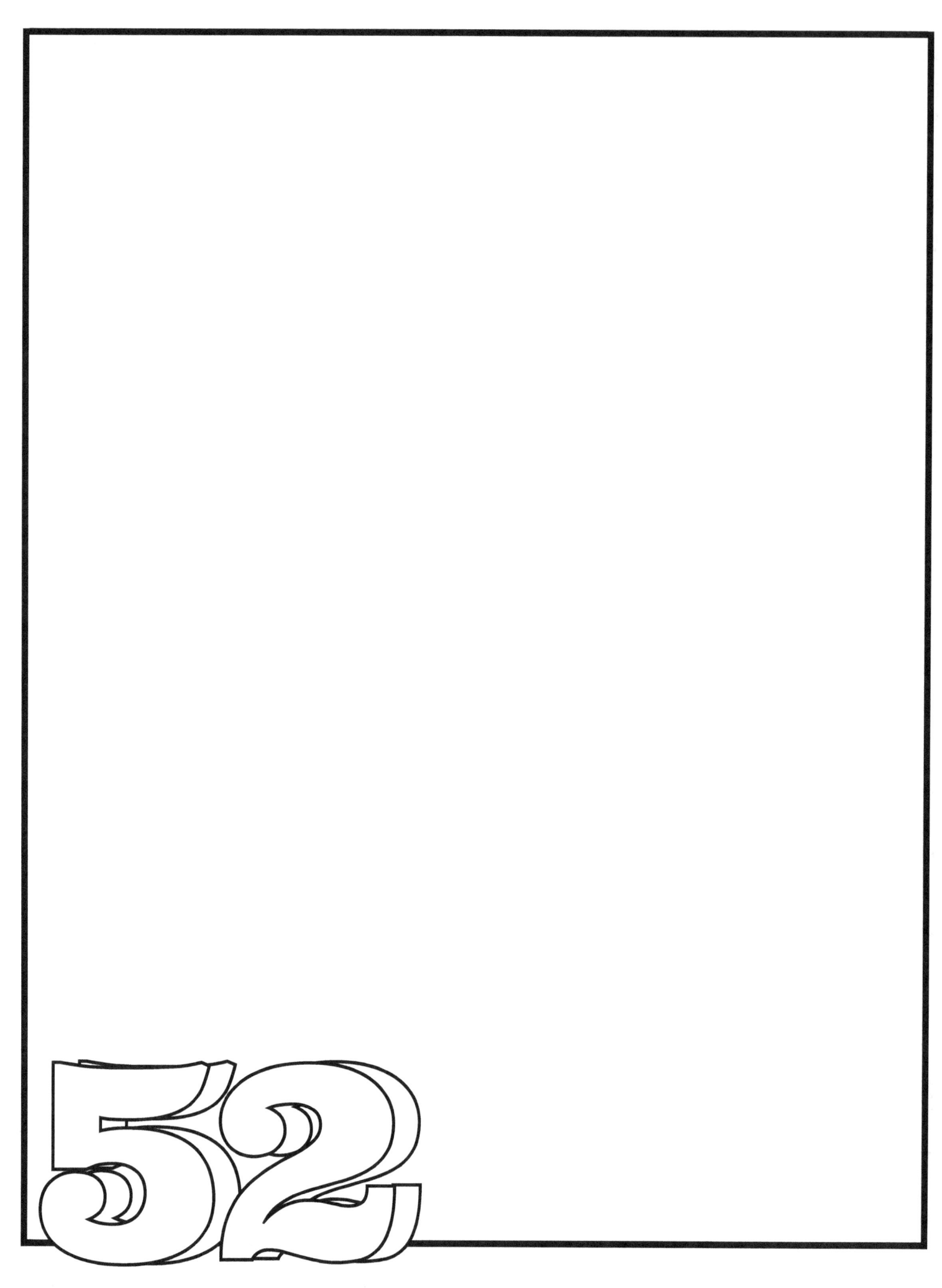

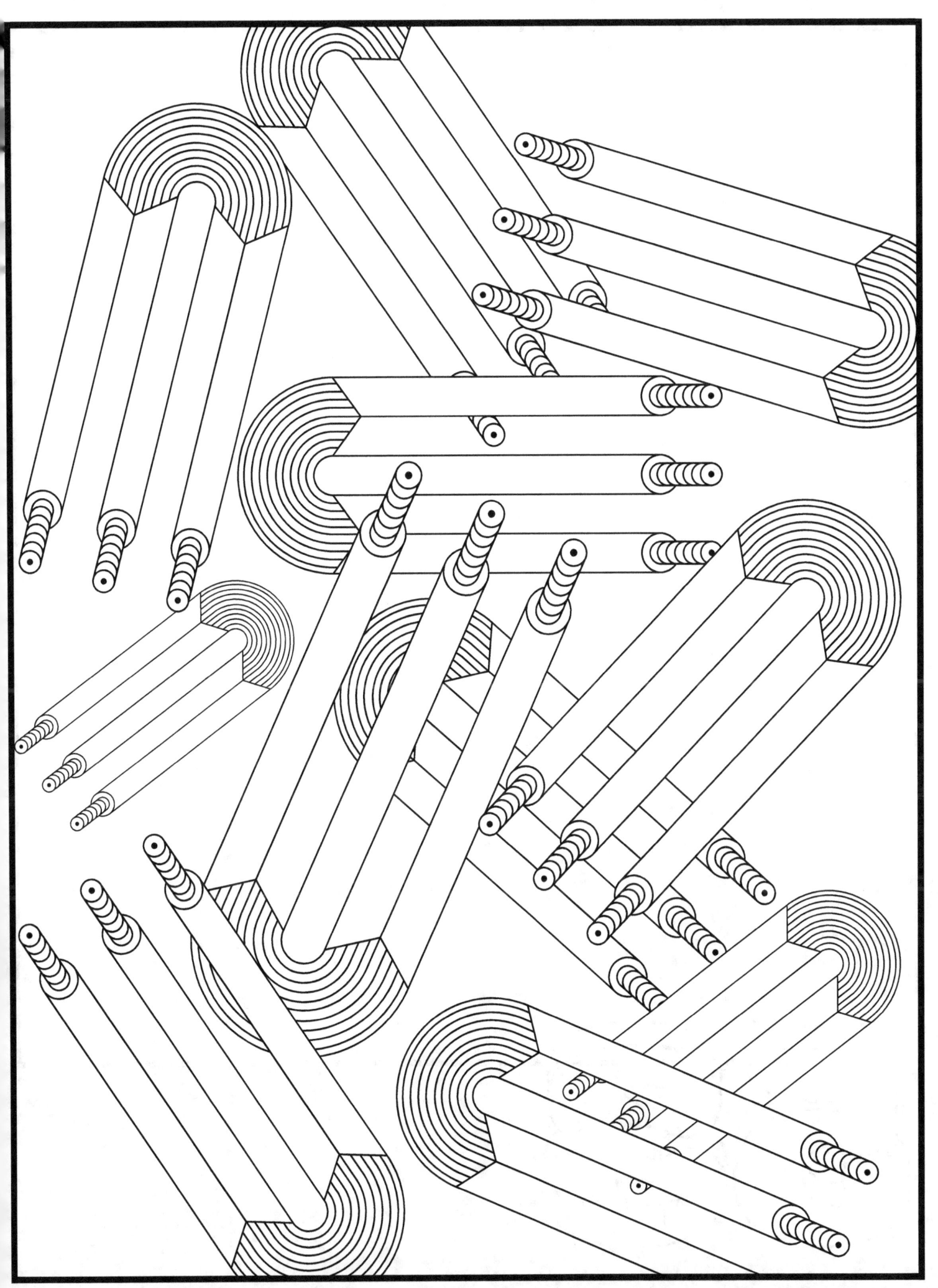

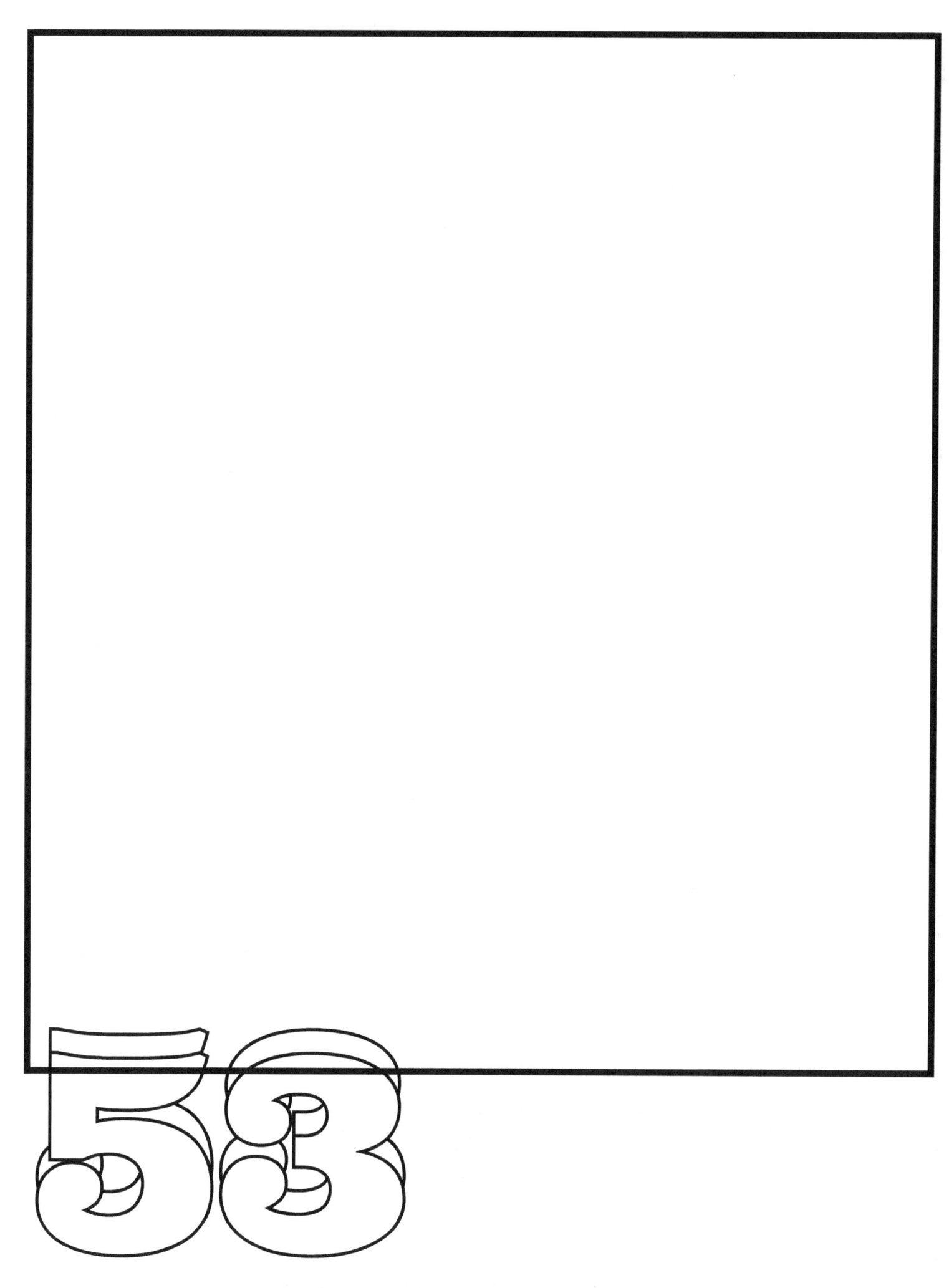

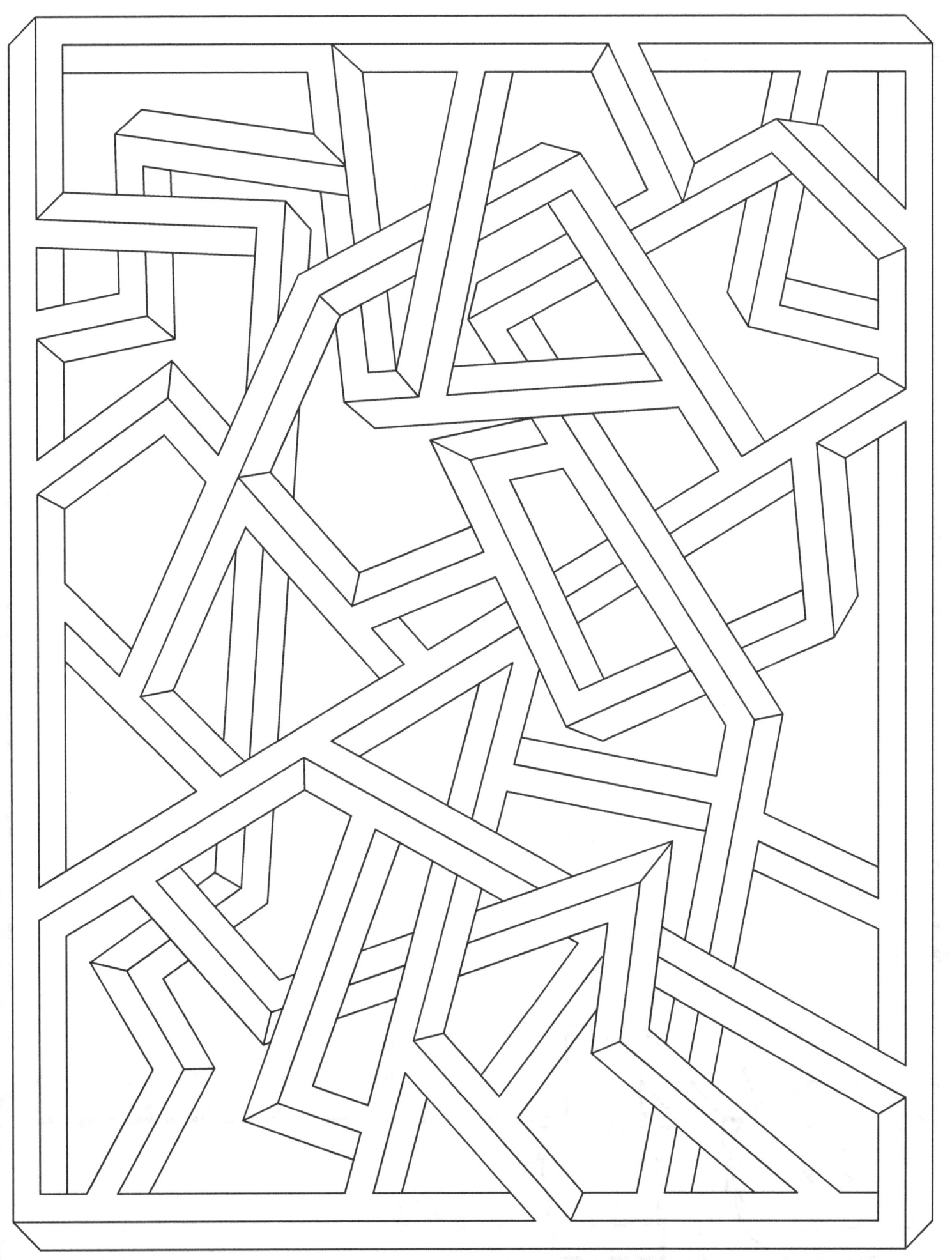

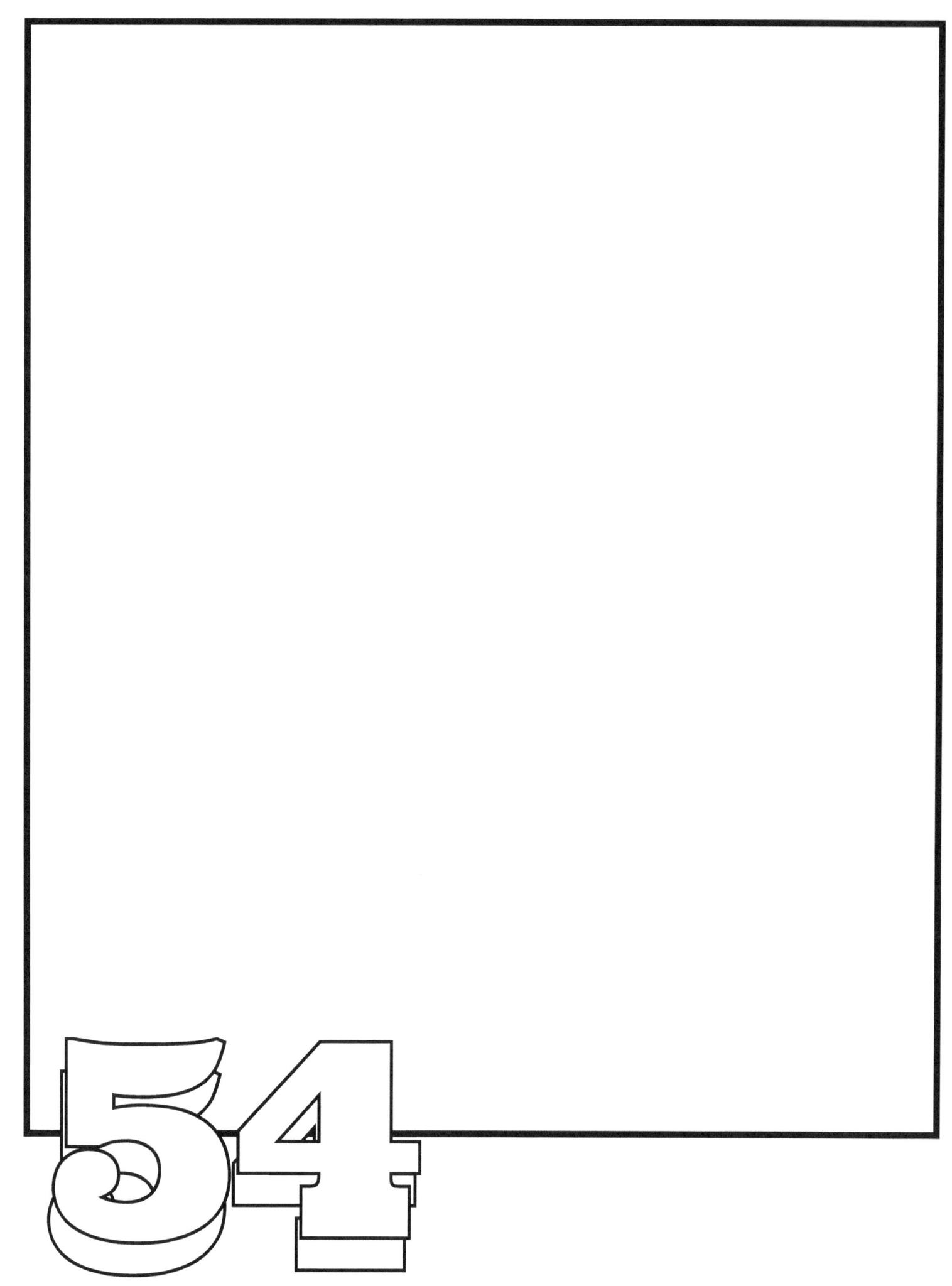

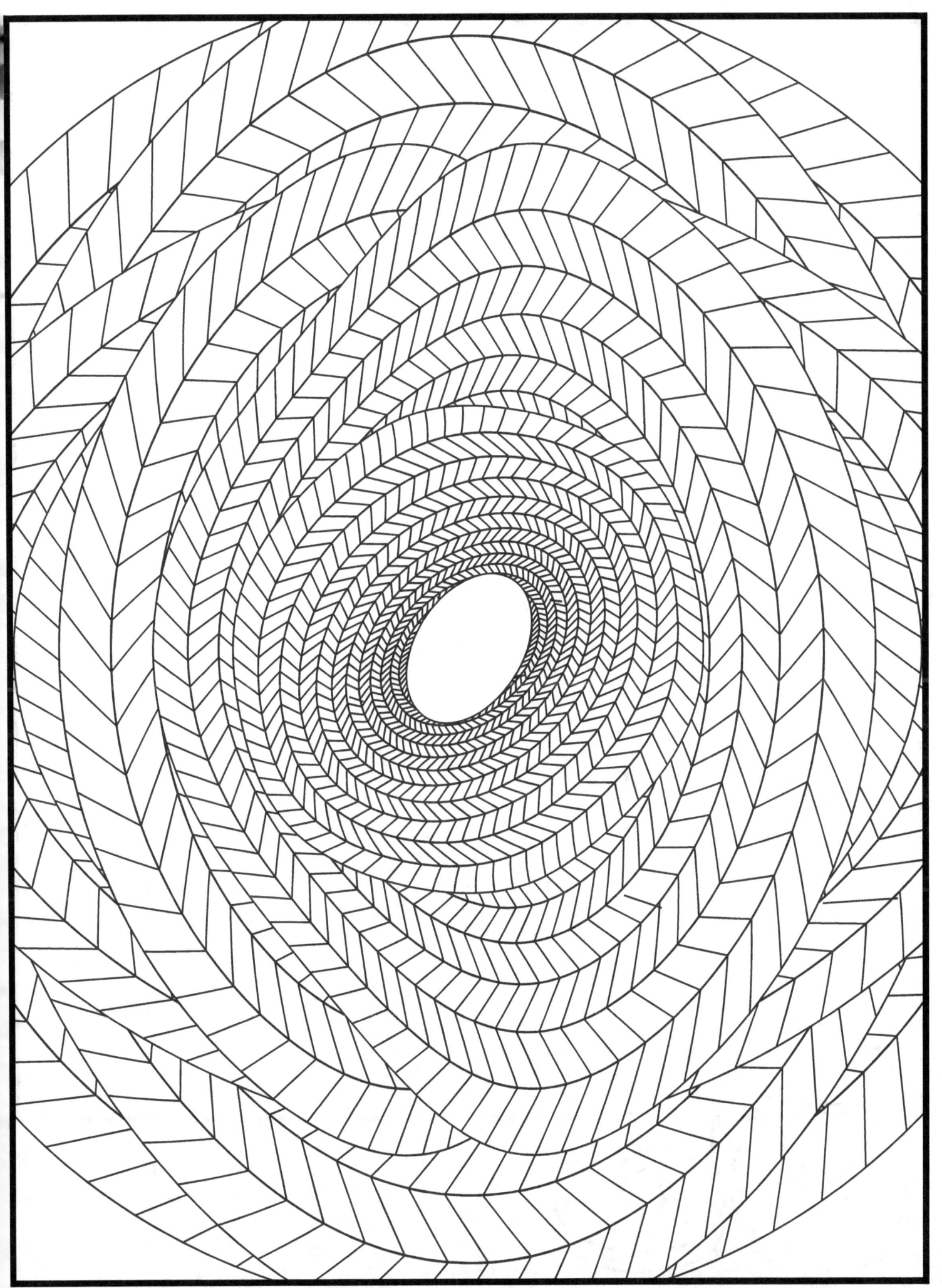

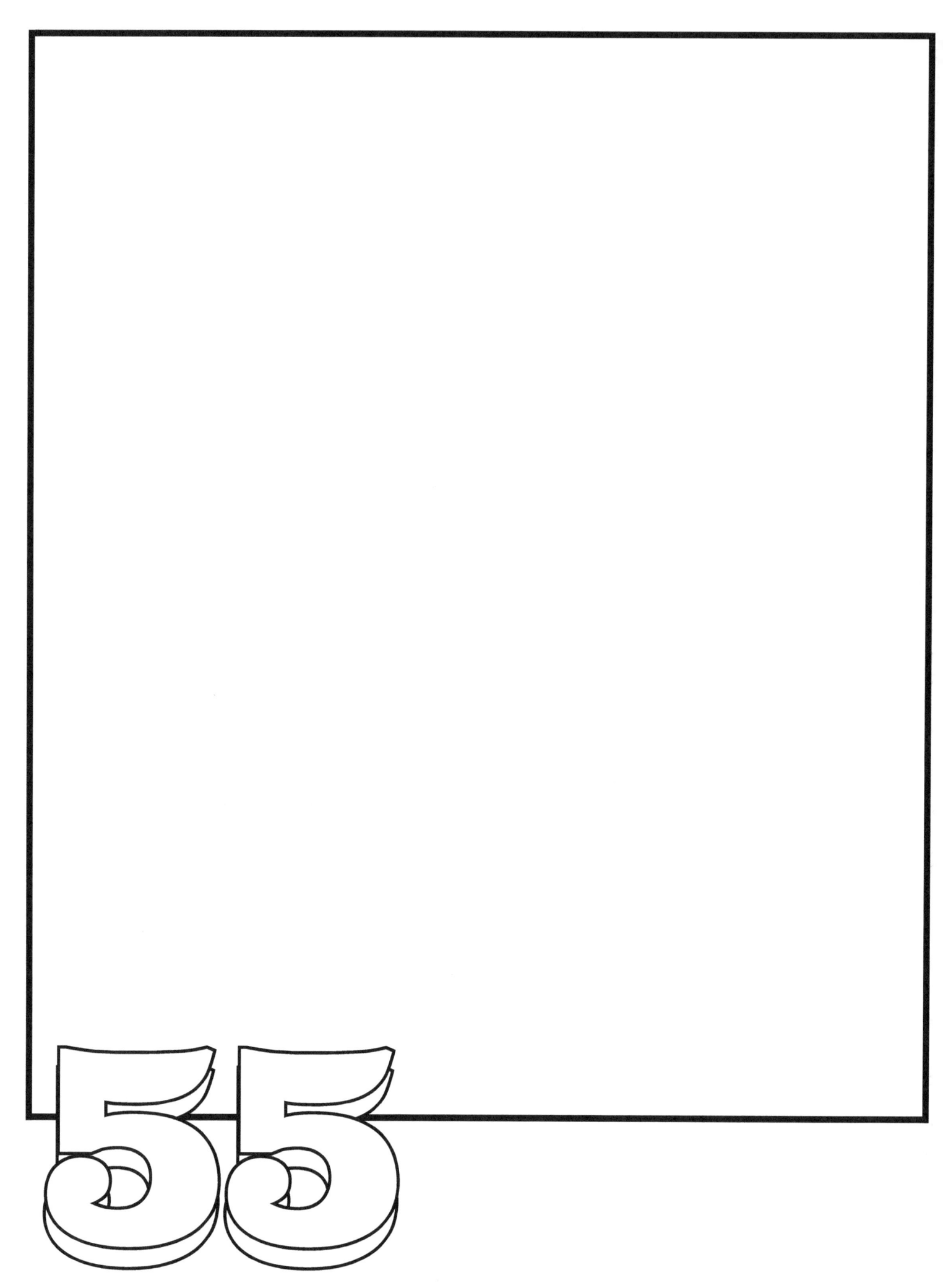

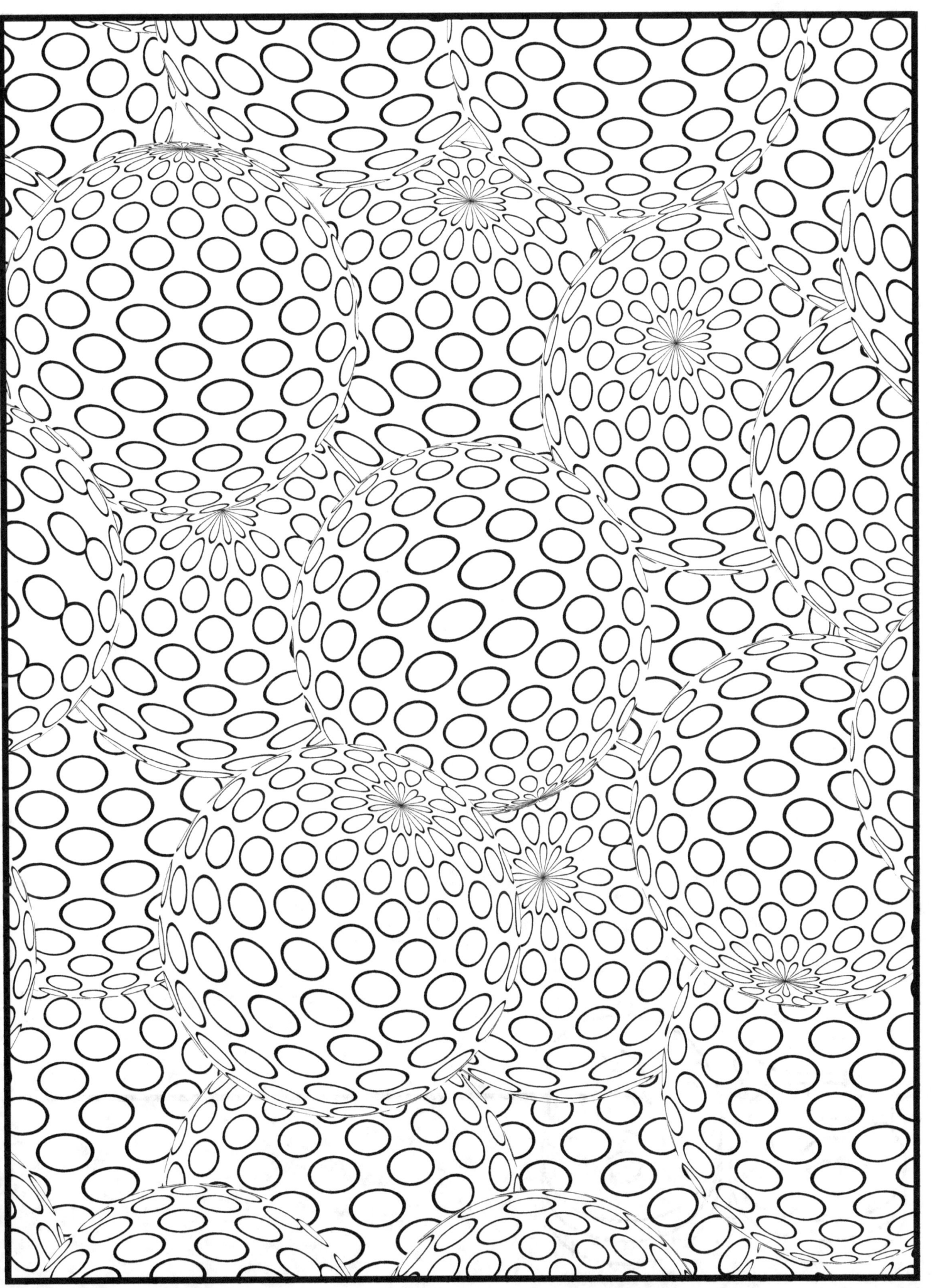

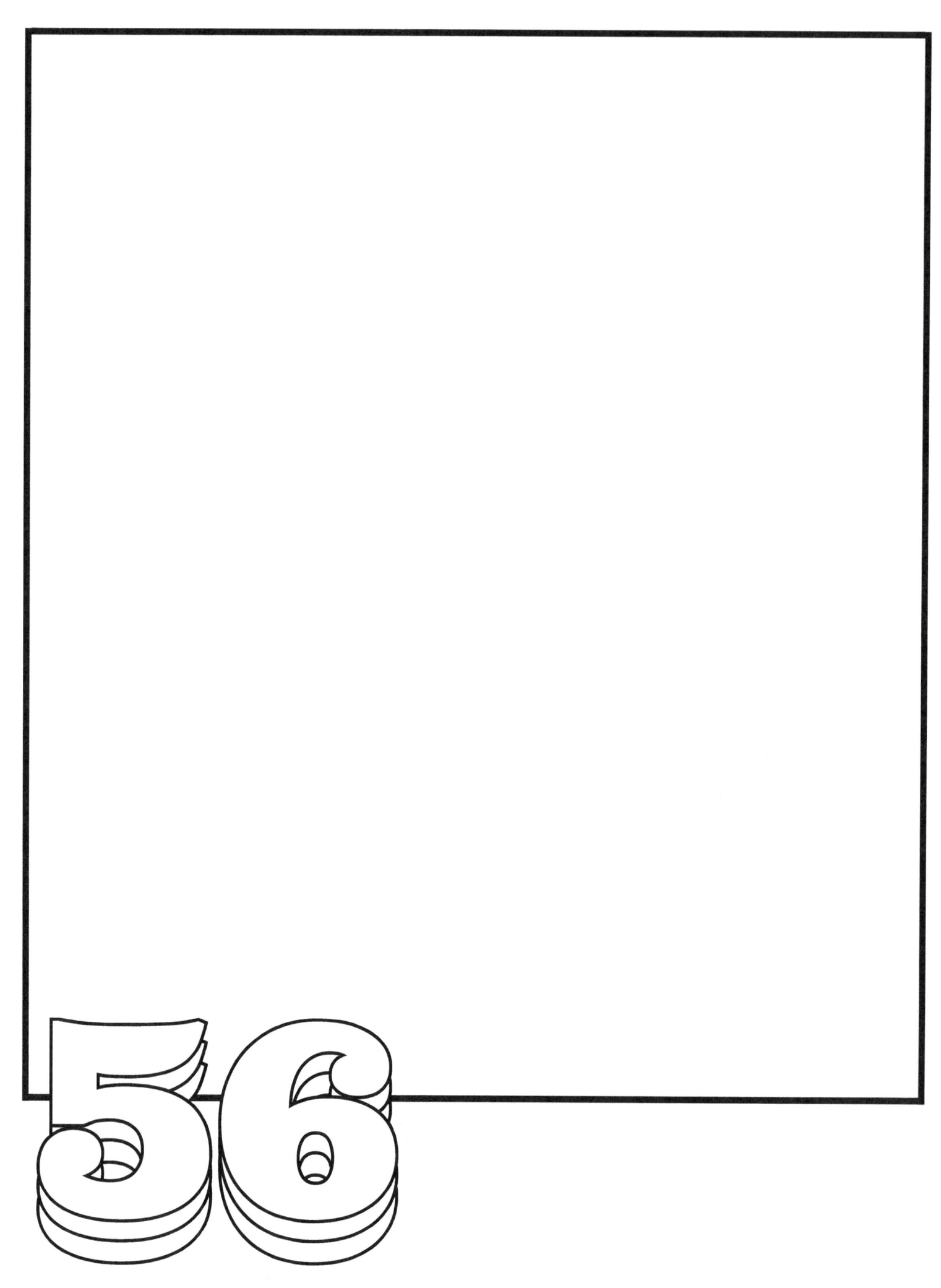

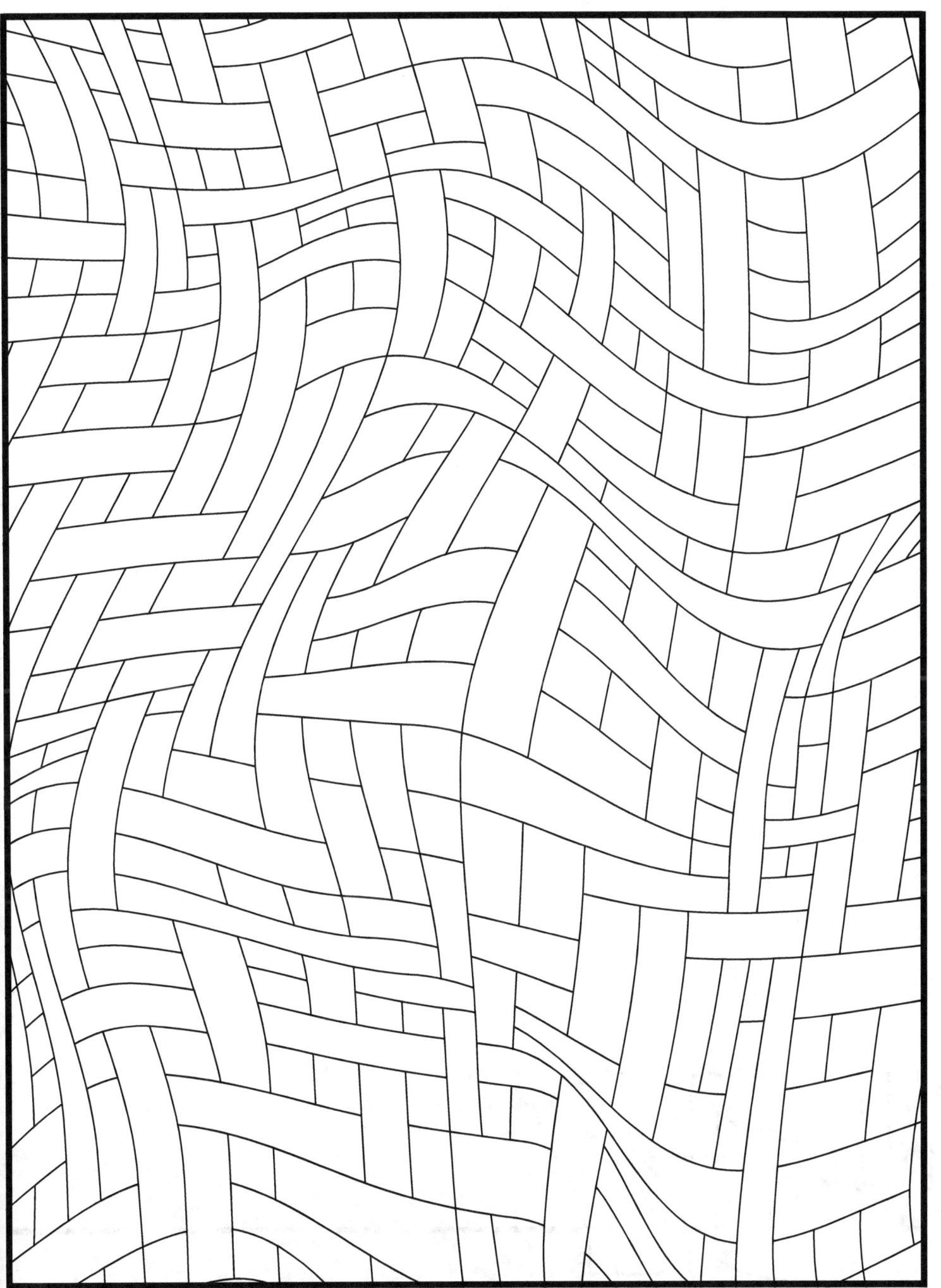

57

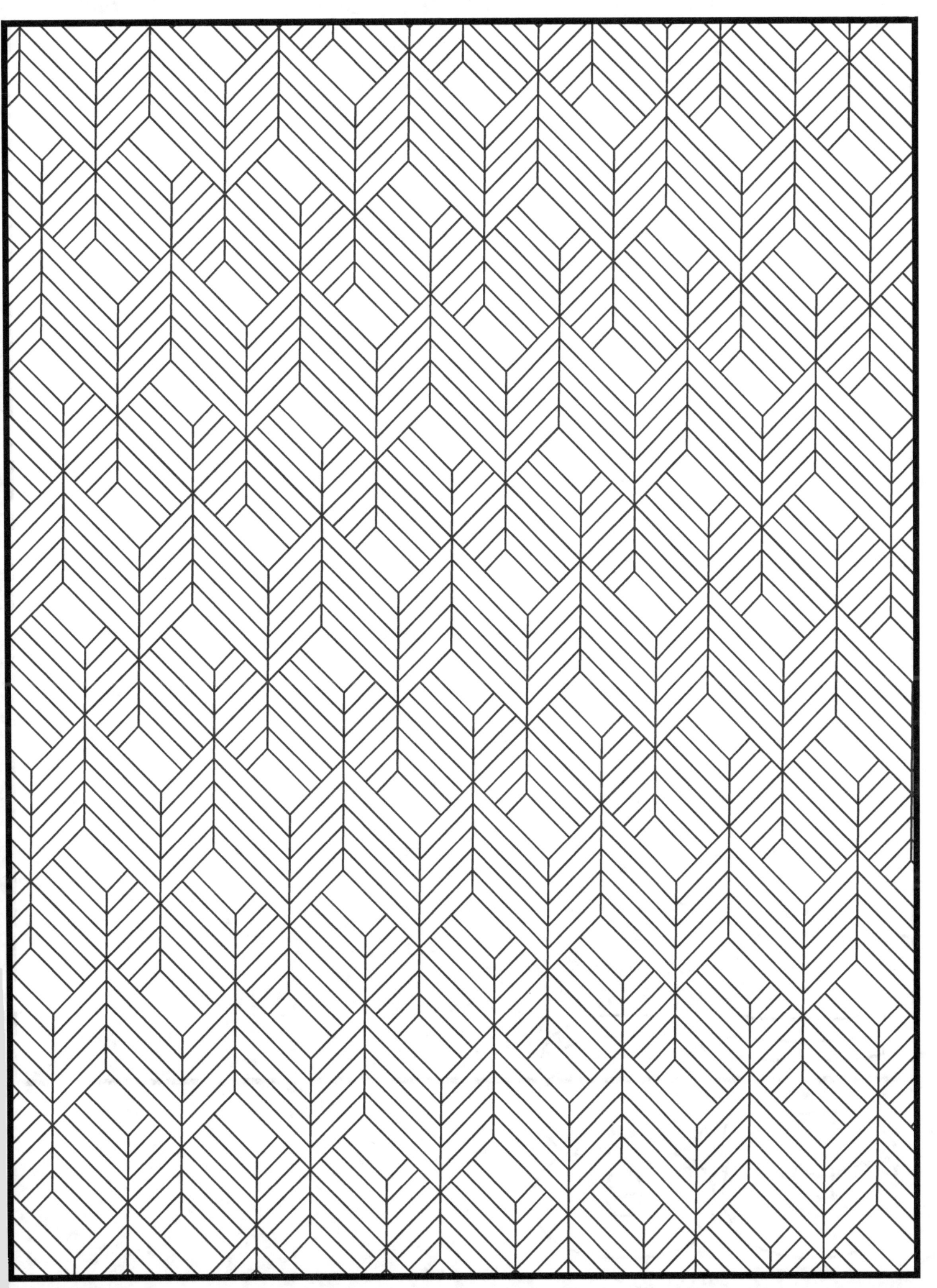

58

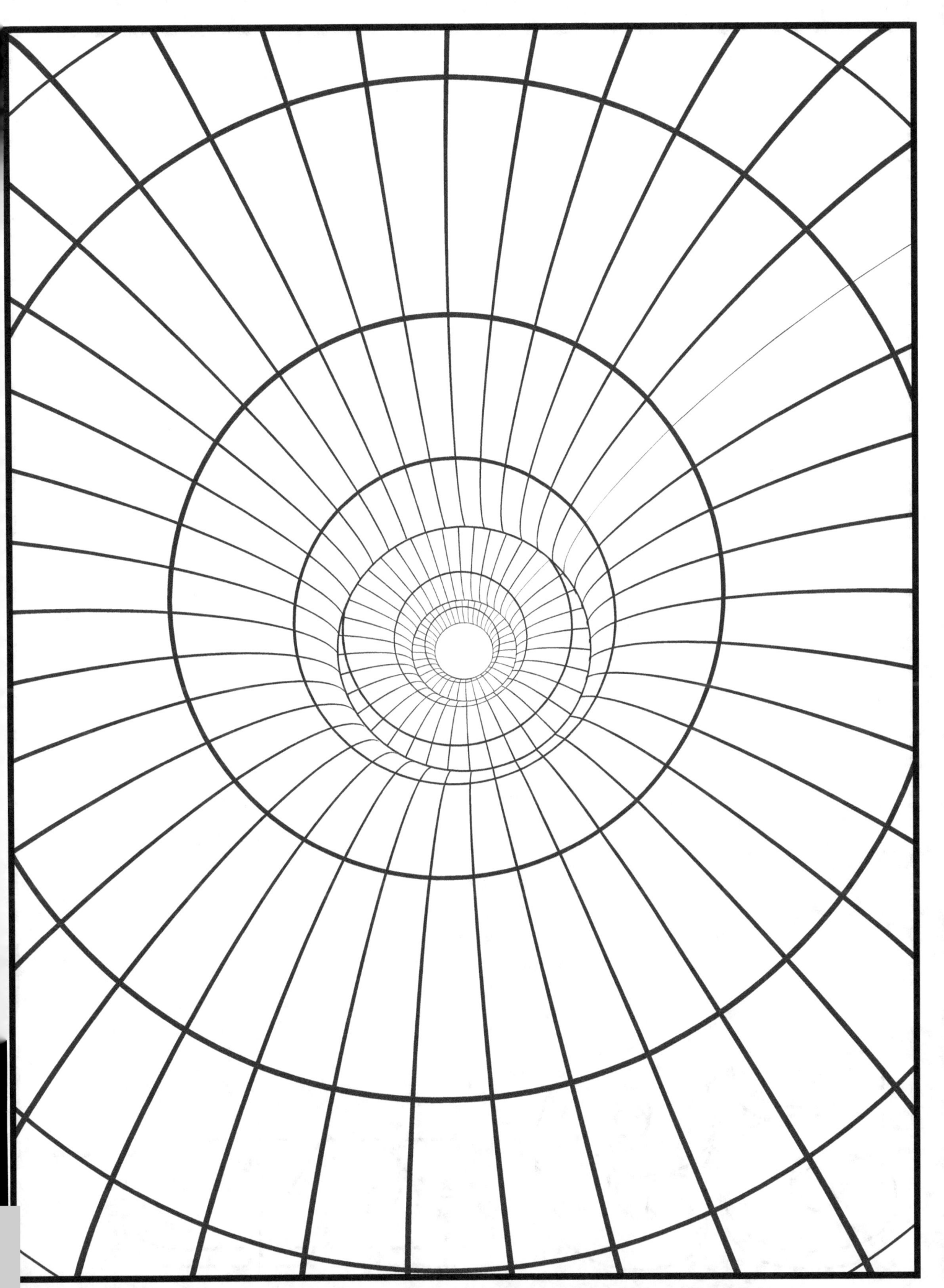

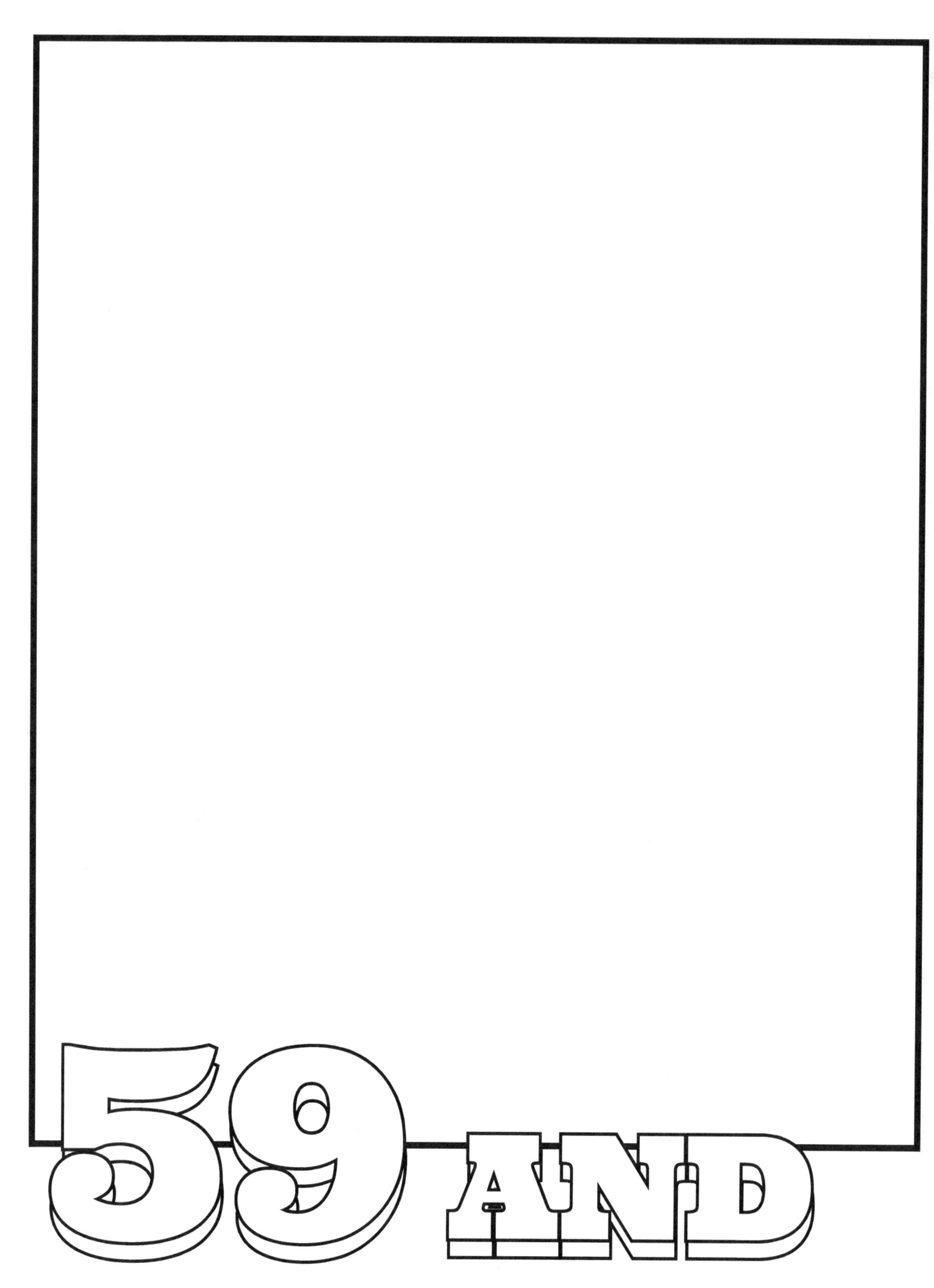

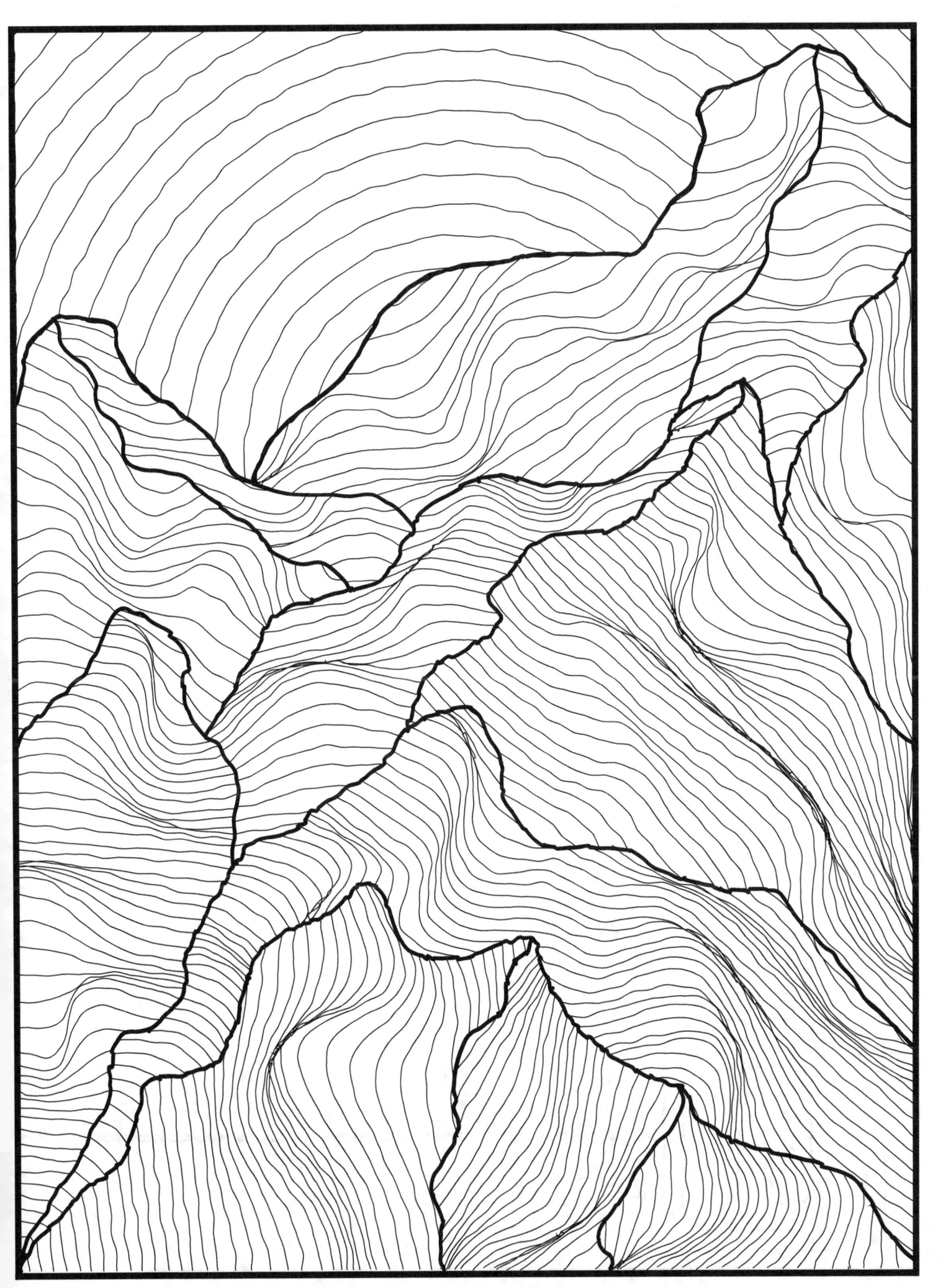

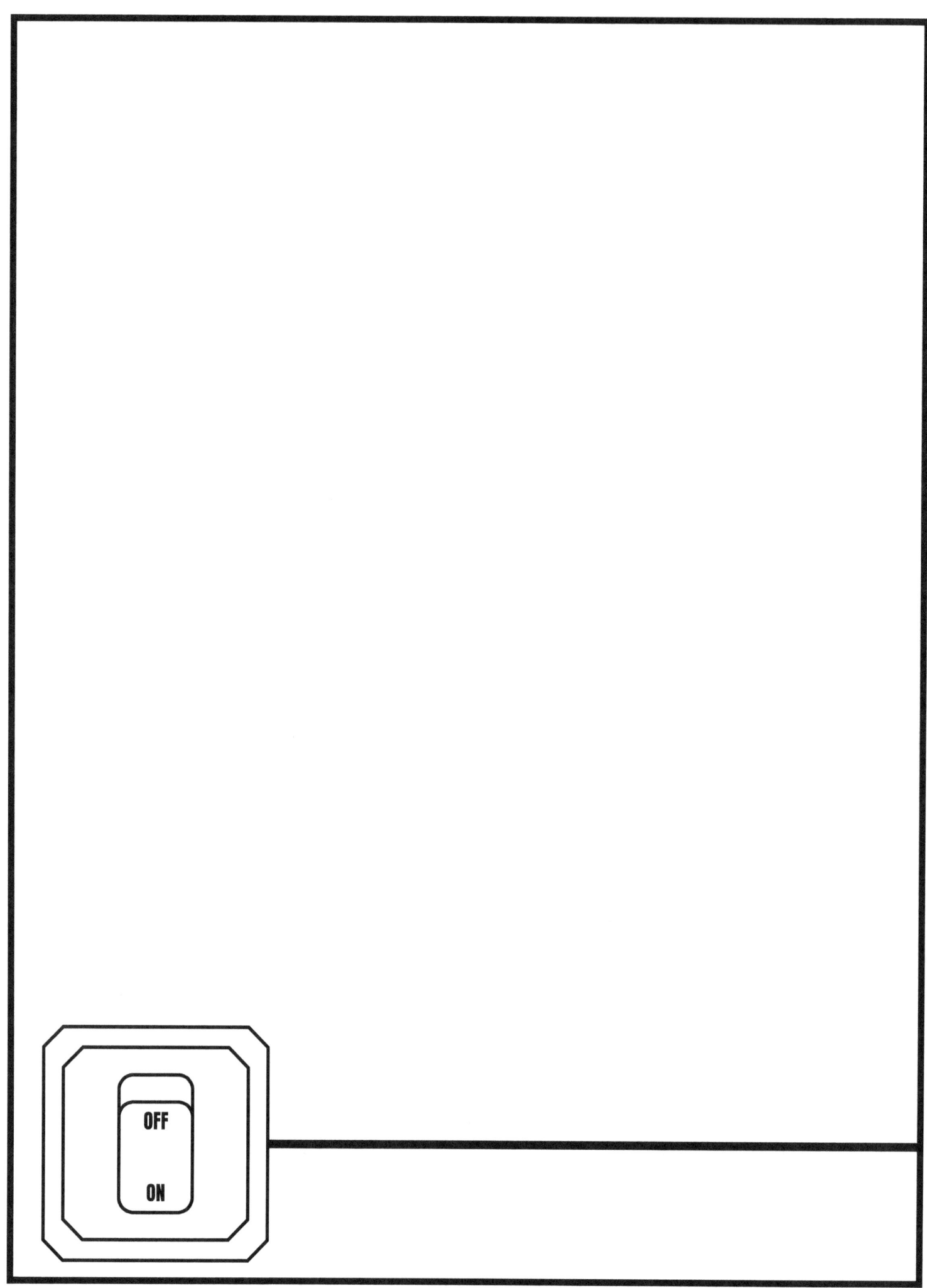

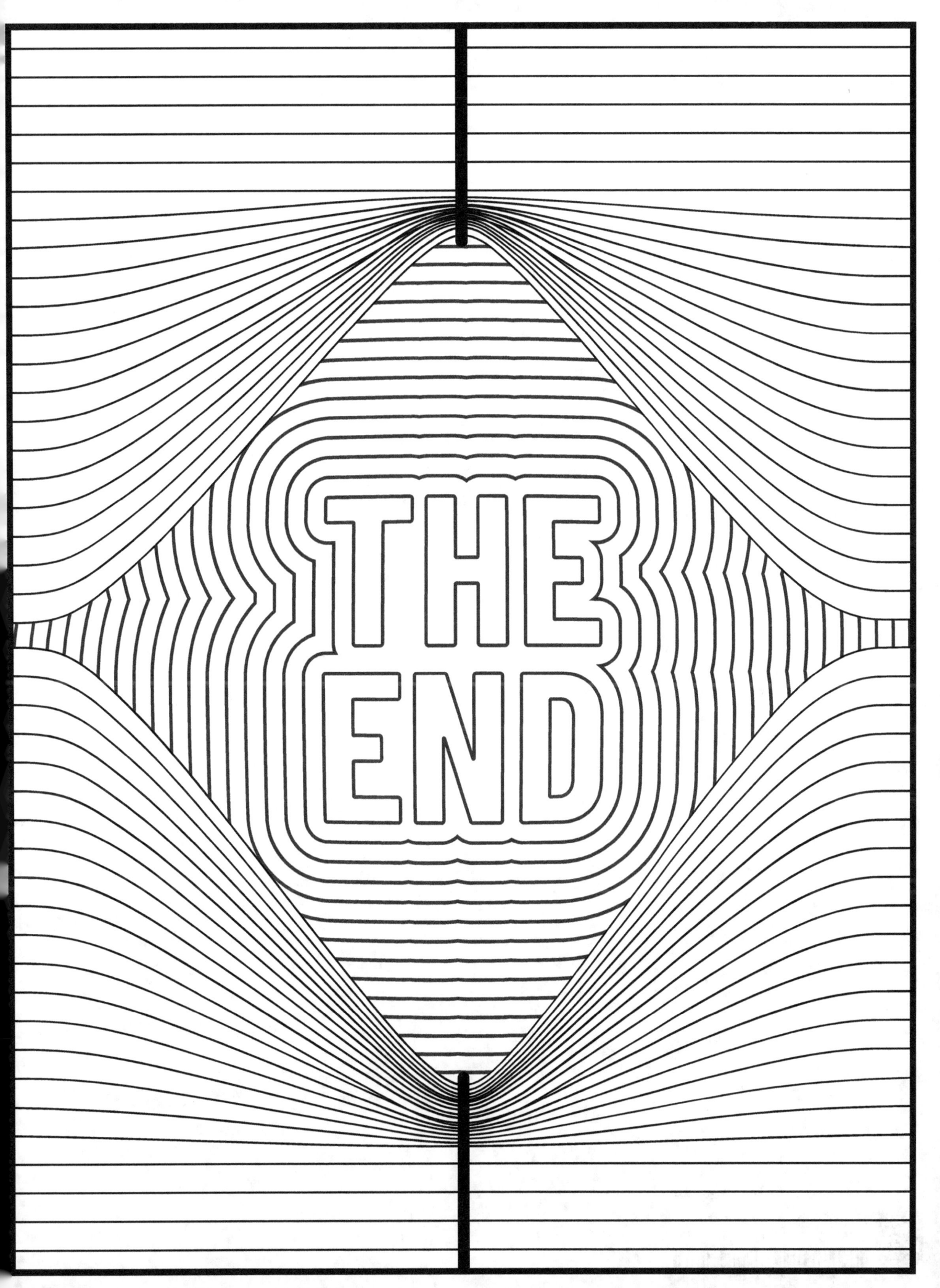

www.ingramcontent.com/pod-product-compliance
Lightning Source LLC
Chambersburg PA
CBHW060419220526
45465CB00008B/2950